GOLF GADGETS

GOLF GADGETS

by Bill Hogan

A Tilden Press Book

COLLIER BOOKS
MACMILLAN PUBLISHING COMPANY
New York
COLLIER MACMILLAN PUBLISHERS
London

A Tilden Press Book
Macmillan Publishing Company
866 Third Avenue, New York, N Y 10022
Collier Macmillan Canada, Inc.

Library of Congress Cataloging-in-Publication Data
Hogan, Bill, 1953–
    Golf gadgets/Bill Hogan.
      p. cm.
    "A Tilden Press book."
    Includes index.
    ISBN 0-02-043601-7 (pbk.)
    1. Golf—Equipment and supplies.   I. Title.
GV976.H64   1988
796.352′028—dc19   86-15363   CIP

Macmillan books are available at special discounts for bulk purchases for
sales promotions, premiums, fund-raising, or educational use. For details,
contact:

> Special Sales Director
> Macmillan Publishing Company
> 866 Third Avenue
> New York, N Y 10022

10 9 8 7 6 5 4 3 2 1

Printed in the United States of America
Book design by Rogers Graphics Design, Washington, D.C.

For my father,
who taught me how to play the game

CONTENTS

INTRODUCTION 1

Chapter One:
YOU AIN'T GOT A THING 7

Chapter Two:
THE ART AND SCIENCE OF PUTTING 43

Chapter Three:
SPECIAL STICKS 61

Chapter Four:
THE PRACTICE RANGE 81

Chapter Five:
KEEPING FIT FOR GOLF 93

Chapter Six:
GOLF GAMES, TOYS, AND SOFTWARE 103

Chapter Seven:
THE LIGHTER SIDE OF GOLF 129

Chapter Eight:
GOLF GIFTS 139

Chapter Nine:
GOLFIANA 149

Chapter Ten:
VIDEO AND AUDIO CASSETTES 161

Chapter Eleven:
THE 19TH HOLE 191

GOLF EQUIPMENT MANUFACTURERS 235
INDEX TO SOURCES 247
INDEX TO PRODUCTS 273

ACKNOWLEDGMENTS

While every book has its share of toil and trouble, this one has, from the beginning, been a genuine labor of love. Many of the people around me have helped make it so, and for that I consider myself an especially lucky soul.

I must first of all recognize my deep debt on several counts to *Regardie's*, the magazine that for nearly ten years now has been my home as a writer and, more recently, as an editor. Had it not been for the encouragement and forbearance of so many people there, this book might still be in the works. For starters I wish to thank Bill Regardie, the magazine's founder and editor-in-chief, who is responsible in no small measure for making me view journalism as such a terrific profession; Brian Kelly, the magazine's editor, who at various junctures generously gave me the time I needed to keep the manuscript in motion; and Bob Vasilak, its managing editor, who in innumerable ways from start to finish made it all possible. I owe thanks to lots of other folks at *Regardie's*, including Steve Gittelson, Kelly McMurry, Randy Bartow, Mike DeSimone, Gregg Leslie, Alex Friend, Paul Caplan, and Hap Attiliis. (Bartow, who receives more mail-order catalogs than anyone I know, was kind enough to stockpile them for me as I worked on the book.)

Along the way many other friends and colleagues provided me with help, encouragement, and inspiration. Among them: Dan Agan, a fellow Hoosier and top-notch golfer; Blair Austin, my friend of more than twenty years and go-for-broke playing partner in the Memorial Weekend Golf Classic; Jim Eastwood; Henry Fortunato, who gave me my start at *Regardie's* and has been a true-blue friend ever since; Eric Fridman, whose good cheer helped keep me in good spirits throughout; Nick Kotz, a gifted journalist whose friendship I treasure and whose counsel I invariably find wise; and John Rosenberg of Online Resources, an intrepid researcher who always manages to find the needle in the haystack.

I'm indebted to several fine writers who helped me craft some of the entries in this book: Alan Green, a good friend and former partner in the freelance business; Laura Bergheim; and John Callan. I'm also indebted to "Dr." Tracy Hazlett of the Washington Golf Centers, who graciously provided many hours of expert consultation.

As I went about researching and writing this book, many people within the golf industry were especially courteous and kind to me. It would be impossible to list all of them here, but I do wish to extend a special measure of appreciation to some of those who went out of their way to help: Steve Gilligan of The Golf Works; Jim "Little Cat" Williams of Practice House Golf; Melinda Mongelluzzo of Activision; Christopher Jones of Caddi-Sak; Loyal "Bud" Chapman of Chapman Studios; Randy Pasternak of Chesal Industries; Jim "The Spalding Man" Cooper; Pat Donovan of Richard E. Donovan Enterprises; Shirley Davis of Kerdad; Garth Wingfield, for MacGregor Golf Company; Elena Mildenberg of 1 Step Software; "Pug" Pilcher of The Pilcher Company; Lee Richards of Practical Computer Applications; Joseph Bradley of Precision Putting Systems; Harold Trimble of Pursuit of Par Enterprises; William Austin, for Reflex Inc.; Leslie Walker of The Sharper Image; Bud Sokol of Swing

Ring; C.D. Moffatt of Tee-Off Company; and Patrick Roper of ThetaMark Home Video.

Two close friends went way beyond the call of duty in helping me put together this book, and without their contributions I might never have finished. Jim Dentzer, a wonderful friend in every respect and formidable competitor on the golf course, was always there when I needed him, which, as it turned out, was often. While his hand in the book may be invisible to others, I can see it in nearly every page. Mike Hill, my collaborator on an earlier book, helped collect and organize the clippings, catalogs, and other raw material that quickly filled two filing cabinets and ultimately became this book. I'm grateful to them both and only hope that someday, somehow, I will be able to repay the debt.

I also wish to thank Graeme Bush of Caplin & Drysdale, who expertly and reassuringly guided me through thickets of fine print, and Joel Makower of Tilden Press Inc., who shepherded the book to completion.

Above all, however, I owe everything to my family— to my father, who taught me how to play the game and to whom this book is dedicated; to my mother, who taught me what life is all about; to my dearest Tatiana, whose love has sustained me and whose faith, even in the most trying times, never wavered a whit; to Ivan and Lydia, who always kept me smiling; and to my two brothers, Mike and Jim, who have understood.

To everyone who helped and believed in the book, including those I've inadvertently overlooked, I extend my thanks and appreciation.

B.H.
June 1989
Washington, D.C.

INTRODUCTION

I love golf like no other game.

If someone were to approach me tomorrow and say that I could spend the rest of my waking hours on the golf course, I believe that I would bless this John Beresford Tipton-like soul, pack up my things, and head for heaven on earth. I've supposed for a while now that my own paradise must be somewhere in Florida, but many aficionados of the game could make a good case for St. Andrews, Scotland; Monterey, California; Augusta, Georgia; Pinehurst, North Carolina; or even Clementon, New Jersey.

Funny thing about it, too: I am by no means a fanatic. I've been playing golf for more than 20 years now, mostly on weekends, and while the game has often confused me it has never consumed me. There are, I've figured, other things in life— my family, my friends (including those who don't play the game), my livelihood, and a host of passions that range from reading and writing to jazz, black-eyed peas, key lime pie, and White Horse scotch.

Then again, though, every time I walk off the 18th green and head to the clubhouse, one thing is certain: I will lovingly and longingly eye the first tee again. If it's early enough in the day the odds aren't bad that, partners and weather willing, we will have another go at it. If not, and if it happens to be a Saturday, I will find no small measure of comfort in knowing that Sunday is a day for golf. And if it happens to be Sunday afternoon and the sun is on its way down, all I can do is wince at the prospect of what's ahead. But I know in my heart that this, too, shall pass. Six days hence it will be Saturday once again.

I blame all of this on my spoon, which nowadays is called a three-wood. When it wants to be, it is the sweetest club in my bag. What a whoosh it delivers— the thrill without the chill— when I'm staring down the neck of a narrow fairway or trying to send my ball, via airmail, over a water hazard. I never blame this club for anything, because it is forgiving and dependable. It is my friend.

Several years ago its brother— my driver— left me. I used to be strong and damn near straight off the tee, rarely crushing the ball but usually letting it sail, with a slight draw, about 240 yards down the middle. Again and again. Then the club started failing me something awful. A few dozen yards vanished, and every drive I hit felt something less than solid. I agonized over what might be wrong with my swing, over what itsy-bitsy adjustment I might make to set things right again. Nothing— and I mean nothing— worked. Finally, out of plain desperation, I did what I should have done months earlier: I sliced its plastic collar open with a razor blade, unraveled the whipping, and stood slack-jawed as I looked at a dozen or so splits running up its neck. There was a moment of elation as the truth dawned: *It wasn't me, it was the club.*

My damaged driver was soon headed halfway across the country, to a rehabilitation center managed by the guy who might actually have built the club in the first place. There it was repaired and refinished in such a way that it looked virtually brand new (right down to a copy of the decal that for so many years had stared at me off the tee). But the poor thing has never really been the same. I've wondered at times whether its bulge and roll was ever-so-slightly altered in the refinishing process, or whether whatever they used to patch up those splits has become unglued. Even I have become unglued. I've tried plenty of other drivers in the time since— including a stiff-shafted, modern-day version of my 1961 Wilson Staff Model— but they just aren't the same. I've thought about having a new driver custom-built from the original specs, but in the meantime I've been doing what millions of other golfers do: hitting my old and reliable three-wood off the tee.

As for my irons, they, too, are oldies but goodies: 1963/64 Wilson Staff Dynapowers. They were a present from my dad, who paid $75 for the entire set (two-iron through pitching wedge) in the late 1960s— about the time I was getting serious about golf. He bought them from a fireman who must have spent more time polishing them than playing with them, and they still have the original wrapped-calfskin grips. A few years back I played with someone who offered to buy my irons right out of my bag, and I figured there must be something more to them than meets the eye— or at least my eye. There was. As it turned out, they're considered genuine classics. And while they're worth far more than what my father paid for them, I can't even imagine parting with them. Sure, you can buy a set of perimeter-weighted irons— "player improvement" clubs, they're called— but hit the crispest four-iron shot you know how and it still, to my way of thinking, feels like mush.

Over the years I've been less faithful to my putters . . . or perhaps it is vice versa. My first one looked as if it had been lifted from the barrel at a miniature golf course. When I grew embarrassed about carrying the thing, I paid $12 for a secondhand Ping Anser

at a local country club. Back in those days there was a PGA event on the golf course next to the Indianapolis Motor Speedway (Arnold Palmer won it one year, as I recall), and as I watched the pro-am one year I noticed at least two players— Gene Littler and Labron Harris, Jr.— using Ping Ansers. At the time Ping putters were highly unorthodox instruments, but within just a few years everyone, it seemed, was carrying one. As it turned out, the one I acquired is known today as a "Scottsdale" Ping, inasmuch as it was manufactured before Karsten Solheim moved his clubmaking operation to Phoenix. I haven't used the putter in years, but thank goodness I didn't get rid of it. Owing to its rarity, it's worth hundreds of dollars.

I then switched to a remake of the putter that Jack Nicklaus made famous: the Bristol "Geo. Low Wizard 600." Mine cost about $25; these days you can expect to pay about 100 times that for an original. For several years I used this flanged blade about as successfully as I'd used my old Ping Anser. Then, one day, fate looked upon me kindly. A fellow who worked down the hall from me was complaining about his putting game— in particular, about his putter. He was ready to get rid of it, he said, because he thought he needed something heavier. I asked him what kind of putter was giving him so much grief. "Some old thing made by Wilson," he told me. I asked him if I could have a look at it, and, lord have mercy, it was a Wilson 8802 in near-mint condition. I explained its value to him, in a manner of speaking, but also offered to buy him the new putter of his choice in lieu thereof. Ever since it has been mine. And unlike the story of my driver, this one has a happy ending. Thanks to the 8802, I have been putting less and enjoying it more.

I am pleased to report, too, that I've never had the "yips." The mere mention of this malady is enough to send shivers down the spine— not to mention the arms and hands— of anyone who's serious about the game. It's golf's most dreaded disease: an unpredictable and inexplicable "seizing up" of the nerves that has prevented some of the best players in the world, and many of the worst, from exerting any real control over the putter as it moves back and through the ball.

Just ask Sam Snead, Orville Moody, Bernhard Langer, or even Ben Hogan, whom many consider to be the greatest golfer in history. Each has suffered, at one time or another, from a severe case of the yips.

"All the technique or practice in the world wasn't going to help me," Hogan said. "It was a nerves situation, and it was embarrassing for me out there in front of people. I couldn't get the putter back."

The yips also can jinx the gentle forward motion of a smooth putting stroke. Listen for a moment to Jim Ferree, who was driven from the PGA Tour in 1966 by a seemingly terminal case:

"You ever seen anyone putt with the yips? It's like somebody goosed you with a cattle prod. I'd take the putter back all right, but then somewhere between there and the ball . . . puchoo! It was like somebody had hit me in the heart. The spots would come. I'd get dizzy. Terrible, just terrible."

Ferree studied the disorder for years, agonized over its potential causes, and tried every purported cure and known form of relief: new putters, new grips, psychiatrists, hypnotists, eye doctors, contact lenses, glasses— you name it, and Ferree, most likely, tried it.

Finally, Ferree resorted to the "Slim Jim," an abnormally long, split-handed putter (his has a 50-inch shaft). The yips didn't vanish entirely, but the new putter did trigger the best golfing streak of his five-year-old career on the Senior PGA Tour. Today, plenty of other players on the seniors tour— among them Orville Moody and Charlie Owens (who invented the Slim Jim)— employ variations on the same scheme.

The lesson? There's no universal cure for the yips, or for any other putting problem, but experimentation, ingenuity, and practice seem to work a lot better than prayers.

That's what this book is all about.

In the pages that follow you'll find not only the Slim Jim putter, but hundreds of other special golf clubs, training and practice devices, gadgets and gizmos— anything, really, that golfers might use to improve their games. Many of us want to believe that there is a secret to the golf swing— something that Ben Hogan and Sam Snead and Arnold Palmer and Jack Nicklaus managed to learn along the line, but something that still, willy-nilly, eludes us. With a little bit of luck, we think, maybe we will stumble on the key swing thought or neuromuscular maneuver that will put our game on track once and for all. "It is this constant and undying hope for improvement," Bernard Darwin, the British golf writer, once observed, "that makes golf so exquisitely worth the playing."

So use this book as your road map to improvement. Along the way you'll also find a host of other goods about golf, from sophisticated computer simulations of the Old Course at St. Andrews, Scotland, to art work and all manner of other memorabilia that capture, in one way or another, the evolution and essence and the best and most challenging game of them all.

No other game, as best I can tell, offers its participants such a panoply of equipment and accessories. No other game attracts so many players— 18 million, at last count, in the United States alone— and allows them to compete, on a more or less even keel, with players 50 years their junior. And no other game offers its devoted flock such splendid and spectacular natural settings.

Although I have never been particularly partial to bowling, it does, I suppose, have one thing over golf: In bowling there is such a thing as a perfect game. In golf there is only a perfect shot— the one that goes in the hole— and nobody has ever come even remotely close to putting 18 of them together.

How to Use This Book

In the chapters that follow you'll find descriptions of more than 500 products that have something to do with golf— everything from swing-training devices, self-hypnosis tapes, and spike wrenches to classic-club reproductions, computer software, and cookbooks. While I've tried to sensibly sort this panoply of products into useful categories, I realized from the outset that many of them could logically go in more than one place. What to do, for example, with Puttband-Swingband, which, as its name implies, is aimed at improving both your putting stroke and your full swing? It wound up in the second chapter ("The Art and Science of Putting") instead of the first ("You Ain't Got a Thing . . ."), mostly, I guess, because the manufacturer didn't name the device Swingband-Puttband. In a few particularly vexing cases, I included different write-ups of the same product in separate chapters. And I decided to lump all of the video and audio tapes

into a single chapter, even though quite a few of them— Ben Crenshaw's "The Art of Putting" being a case in point— might just as well have gone elsewhere. So if you don't see exactly what you're looking for in one chapter, please browse through the others. If nothing else, chances are that your wish list will grow as you go.

In putting this book together I wrote to more than a thousand companies that manufacture, distribute, or market golf-related merchandise; combed through a veritable mountain of mail-order catalogs, golf magazines, brochures, price lists, and other product literature; and talked to as many people in the business as time would permit. Then, from a universe that must surely number in the tens of thousands, I picked the products that seemed to me to be the most useful, interesting, or unusual— with an emphasis, perhaps, on the kinds of items that the typical pro shop isn't likely to carry. I also tended to lean toward products that fit under the generic umbrella of training, teaching, and practice devices, on the theory that most golfers are interested first and foremost in lowering their handicaps.

Every book must have an ending as well as a beginning, however, and I know that many nifty, novel, or otherwise noteworthy products managed to slip through the cracks. Some I was forced to leave out simply because I couldn't find a mail-order source for them. (Many manufacturers and distributors sell their products at wholesale only or exclusively through golf professionals.) Others went by the wayside because their manufacturers went out of business or dropped them from their catalogs. And while I've tried to make this book as comprehensive as possible, I'm still haunted by the thought of the good ones that got away.

I'd be especially grateful to hear about them for the next edition and invite any interested readers to drop me a line in care of *Regardie's Magazine*, 1010 Wisconsin Avenue, N.W., Suite 600, Washington, D.C. 20007.

Please don't try to order products directly from this book. Prices and product lines tend to change faster than the weather, so it's always advisable to obtain a catalog, brochure, or price list first. Mail-order firms frequently drop slow-selling items from their catalogs to make way for new products, and what's here today may be gone tomorrow— or at least sold at a different price. Most of the companies listed as sources in this book have toll-free telephone numbers, which makes getting up-to-date price and product information a snap; otherwise, a postcard or letter will do the trick.

Most of the products described in this book are available from more than one company, and I've listed as many mail-order sources as I could find. (You may also be able to find a good number of them at pro shops, golf stores, or other local retail outlets.) Some of the industry's top-selling golf videos, for example, are darn near ubiquitous. So don't be bewildered if see more than a dozen different sources at the end of a listing. As a matter of style I've generally tried to list the manufacturer or primary mail-order source first, with additional sources listed in alphabetical order after a semicolon. Failing that I've relied on printed prices (from catalogs, brochures, or advertisements) as a rough dividing line, listing what seemed to be the least expensive source or sources first. But the whole matter of prices, like the game of golf itself, isn't as simple as it seems.

For starters, prices change. And they don't always go up. Most golf videos, for example, aren't nearly as expensive as they used to be, thanks to price-cutting trends within the marketplace and heavy competition from the industry's deep discounters. Computer software for golfers— games, simulations, and handicapping programs— has followed the same trend. What's more, many of the mail-order companies listed in this book frequently offer seasonal or quantity discounts, special close-outs, and the like. Yet other discounts sometimes apply; the National Golf Foundation, for example, offers its members special prices on every item in its catalog. And keep in mind, too, that some suppliers include shipping and handling in their prices while others don't. So it pays to shop around a little bit, by telephone or by mail, before you order.

Many of the sources listed in this book offer money-back guarantees with no questions asked, but others will accept returns only if the merchandise you order is damaged or defective. Some charge "restocking fees" if you return or exchange certain kinds of merchandise (books, videos, or computer software, for example). So read the fine print in the catalogs carefully to avoid surprises later on.

This book has two indexes: an alphabetical listing of sources, with their corresponding product entries, and an alphabetical listing of all the products and product categories in the book. The first index, which cross-references products and suppliers, may come in especially handy if you want to order more than one item at a time; by scanning a company's offerings you may see several other products in which you're interested. (And because this book doesn't list each source's entire product line, a little telephone scouting among the major mail-order outlets may enable you to consolidate your wants in a single order.) The second index is designed to let you quickly find the products described in the book and to see at a glance who sells them.

In case you're in the market for a new set of golf clubs— or such standard items as golf bags, carts, shoes, and the like— the book also includes an appendix that lists major manufacturers of golf equipment. Virtually all will send catalogs or other literature free to interested consumers; a handful charge for their catalogs, and I've included such prices wherever possible.

Finally, this book is intended to be a guide to the products and sources listed— not an endorsement of them. So call or write first. Exercise the same judgment you would in making other purchases. And do let me know if you find anything out there that'll give me a fighting chance to win a spot on the Senior PGA Tour by the time I turn 50.

CHAPTER ONE
YOU AIN'T GOT A THING . . .

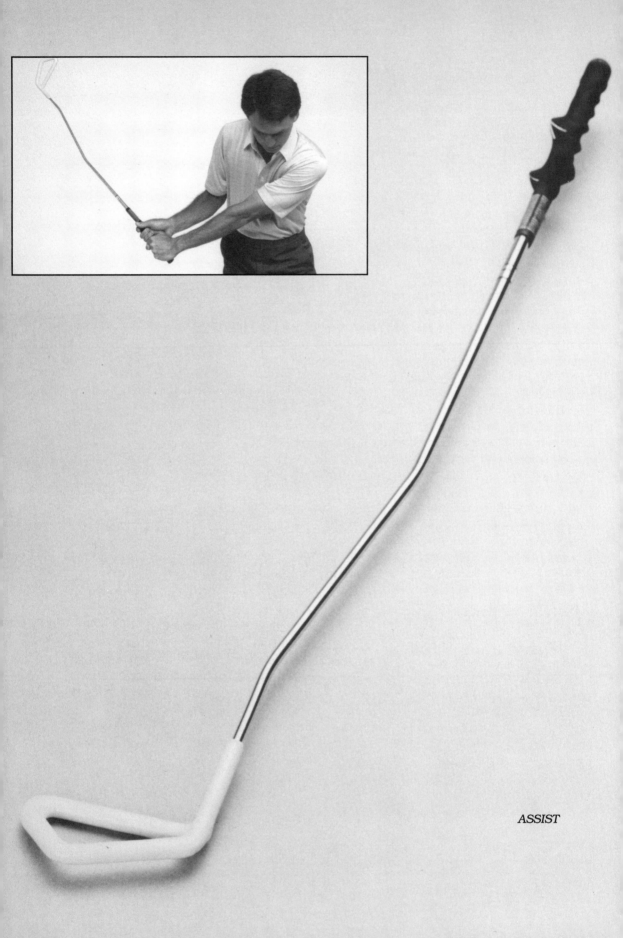

ASSIST

BUILDING A BETTER SWING

ASSIST

ASSIST, an odd-looking training club developed by the late Toni Olsen, stands for "All Season Self-Improvement Swing Trainer." It features a heavy, plastic-coated head that promotes full extension and builds up the muscles used in the golf swing. But the heart of the ASSIST's success lies in its patented, precision-tuned angular shaft, which automatically produces proper wrist action through the hitting area and accentuates the feeling of release. In addition, a special training grip guarantees that the hands are placed properly on the club. The men's model of the ASSIST is 37 inches long; the women's and juniors' model, which features a lighter head and smaller grip, is 35.75 inches long.

$45 from Matzie Golf; also from Austad's, The Golf Works, Las Vegas Discount Golf, Polar Golf, and J. White Industries.

THE JIMMY BALLARD SWING CONNECTOR

You'll never hear Jimmy Ballard, one of golf's top teaching pros, say "keep your head down" or "keep your left arm stiff." But if you've read his book, *How To Perfect Your Golf Swing*, you undoubtedly know that Ballard's idea of perfection in the golf swing has to do with the principle of "connection"—keeping the leading arm and upper body working as a unit.

If you want to practice what Ballard preaches, the Swing Connector just may be the answer to your prayers. Simply strap this six-inch-wide band around your chest (there's a Velcro fastener) and insert your lead arm through the smaller band that's attached to it. With the Swing Connector in place, the lead arm moves back in perfect sync with the turn of the shoulders and upper body. As the club moves to the top of the backswing, the lead arm is forced to stay in a "connected" position close to the chest. Then, as the club moves down and through in the forward swing, the arms continue to work in tandem, with the elbow of the lead arm staying down as the swing is completed.

$60 from Banff Golf.

THE BERTHOLY SWING PIPE

Paul Bertholy builds golf swings for a living. He's built more than 65,000 of them, in fact, at his Bertholy-Method Golf Schools in Foxfire Village, North Carolina, and at PGA workshops across the country. His own swing was cloned from Ben Hogan's in the early 1940s, Bertholy says, and now— with an assist from the Bertholy Swing Pipe— you may be able do a little bit of cloning yourself. It's a double-weighted exercise tool that's supposed to feed the precise sensations of a great golf swing into your kinesthetic muscle memory.

The Bertholy-Method identifies "the seven cardinal positions" of the golf swing and implants each position into muscle memory through a conditioning program of precise repetitions and 10-second isotonic holds. It won't lower your handicap overnight. But it may help you build a smooth, solid swing that's nearly second nature.

The Bertholy Swing Pipe is $35 from Paul Bertholy; the entire Bertholy-Method kit, which includes a 250-page manual, is $60.

Correct Swing

Back in 1937 Ernest Jones outlined the mechanics of the golf swing in what was to become one of the game's classic instruction books. "Swinging and levering are diametrically opposed methods of applying power," he wrote in *Swinging Into Golf.* "In a swing the connecting medium between the power and the object swung [golf club] has both ends moving always in the same direction. In levering, the two ends always move in opposite directions. It is no more possible to join up the two in one unified application of power than it is to mix oil and water."

Jones went on to describe the teaching drill he used to convey the feeling of the correct swinging motion. "Moving a weight back and forth on the end of a string is possibly the simplest demonstration of a swinging action," he wrote. "A pocketknife attached to the

Dynasight

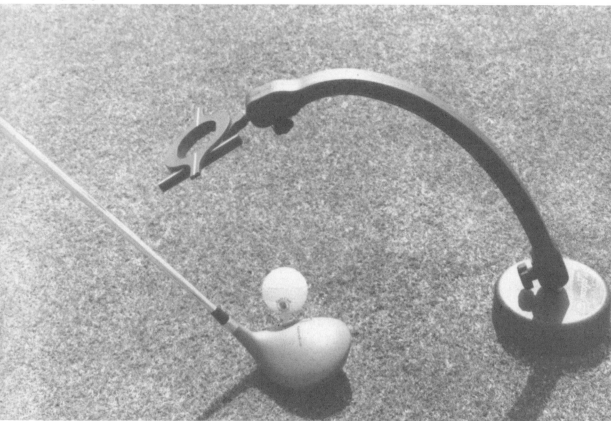

Flying Elbows

corner of a handkerchief serves the same purpose. Since the handkerchief is flexible, it can transfer power through swinging, but not through levering."

Some 50 years later Jones's lesson has been revived in the form the Correct Swing kit. The Correct Swing teaching aid consists of a cord-on-a-grip that can be connected to either a light or heavy golf ball. It helps you develop the proper tempo and timing by forcing you to develop the feel of swinging— not levering— the club with centrifugal force. Peter Jacobsen, a leading player on the PGA Tour, illustrates the action in an accompanying videotape.

$69.95 from Correct Swing.

DYNASIGHT

Do you sway as you swing? If so, Dynasight will let you know in no uncertain terms. Simply adjust the device so that you're looking at the golf ball through an oval sight opening. Any excess head or body movement as you swing will cause the ball to "move" away from the center of the opening. The immediate visual feedback helps you develop solid, square contact with the ball, and by adjusting the guidelines on the oval sight opening, you can practice hitting draws and fades. Dynasight is made of fiberglass-reinforced plastic and can be adjusted for any swing; two retractable steel spikes in its base provide greater stability on grass.

$50 from Lion Tool & Die.

FLYING ELBOWS

If your right elbow "flies" during your backswing, this training device just may be what the golf doctor ordered. Its two adjustable arm loops, connected by a Velcro strap, are designed to keep the elbows from moving out of position at any point in the full golf swing— especially at the top of the backswing. (If too much outward pressure is exerted by the trailing arm, the Velcro gives way.)

$12.50 from The Golf Works; also from Banff Golf.

FOOT WEDGE

This, thank goodness, isn't what you think. It's a simple training aid designed by Gary Wiren to keep the right foot from rolling to the outside at the top of the backswing— a common error that makes a powerful downswing virtually impossible. The Foot Wedge is made of durable maple, and a retractable tee-length metal spike keeps it from slipping during use.

$8 from The Golf Works.

GOLF SWINGER

Back in the early 1970s Wally Davis built his first prototype of the Golf Swinger by attaching a sawed-off golf shaft to a plastic bottle that he'd partially filled with water. After months of experimentation, however, Davis switched to a metal "clicking" mechanism and settled on the version his company has sold ever since: a practice club and exerciser that when swung correctly clicks at the bottom of the downswing and automatically resets on follow through.

If the Swinger clicks prematurely, it means that you're "hitting from the top" and losing both distance and accuracy. If it resets too early after the click, you're not executing a full follow-through with arms extended. The Swinger is perfect for indoor practice— it's only 25 inches long— and is avail-

Foot Wedge

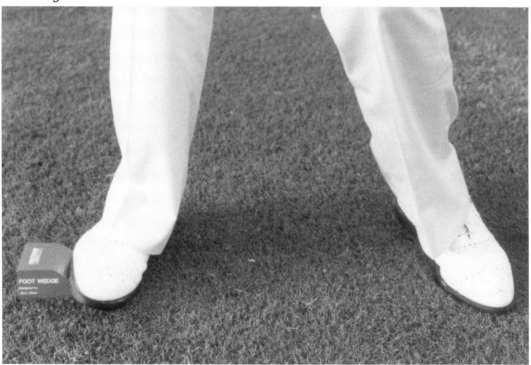

able in two weights: heavy (26.5 ounces) and medium (21.5 ounces).

$47.25 from Kerdad; also from Las Vegas Discount Golf and Polar Golf.

GolfTek Swing Analyzer/ Pro III Model

Back in 1977, when GolfTek introduced the world's first electronic golf-swing analyzer, who could have imagined that before long the market for such high-tech, high-end devices would be clogged with competition? Mitsubishi, the Japanese electronics giant, may have been the first to invade GolfTek's turf, and a handful of other firms— including Miyamae, another Japanese electronics firm, and Sports Technology, a Connecticut-based company— weren't far behind. But GolfTek's engineers and computer whizzes have persevered in their search for the perfect swing analyzer, and the Pro III Model is their best and brightest yet.

The GolfTek Swing Analyzer utilizes an array of 32 light sensors that track eight critical characteristics of the golf swing and obviate the need for attaching magnetic strips to clubs. The unit's half-inch-high digital displays show the path of the clubhead (outside-in or inside-out, in two-degree increments), the angle of the clubface (closed or open, in one-degree increments), clubhead speed (in miles per hour), ball carry (in yards), the point of impact (five clubface positions from heel to toe), and swing tempo (accurate within a tenth of a second). The unit also signals one of nine possible flight paths (from straight down the middle to pull-hooks, push-slices, and everything in between), as well as one of three possible landing areas (fairway, left rough, or right rough).

The GolfTek Swing Analyzer sells for $1,650 and is available in both right- and left-handed models. The software cartridges that are included enable the system to produce animated reproductions of any golf shot (on either of two typical holes) or of the clubhead as it moves through the impact area.If you'd like, you also can add a number of higher-tech options to the base unit. The GolfTek Graphics System ($1,615) uses a Commodore computer, 20-inch color video monitor, and dot-matrix printer to store, display, and print out a golfer's vital swing statistics. The GolfTek Video System ($2,600-$3,900), thanks to its high-speed color camcorder and digital-effects VCRs, lets you see and study your golf swing— or anyone else's— in ways that would have been unimaginable just a few years ago. Add a Video Graphics Printer ($1,400) and you can generate black-and-white reproductions of any video image in just 10 seconds.

All from GolfTek.

GolfTek Personal Model Golf Computer

If you don't want to spend an extra thousand bucks on a few extra bells and whistles, you may wish to consider this portable, lower-cost cousin of the GolfTek Swing Analyzer (see above). It won't project your golf shot's likely flight path or ultimate destination, it leaves out the degrees in measuring the path of your clubhead, and it shows only three possible impact positions (center, heel, and toe) instead of five. Otherwise, however, it tracks and displays every swing characteristic the Pro III Model does. The GolfTek Personal Model Golf Computer, which is for right-handed use only, runs on batteries (four alkaline "D" cells), works with either woods or irons, and can be used indoors under a 150-watt reflector flood lamp or outdoors in the shade (direct sunlight affects the sensors in its base).

$500 from GolfTek.

GRAPH-CHECK SEQUENCE CAMERA

If you've ever wanted to compare your swing to Jack Nicklaus's— or, for that matter, to any of the other top players whose swings are shown, frame by frame, in the golf magazines— here's the right camera for the job. With eight separate shutters of adjustable speed, the Graph-Check Sequence Camera can capture your entire swing— or just part of it— in a series of eight stop-action photographs. Best of all, you won't even have to wait for the lab to let you know whether your right elbow flies or your head dips; the Graph-Check uses Polaroid film.

$800 (add $100 for a custom-made carrying case) from Banff Golf.

GROOVE-E-SWING TRAINER

Even if your clubhead isn't flying as fast as a speeding bullet, you'd need the eyes of Superman to see whether it's passing through the impact zone on the proper path. While the Groove-E-Swing Trainer won't help you *see* the clubhead as it meets the ball, it will let you know precisely where it was before, during, and after the moment of impact. This

plastic practice platform has six upright pins that are positioned at various points along a strip of artificial turf; as your clubhead passes through the hitting area, the pins— by falling down on the job, as it were— capture its path for posterity. If you're plagued by a chronic slice or hook, practicing with this device may put your swing on the path to recovery. You can use it indoors or out, with either woods or irons.

$17.95 from Everything for Golf

HEAD FREEZER

Why is it that an eensy-weensy swing change can sometimes make such a dramatic difference in your game? Back in 1986 Betsy King, one of the top players on the LPGA Tour, started concentrating on keeping her head steady at the start of her downswing. She finished in the top three in four straight tournaments, including victories in the Henredon and Rail Charity Golf Classics. "I had been pushing shots to the right because my clubface was open at impact," King later told *Golf Magazine.* "Discouraging my upper body from getting ahead of the ball encourages a free arm swing and allows me to return the club consistently to a square impact position."

If you start your downswing with anything but a steady head, here's a nifty training and practice device that may help you keep everything in focus. The secret lies in two colored beads that are suspended on parallel wires in the mouth of a U-shaped frame. Simply clip the Head Freezer to your golf cap or visor, flip it down as you address your ball, and you'll be treated to a dandy optical illusion: the ball is framed in a rectangle of four dots (the double images of the beads). As long as you keep the ball and your intended target line centered within the rectangle of dots, your eyes and head will be aligned for a perfect hit. But move your head during any part of your swing and you'll instantly know that something's askew. After practicing with the Head Freezer for awhile, the theory goes, you'll automatically swing with a cool and steady head. And if a wandering head is throwing your putts off line, you can even use the device on the practice green to make sure everything stays square.

$14.95 from Head Freezer.

HEAD TRAINER

If lots of topped shots per round have left you with a sky-high handicap, chances are you're repeatedly "looking up"—lifting your head before the club contacts the ball. One cure for this dread disease may be the Head Trainer, which forces you to keep your head down and your eyes on the ball during the entire swing. It consists of an adjustable headpiece that's connected to one end of a telescoping tube (the other end is stuck in the ground far enough from your body to allow you to swing freely). "With practice," the manufacturer says, "the brain gets the message."

$29.95 from Head Trainer.

HEAD UP PREVENTER

Do you have problems "keeping your head down" during the golf swing? If so, this battery-powered practice aid may be just the solution you've been looking for. Here's how it works: Next time you're on the practice range, or just swinging away in the backyard, place this little miracle-worker near the ball but away from the line of flight. If your head is in the proper position at the moment of impact, you'll see a red light on the Head Up Preventer flash for a split second. If your head has moved from its original position at address, however, you won't be able to see the flash.

$18.95 from The Golf Works; also from Austad's, Miya Epoch and J. White Industries.

HIT & TELL DECALS AND IMPACT DECALS

Do you consistently slice or hook your shots? Do they feel unsolid? These impact marking decals will help you determine exactly how and where the clubface meets the ball. Simply apply one of them to the clubface, hit a ball, and then evaluate the bright red impression left on the decal. An elliptical impression means that the ball hasn't been hit squarely, for example, and a mark toward the heel of the clubface usually signifies a shot that starts out left, loses distance, and fades. An invaluable self-teaching aid for golfers at any handicap level.

Hit & Tell Decals are $4.50 per package (a package contains 10 for woods and six for irons) from Golf Day Products; Impact Decals are $3.50 per dozen (specify either woods or irons) from The Golf Works.

Impact Bag

IMPACT BAG

There's only one moment of truth in the golf swing: the split second when the clubface meets the ball. All golfers yearn for the sweetest of all sensations on the tee— the smooth whoosh of a squarely hit golf ball— but many miss simply because they've let their left wrist break down or their left arm collapse.

Enter the Impact Bag, which is designed to help golfers safely learn the correct position of the left arm and wrist at the moment of impact. (The left arm should be extended, with the left wrist bowed and slightly arched.) Just gather any old cloth materials— towels, sheets, or rags, for instance— and stuff the Impact Bag full but not tight. Then zip it up, place it against a heavy object (a

tree, the wheel of a golf car, etc.), and you're ready to go.

$39.95 from The Golf Works or Gary Wiren's "Golf Around the World"; also from Austad's.

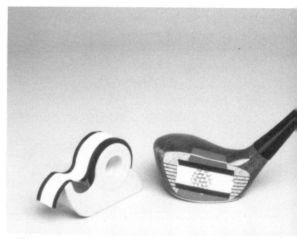

Labelon Tape

LABELON TAPE

As an alternative to Hit & Tell Decals or Impact Decals (see page 15), apply a two- or three-inch strip of Labelon Tape to the face of a wood or iron. Then, after hitting a few balls, you can clearly see exactly *where* on the clubface you're striking the ball. And by peeling the strips off and saving them, you have a permanent record of your progress on the practice range.

$6 for a one-inch-wide roll (with dispenser) from The Golf Works; also from Golfsmith.

THE LONE EAGLE SWING PLANE TRAINER

This isometric exerciser is designed to help your muscles "memorize" the feeling of a proper swing plane. Attach the Lone Eagle's suction-cup mounting device to the wall (or any nonporous surface), adjust the length of the cord for your own swing path (flat, upright, or in-between), and swing the special practice club slowly and repeatedly. By attaching the suction-cup device to a mirror, you can even check your swing at different positions in its ideal plane.

$49.95 from The Golf Works.

MITSUBISHI GOLF TRAINERS

High tech comes to the practice range. Tee a ball up on one of Mitsubishi's machines (or simply place it on the strip of artificial turf), swing away, and a series of electronic sensors "read" the moving club— from driver to putter— at the point of impact. (The sensors actually track a special magnetic strip that's attached to the clubhead.)

The GL-300 Golf Trainer provides instant visual displays of six vital swing checkpoints: clubhead speed at impact,

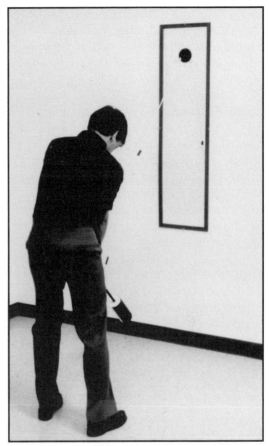

The Lone Eagle Swing Plane Trainer

Mitsubishi GL-300 Golf Trainer

carry, face angle (square, open, or closed, in degrees), shot direction, "duffing," and probable out-of-bounds shots (more than 44 yards wide of the target). The GL-500 Golf Trainer displays data on three additional checkpoints— hitting area (whether the ball was struck on the club's sweet spot, or toward the toe or heel), swing path (inside-out, straight, or outside-in), and accuracy— and also features a rechargeable battery and carrying case. Both units incorporate the same microchip technology and are intended only for right-handed use.

Suggested retail prices are $229.95 for the GL-300 and $419.95 for the GL-500. Information from Mitsubishi Electric. Available from Austad's, Golfsmith, Las Vegas Discount Golf, Nevada Bob's Discount Golf, Polar Golf, Edwin Watts Golf Shops, and J. White Industries.

MIYA COMPUTER SHOT ANALYZER

For a while it seemed as if Mitsubishi had cornered the market on electronic swing analyzers, but Japan's Miyamae Company has recently been giving its rival a run for the money. The Miya Computer Shot Analyzer can be used indoors or out, with or without a golf ball. This portable, user-friendly unit tracks and displays clubhead speed, carry, face angle at impact (square, open, or closed, in degrees), swing path (inside-out, straight, or outside-in), the position of the ball at impact (toe, center, or heel), and probable out-of-bounds shots. Unlike the Mitsubishi units, this one requires no magnetic strips.

$239 from Miya Epoch.

ONCOURSE INSTRUCTOR

You're in deep rough and don't know what to do. Just last week you flubbed the same shot with a four-iron, which leaves you unsure of the club and type of swing that will get you out of trouble this time. Thank goodness that your playing partner today is Bill MacWilliam, a real pro. He succinctly tells you exactly how to approach and execute the shot: "Use three-quarter upright swing. Ball in center of stance. Hit down and through ball. High finish— face target. Hands lead during impact. Strike behind the ball." You follow his advice and loft your ball out of the long grass and onto the putting green.

Thanks to the marvels of microchip technology, MacWilliam, a leading Canadian golf instructor, will faithfully follow you on your appointed rounds, providing professional advice whenever and wherever you need it. His pointers are permanently stored in the 4K memory of Oncourse Instructor, a hand-held computer that covers more than 130 different shot-making situations (everything from playing a one-iron to pitching from a buried lie). You punch in some data about the situation you face: How's the wind blowing? Is your ball in a fairway bunker or greenside trap? What kind of lie do you have— uphill, downhill, sidehill, or buried? Light or heavy rough? Are you chipping, pitching, or putting? What club do you intend to use? Oncourse Instructor then dispenses MacWilliam's advice, which scrolls across a 1.75-inch-wide liquid crystal screen. Because it's just a half-inch thick and weighs only 3.2 ounces, this little unit is as wieldy as a pocket calculator. It runs on two watch-type batteries and comes with a vinyl carry-

Right: Power Trainer

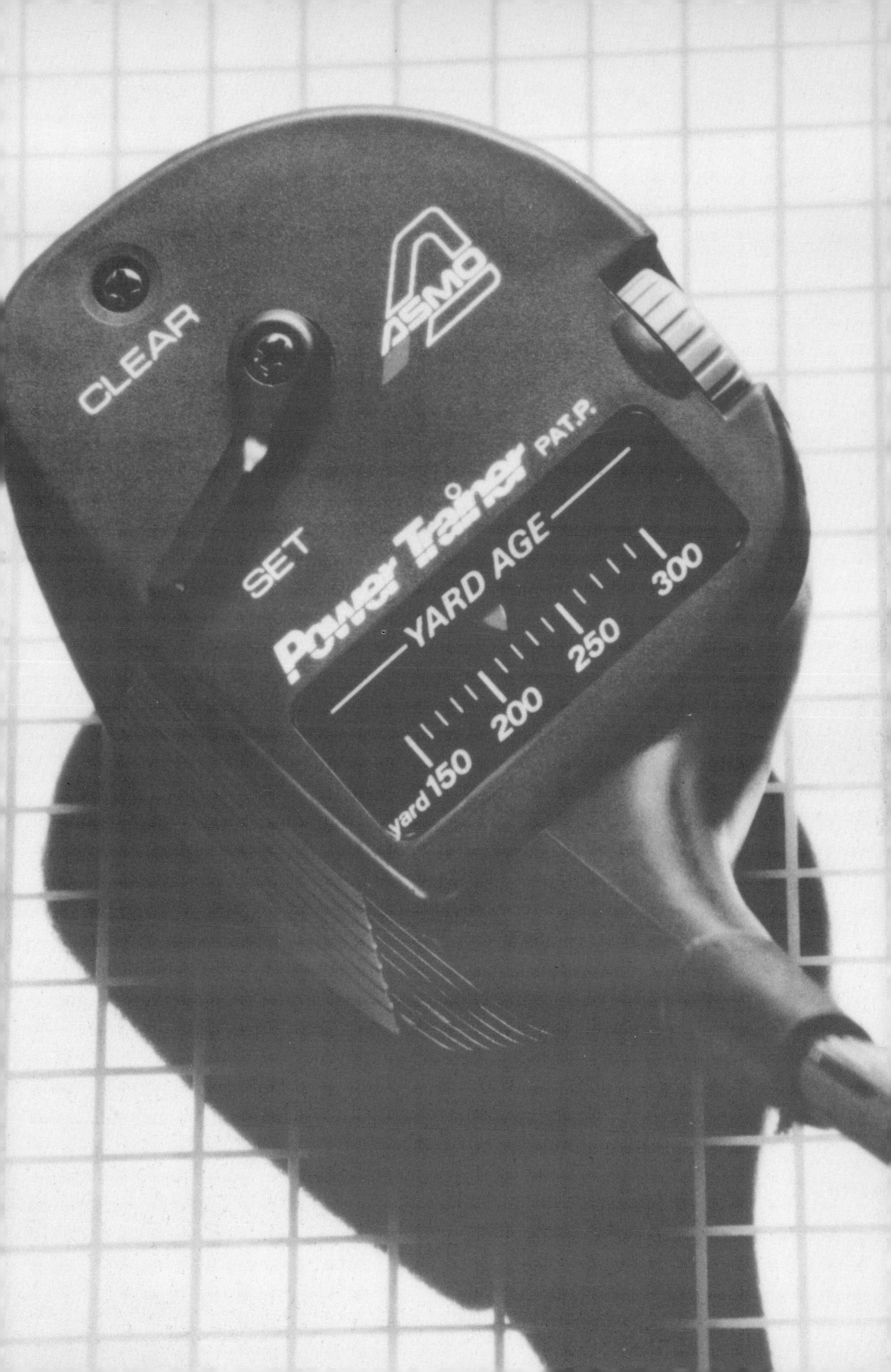
CLEAR
SET
ASMO
Power Trainer PAT.P.
YARD AGE
yard 150
200
250
300

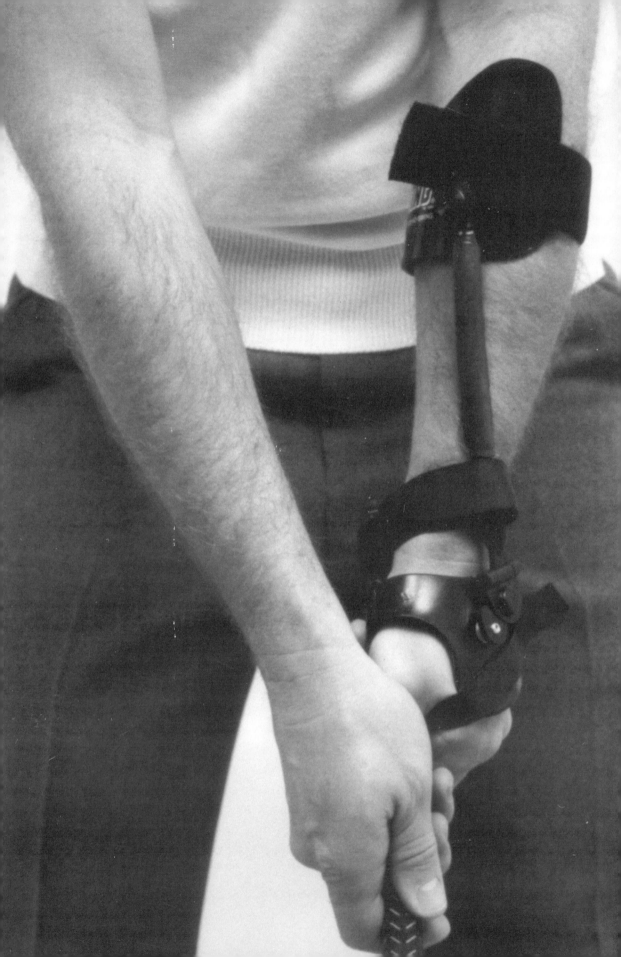

ing case that, when clipped to your golf bag, keeps your Oncourse Instructor within easy reach during play or practice.

$59.95 from Las Vegas Discount Golf; also available from Hammacher Schlemmer.

POWER TRAINER

If you've grown tired of plowing through endless buckets at the driving range, here's a way to dramatically improve the distance and accuracy of your drives—without hitting a single ball. The Power Trainer is a self-contained practice club with an internal spring-release mechanism that monitors the timing of your swing release plus a yardage display that shows how far you would have hit the ball. If the Power Trainer clicks too early— or too late— it means you're not swinging with the proper tempo. And once your timing's right, you can gradually build distance by turning a thumbwheel on the back of the club that controls the level of force needed to produce the click. The Power Trainer is 43 inches long and has a lightweight graphite shaft.

$99 from The Sharper Image; also from Austad's.

PRO-SWING

This strap-on training device is designed to help your muscles "memorize" the feel of proper wrist action during the backswing, while striking the ball, and in the follow-through. Using Pro-Swing

Left: Pro-Swing

during practice keeps the clubface square through the backswing and rotates the wrists for proper release of the club on impact. It may be adjusted for any kind of golf shot— from driving to putting— and includes written instructions as well as a 3.5-minute instructional videotape (VHS format). Available in a regular size for men and a small size for women and juniors.

$69.95 from The Golf Works.

PRO-TATER

Pity the poor push-slicer, for his typical tee shot is one of the sorriest spectacles in all of golf. It almost invariably starts to the right of his intended target line; then, as if to add insult to injury, it continues curving even farther rightward. If he aims way to the left he'll be able, with a little luck, to play his long second shot from the right rough. If he aims straight down the middle his ball will probably wind up one fairway over— if the trees don't stop it first. If he aims to the right, God help him.

The chronic push-slicer is, in all likelihood, at wit's end. He can't win. He's come to believe that his slice is the symptom of an outside-in swing path— and who could blame him?— but his continuing attempts to turn his swing inside out only seem to make matters worse. What he's never realized is that all along he's been swinging the club down on the proper, slightly inside-to-square, path. His real problem? The clubface is wide open at the moment of impact.

The most common cause of the push-slice is a failure to properly release the hands through the hitting zone (frequently called "blocking"). If all goes well in the golf swing, the right hand should gradually and naturally roll over the left hand through impact, causing the toe of the club to draw even with— or slightly pass— the heel as it strikes the ball. The clubhead thus meets the ball squarely and imparts an iota of counterclockwise sidespin, which in turn generates a gentle draw.

If pushes and slices are part and parcel of your golf game, the Pro-Tater— a bent, sawed-off steel shaft with a training grip on one end and a plastic-coated weight on the other— may help you straighten everything out. It's designed not only to promote the proper pronation of the forearms through the downswing and a full release of the hands and wrists in the impact zone, but to strengthen some of your golf swing's key muscle groups at the same time. Swinging the Pro-Tater just as you would a golf club teaches you the correct rolling action of the forearms and hands as well as the importance of tempo and timing in generating club-head speed. Swinging it with just the left arm helps train your leading side to control the downswing. Swinging it with just the right arm helps you memorize the sensation of a full release. Because the Pro-Tater is only 24.5 inches long, you can practice with it just about anywhere, indoors or out. And thanks to a molded-rubber training grip (see page 32), you don't even need to worry about how you hold it.

$39.95 from Austad's.

Sony CaddyCam

If your golf swing isn't yet picture-perfect, this portable video system from Sony may well represent the state-of-the-art solution to your problems. The CaddyCam Video 8 unit (so named because it uses compact 8mm videocassettes) contains everything you need to record, play back, and analyze your golf swing— whenever, and just about wherever, you'd like. As video cameras go, Sony's variable-speed, automatic-focus Handycam is the cat's meow. Its five different shutter speeds (1/60, 1/100, 1/150, 1/1,000, and 1/2,000) let you record for real-time, slow-motion, or freeze-frame replay, and its automatic-focus feature takes the worry out of capturing golf swings and other moving targets. What's more, its six-power zoom lens enables you to zero in on any part of your swing— your shoulder turn or impact zone, for example. And as compact color monitors go, Sony's eight-inch Trinitron, which swings into action from the unit's flip-up lid, can't be beat; it has a glare-free screen for easy outdoor viewing and an infrared remote control. Best of all, you can take the entire 110-pound system with you to the golf course or practice range; all of the components are built into a mobile, 42-inch-high pull cart with a tubular-steel frame and 14-inch wheels. And when the CaddyCam's 12-volt battery runs low, you can simply plug it into any standard household outlet for recharging.

$5,200 from Hammacher Schlemmer.

The Spiro Swinger and Swing Rite

Miller Barber, who's known as "Mr. X" to his colleagues on the Senior PGA Tour, has one of the least graceful— but most profitable— swings in professional golf. "When Barber swings," Ben Crenshaw once cracked, "it looks as if his golf club gets caught in a clothesline."

Barber's the guy whose "flying" right elbow makes even Jack Nicklaus seem as if he's swinging in a straightjacket. Although the ailment hasn't hurt Barber any— over the years he's kept his swing in a reliable, repeating groove— it could very well be the culprit behind your chronic slice. If so, you may be able to cure your case of flying elbow by practicing with either of these training devices. Both The Spiro Swinger and Swing Right consist of wide, twin-looped elastic bands that keep your elbows in proper position and your arms working as a unit throughout your swing. And if muscle memory counts for anything, you'll soon have a slice-free swing on the course, too.

The Spiro Swinger is $5.95 from Austad's; also from J. White Industries. Swing Right is $5.95 from Golfsmith.

SPORTECH GOLF SWING ANALYZER

Deane Beman, the commissioner of the PGA Tour, calls this "the finest teaching aid on the market." While Beman isn't exactly a disinterested party— the Sportech Golf Swing Analyzer is the only device of its kind ever endorsed by the PGA Tour— he's probably right. The Sportech unit utilizes 55 ultrasensitive weight and light sensors to collect data on key points of the golf swing undetectable to the human eye; a high-performance computer system then processes and displays the data on a color video monitor and, if desired, automatically reproduces anything shown on the screen on paper printouts.

When you step onto the platform facing the Sportech unit and swing, independent scales under both feet measure shifts in weight distribution while the sensors track your clubhead from takeaway through impact. At the completion of your swing, the color monitor displays the relative paths of your backswing and downswing (illustrated by dotted lines and listed in degrees inside-out or outside-in), the relative speeds of your backswing and downswing (in feet per second or miles per hour), the angle of your clubface at impact (square, open, or closed, in degrees), and your weight distribution at address, top of the swing, and impact. Measurements can be displayed individually, in any desired combination, or collected behind a blank screen for later retrieval. (By storing data from previous swings or practice sessions, for example, you can generate cumulative averages.)

Because the Sportech Golf Swing Analyzer is aimed primarily at country clubs, golf schools, golf shops, and driving ranges, it also features a club-fitting program. By hitting a series of shots with any number of different clubs— with varying lengths, shaft flexes, swing weights, and so forth— you can then compare the averages for each club tested, ranking them from "best" to "worst." The process can be repeated until you settle on the clubs that produce the best results for you.

An optional game package ($250) adds a driving contest and a simulated 18-hole golf course. Computerized reproductions of several PGA Tournament Players Club courses are planned.

$5,950 from Sports Technology. (If this one's out of your price range, why not order the coin-op model and let all your golfing friends pay as they play?)

The Stable Flexor

If your right knee stiffens or bows to the right on your backswing, you're probably asking for trouble. Maybe you should be asking instead for the Stable Flexor, which promotes stability and proper leg action by keeping the right knee in a slightly flexed position. Wear it during practice sessions and you'll begin to feel the lower-body action that's needed to "trigger" the downswing and produce consistent shot-making. The Stable Flexor fits comfortably on the back of the right knee and is held in place by straps attached to the thigh and calf.

$31 from Banff Golf.

Swing Memory

Swing Groover

Swinging a golf club through thin air is fine for limbering up, but it's the behavior of the ball that tells you whether your clubface was square, open, or closed at impact. So what do you do if you can't hit real golf balls in your backyard? One answer is to invest in a practice net or electronic swing trainer; another is to sink a little bit of money into the Swing Groover, which basically consists of a solid practice ball that hangs from— and, when hit, orbits around— a metal upright. (The upright is in the shape of an inverted "L," so you can swing away without worrying that you'll strike anything but the ball.) The longer and straighter the ball orbits around the overhanging arm, the longer and straighter your shot would have been. But if the ball orbits on any kind of errant path, it's a sure sign that your clubface was open or closed at launch time. And because you don't waste any

time shagging balls, you can spend more time fine-tuning your swing. Four ground stakes keep the unit anchored in place while you practice, and a simple adjustment allows you to hit either tee or fairway shots. You'll need four tools to put the Swing Groover to work: a screwdriver, a wrench, a hammer, and, of course, the club of your choice.

$26.95 from Austad's.

Swing Memory

With just five minutes of use a day, Swing Memory is supposed to help your muscles "memorize" the optimal swing plane and arc for your body type. Simply secure the unit to a wall or other flat surface at eye level (using either a suction-cup device or a permanent mounting plate), attach the swiveling rod and special practice club, and begin swinging on your correct plane and arc. Swing Memory puts an end to such swing no-nos as flying elbows, excess body swaying, and overactive hands.

$79.95 from The Golf Works; also from Austad's and Banff Golf.

SWING MIRROR

Here's a nifty way to see your own golf swing in action—without a video camera and recorder. This 9.5-inch convex mirror provides a wide field of vision, and its positioning crosshairs let you observe your own swing adjustments.

$35.50 from The Golf Works.

Swing Mirror

SWING-O-METER

Ever wonder why Davis Love III is one of the longest drivers on the PGA Tour? It's mostly a matter of clubhead speed. He can swing a golf club at 120 miles per hour, faster than any human being ever clocked. (Love is so long off the tee, in fact, that he consistently outdrives other pros with his one-iron.) Now, thanks to the Swing-O-Meter, you can clock the speed of your own golf swing at home or on the range. Simply clamp this device to the shaft of any golf club (just above the whipping on your driver, for example) and let 'er rip. It will instantly measure and record your clubhead speed (from 50 to 110 mph) and your projected distance (from 125 to 275 yards). You can use the Swing-O-Meter indoors or out, although the manufacturer cautions against hitting real balls with the device attached to a club. While your swing may never quite be up to Love's speed, at least you'll be able to say that you've really clocked some of those drives.

$49.95 from Swing-O-Meter; also from The Golf Works.

SWING PLANE TRAINER

No, this isn't for practicing in the dark. The Swing Plane Trainer—a short shaft with a golf grip affixed to it—features built-in flashlights that project small beams of light from both ends. The beams of light let you check your alignment and swing plane from the beginning of your backswing to the end of your follow-through. If your swing is sound, the lights from both ends of the shaft will in turn point to (or be parallel to) the same straight line on the ground: your intended line to the target.

$49.95 from Swing's the Thing.

Swing Ring

Here's the ultimate swing doughnut: a two-piece, nickel- or gold-plated weight that can be fitted in seconds to any wood or iron—even to a putter. Because its adjustable interior ring is made of rubber, the Swing Ring can be securely fitted to any section of the shaft (above the whipping on a driver, for example), thus protecting your clubs from the

kind of damage that conventional swing doughnuts can cause. In addition to toning up and tuning up your golf muscles, the added weight of the Swing Ring promotes a smooth, slow takeaway; encourages a full shoulder turn and swing arc; and inhibits overswinging and hand separation. It's available in three different weights (7.5 ounces for professionals, 5.5 ounces for men, and 4.5 ounces for women and juniors) and includes a carrying case that can be easily attached to your golf bag.

$9.95 (nickel-plated) or $12.95 (gold-plated) from Swing Ring.

Swingrite

At first glance Swingrite looks like a conventional driver, but it's only for

Swing Ring

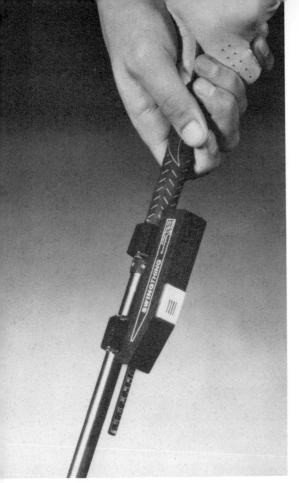

Swingthing

ious battery-powered training aid that lets you "hear" your speed and timing throughout each swing. Simply secure Swingthing to any club (with two Velcro straps), set its adjustable speed control to the desired swing speed (in miles per hour), and swing away. A built-in buzzer beeps steadily whenever your swing speed exceeds the selected setting. Gradually increase the setting to find your top speed and the point in your swing at which it occurs (preferably 10 to 15 inches after impact). Then set it 25 to 35 miles per hour below your top speed to check timing and acceleration. A beep before the ball? You're hitting too early ("casting"), which leads to an outside-in swing and produces pulls or slices. If your swing accelerates properly, the beep is delayed until the clubhead reaches the ball and continues well into the follow-through. The later and longer the buzzer sounds, in fact, the greater your distance and control. Swingthing can be used with any club, either while hitting balls or taking practice swings. It automatically resets after each swing and has no noticeable effect on a club's swingweight.

$44.95 from Edwin Watts Golf Shops; also from Golf Day Products, Las Vegas Discount Golf, and J. White Industries.

practice. A weighted mechanism in the clubhead "clicks" at the exact moment your wrists release before impact, vividly demonstrating exactly what release is and where it occurs in your downswing. The Swingrite training club features an adjustable power setting to accommodate players of any strength, and it can easily be reset (recocked) after each swing.

$49.95 from The Golf Works or Golfsmith.

SWINGTHING
Ever listened to your golf swing? That's the idea behind Swingthing, an ingen-

TEE-OFF
Ever dreamed of sending your golf ball into orbit? Tee-Off will do it for you, and in the process show whether your ball would have hooked, sliced, or sailed down the middle of the fairway. This practice aid features a wiffle-type ball that's suspended from a steel arm by unbreakable nylon cord; when hit with

Tee-Off: outdoor (top) and indoor models.

any wood or iron, the plastic ball orbits around the overhanging arm on a straight, inside-out, or outside-in path. The longer and straighter the ball orbits, the longer and straighter your shot would have been. Best of all, the ball is automatically "re-teed" after each hit.

The outdoor model ($14.95) has spikes that anchor it in the ground; the platform model ($21.95) can be used on any flat surface, indoors or out.

From Tee-Off; also from Golfsmith and J. White Industries.

TEMPO TRAINING CLUB

May the force be with you— centrifugal force, that is. If it isn't, you'll "hit from the top," close the clubface too early, and lose distance and control. The Tempo Training Club may look like a standard driver, but its highly flexible fiberglass shaft unmistakably demonstrates the perils of hitting from the top. Steady practice with the club should help you build a smooth, late release by letting you feel the sensation of centrifugal force working for you instead of against you. The men's Tempo Training Club is 43 inches long; the women's model is 41.5 inches long.

$44.50 from The Golf Works.

THE TOSKI TRAINER

Bob Toski, one of golf's top teaching pros and a regular on the Senior PGA Tour, doesn't look like your average ninja warrior. But Toski's betting his good name that learning to swing what amounts to a pair of *nun chuks*— the chain-and-stick weapons used in the martial arts— can fix three of the most common faults in golf: spinning the right shoulder out and around, rather than in and under, at the beginning of the downswing; "casting" the club (hitting from the top of the swing); and failing to properly rotate the hands through the impact zone. Toski collaborated on "Ninja Golf," as it's come to be called, with Ted Pollard, a martial-arts expert, three-handicap golfer, and onetime double for the late Bruce Lee.

The Toski Trainer consists of two weighted sticks that can be connected at the grip end with a strap. Each stick

Right: The Toski Trainer

is just over two feet long and has a ball attached by an unbreakable cord to the end. Simply hold the sticks, one in each hand, and swing with your hands close together—just as if you were swinging a club. If your shoulders or wrists rotate incorrectly, the sticks will click together or the balls will collide or gyrate wildly. But if you swing the sticks smoothly and correctly, the balls will effortlessly follow each other through the stroke. And warming up with the weighted sticks is supposed to help develop strength, flexibility, and control.

$99.95 (includes Toski's 20-minute VHS training cassette and a 56-page reference manual) from Objective Golf; also from National Golf Foundation.

TruSwing

This practice unit may provide unwelcome proof that your swing is something less than Sam Snead's. Four rotating plastic "flags" (one of them yellow and the rest blue) track your swing path, and a swiveling golf-ball-sized target checks your clubface position at impact. With an inside-out swing and square clubface contact, you'll move only the yellow flag. But if you swing from outside-in, or hit the ball with either the heel or toe of your club, one or more of TruSwing's blue flags will let you know the awful truth.

$34.95 from The Golf Works; also from Austad's.

Wrist-Magic

Study one of those stop-action photographs of a top player's swing at the moment of impact and you'll see that

TruSwing

the back of his left hand squarely faces the target and is slightly ahead of the clubhead. The typical high-handicapper, however, almost never manages to strike the ball with his leading hand and wrist in the proper position. As he enters the hitting zone his left wrist collapses, instantly changing the arc and plane of his swing, throwing the clubhead ahead of his hands, and draining his shot of power and accuracy. What's more, the top player, with his hands just a shade ahead of the clubhead at impact, actually reduces the club's effective loft—making his five-iron, for example, behave like a four-iron. The high-handicapper, whose hands trail the clubhead at impact, turns his five-iron into the functional equivalent of a seven-iron. If you've ever wondered why so many of your shots are high and weak, maybe you should try this shoehorn-shaped plastic brace on for size (and one size fits all, right- or left-handed). Simply slip Wrist-Magic under your golf glove as you practice—wearing it during play is a no-no under the Rules of Golf—and you may be able to break the curse of wrist collapse.

$4.95 from Everything For Golf.

GETTING THE
RIGHT GRIP

BLUE FINGER

If your golf game needs straightening
out, the folks who manufacture Blue
Finger claim they have the cure. Wrap-
ping this Band-Aid-size strip around
your index finger, they say, will keep
your clubs from sliding or twisting (even
in the rain), virtually eliminate your
slice, prevent blisters, and generally
improve your grip. Who could ask for
anything more?

*$2.99 for a package of 10 from Consoli-
dated Service Group.*

THE HOOKER GOLF GLOVE

Ben Hogan, perhaps the finest ball-
striker the game has ever known, once
wrote that he wished he had three right
hands with which to hit the ball.
Hogan's swing was a thing of beauty
and precision, and he approached the
hitting zone from the inside with awesome— but controlled— power. For many
middle- and high-handicap players,
however, right-hand dominance of the
golf swing spells nothing but disaster; it
generally produces an outside-in swing
path and almost inevitably leads to a
slicing problem. The idea behind The
Hooker Golf Glove is to restrain— and
retrain— the right hand and wrist by
harnessing them in proper position
throughout the swing (three Velcro
straps do the trick). It'll tame any last-
minute impulses to swipe at the ball
and otherwise prevent your right hand
and wrist from overpowering your

swing. Wear this glove on the practice range (it doesn't conform to the Rules of Golf) and you may soon see what it's like to play the game from the fairways. For what it's worth, The Hooker Golf Glove (which is available for right-handers only) carries the endorsement of Calvin Peete, who for many years has been one of the most consistently accurate players on the PGA Tour.

$18.95 from Las Vegas Discount Golf.

SHOTMAKER GOLF GLOVE

A sound swing starts with a sound grip, and now there's a simple way to make sure that your left hand is correctly placed on the club— whether you're hitting a driver or a sand wedge. The secret behind the Shotmaker Golf Glove is a rodlike insert that's sewn permanently into its palm. The insert locks your clubs in the same position every time you swing— so they can't slide, turn, or twist— and strengthens your grip at the same time. The Shotmaker Golf Glove is made of soft, supple, tan-colored cabretta, and is available in five men's sizes (small, medium, medium-large, large, and extra-large) and three women's sizes (small, medium, and large). While the glove doesn't conform to United States Golf Association rules, wear it enough at the practice range and soon a proper grip will be second nature.

$16.95 from Competitive Edge Golf; also from Austad's and Golf Day Products.

TRAINING GRIP

When you grip a golf club, is your right thumb directly on top of the shaft? If so, you're sorely in need of some remedial education (the right thumb and forefinger should cradle the grip in an inverted "V" position), and this Training Grip may just fit the bill. Its molded thumb and finger positions force you to properly place your hands on the club— and to keep them there throughout your swing. Although it doesn't conform to USGA regulations, the Training Grip is a terrific time-saver for beginners, slow learners, and anyone else who can't seem to master the first fundamental of a sound swing. Simply install one on a practice club and soon the proper grip will be a matter of muscle memory.

$5.50 from Florida Golf Warehouse; also from Austad's, Golf Day Products, The Golf Works, Golfsmith, Las Vegas Discount Golf, Northern Golf Ball Company, and J. White Industries.

LINING UP AND
LETTING GO

BALL FLIGHT VISUALIZER

Invented in Sweden by Björn "Basse" Friberg and field tested by 60 Swedish golf professionals, the Ball Flight Visualizer clearly demonstrates the causes of hooks, slices, pushes, and pulls. Here's how it works: The device's "tee zone" can be rotated to show the effect of different swing paths; a separate magnetized clubhead is used to show the effect of a square, open, or closed clubface. Two magnetized golf balls— one placed on the center of the tee and the other at the appropriate end point— illustrate the resulting flight path. Made of extremely tough water-resistant plastic, this teaching aid can be used indoors or out— or even mounted on a wall. (Left-handers simply use the reverse side.)

$105 from The Golf Works; also from Banff Golf.

CHALK IT

Are you sure your alignment is correct? With Chalk It, a convenient aerosol spray, you won't be guessing anymore. Just draw an alignment arrow pointed at the target and a cross line for ball positioning. It's also an ideal way to draw a target area for chipping or pitching practice. When used as directed, Chalk It won't harm grass.

$3.25 from The Golf Works or Practice House Golf; also from Golf Day Products.

JACK GROUT TEE-SQUARE

He set Jack Nicklaus straight early on, and now he'll do the same for you. With the Jack Grout Tee-Square, you can study the golf swing— from fundamentals to fine points— with the man who's been Nicklaus's lifelong teacher and trouble-shooter. The lesson begins with theTee-Square, an adjustable alignment aid that teaches you the proper positions of your feet, ball, and club (driver through wedge) in relation to your intended target line. By using the Tee-Square in tandem with Grout's 131-page book, *On the Lesson Tee*, and his 43-minute video, "Keys to Consistency," your session with the master swing-builder can last as long as you'd like.

$79.95 from Ardent Video Publishing; also from Richard E. Donovan Enterprises and The Golf Works.

MAGNETIC LIE ANGLE TOOL

If you consistently pull or push your iron shots, this simple teaching aid— a red-tipped metal rod that's mounted on a magnetic base— may show you that the fault lies in the way you align and sole the clubface at address, not in the way you swing. When the magnet is attached to the face of any iron, the rod illustrates how a golf ball would leave the clubface after impact. If the clubhead is properly aligned and soled at address, the rod will point directly at your target; if the clubface is open or closed, however, or if the iron is soled improperly (too flat or too upright), the rod will point to the right or left. The Magnetic Lie Angle Tool is especially effective in demonstrating how to play uphill, downhill, and sidehill lies.

$6.95 from The Golf Works.

Magnetic Lie Angle Tool

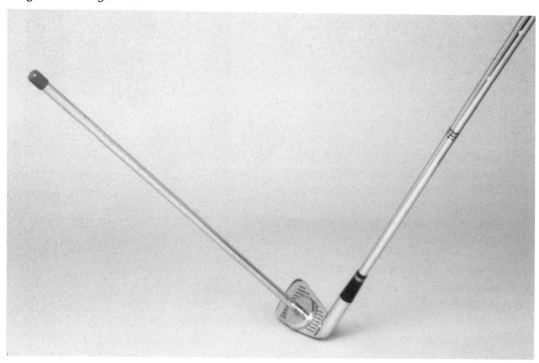

Pro-Align

PRO-ALIGN

Developed by David Bisbee, a former
touring pro now with John Jacobs'
Practical Golf Schools, this three-in-one
practice aid teaches proper alignment,
aim, and swing path. Its adjustable
alignment track positions your feet and
shoulders the proper distance from the
ball, whether you're driving or putting.
A "loft align" indicator behind the
impact zone trains you to set up with
the clubface square to the target. And
the Pro-Align's "pathfinder" track (which
can be used separately, if desired) uses
negative reinforcement to help you
groove the all-important "inside-to-
square" swing; errant swings will cause
your clubhead to hit the unit's plastic
flag with a resounding whack.

*$32.95 from The Golf Works; also from
Banff Golf and Golf Day Products.*

SAM SNEAD'S POWER STANCE MAT

This portable, rubber-backed mat lets
you step into Sam Snead's golf shoes
anytime you want, at home or on the
practice range. It illustrates his exact
alignment, stance, and ball position for
each shots— from drives to chips and
pitches.

*$12.95 from The Golf Works; also from
Gary Wiren's "Golf Around the World."*

SET-UP MASTER

Are you always square to the target
when you set up for a shot? This portable training unit folds out to show the
proper position of both feet in relation
to the golf ball and can be adjusted for
any wood or iron in your bag— from
driver through sand wedge. The Set-Up

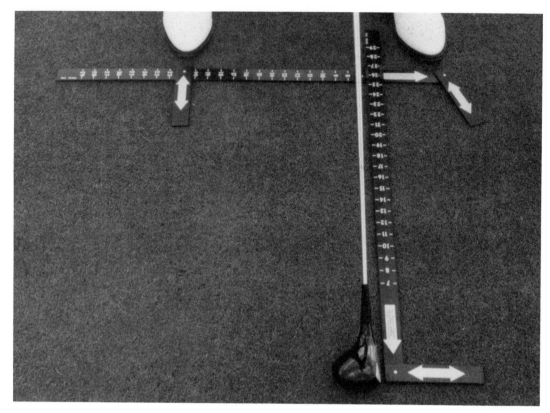

Set-Up Master

Master's target indicator lines up parallel with your shoulders and is aimed along the intended line of flight.

$12.95 from The Golf Works.

THE SLICEBUSTER

Add lots of garlic and some bicarbonate of soda to your spaghetti sauce, the old joke goes, and you can both create and cure indigestion at the same time. The Slicebuster brings the same concept to the practice range. This two-in-one training aid not only can help you cure a chronic hook or slice, but also can help you learn how to hit intentional draws and fades. While an expert shotmaker has the ability to move the ball from left to right or vice versa on demand (around a sharp dogleg, for example), the typical high-handicapper is forced to compensate for his uncontrollable curve ball. As the legendary Bobby Jones once put it: "The dub allows for the hook or slice only because he has always had it before; he does not know why he has it, nor how to stop it; above all, he does not know how much he will get, or if he will get it at all."

The Slicebuster consists of a rectangular metal base, an upright arm in the shape of an inverted "L," and an adjustable crossbar that's suspended above the ball. If you want to cure a hook or slice, simply adjust the crossbar so that it's parallel to the base of the unit and aimed along your target line; then, as you address the ball, squarely align your shoulders, hips, knees, and feet with the crossbar. As you swing, it enables you to better visualize your target line and to keep your clubhead moving on the proper path through the hitting zone.

If you want to create a draw, fade, hook, or slice, adjust the crossbar so that it's aimed not along your target line, but along the initial flight line you're seeking to achieve. (If you want to fade the ball, for example, the crossbar would point to the left of your target.) As you address the ball, line yourself up with the crossbar. Next, without changing your grip or body position relative to the initial flight line, open or close the clubface as little or as much as you need to produce the desired curvature. Then simply swing the club as you would for any other shot. Your body alignment and swing path will start the ball off in the right direction, and the angle of the clubface at impact will impart the left-to-right or right-to-left spin that causes the ball to curve back toward its ultimate target. The Slicebuster can be set up in just a couple of minutes and comes with a step-by-step instruction booklet.

$14.95 from Everything for Golf.

STANCE GUIDE

"It's so simple that even I can't believe how well it works," says Bob Delgado, the inventor of Stance Guide. "When you look at it, people say this can't be all there is to it."

"It," as it turns out, is a pair of bright-colored, adhesive arrows that, when properly applied to the toes of your golf shoes, point in the same direction as your intended target line. With every shot— from drives to putts— the omnipresent arrows help you make sure that your feet and body are perfectly aligned to the target. Because they're waterproof and soil-resistant, a package of Stance Guides (three sets of stickers) should last at least a season; a special golf ball that's designed to improve your alignment on the putting green is also included. Yes, your golfing companions may joke about those funny-looking arrows on your shoes, but so what if really they help your game?

$10 from Golf Rite Products.

STRETCH-ALIGNER

If you ever check your alignment by placing clubs on the ground, this versatile little practice aid is bound to come in handy— whether you're in your backyard, at the driving range, or on the practice green. The Stretch-Aligner's elastic cord lets you lay down a stance or target line up to 10 feet long, and by using its ground pins and guide markers you can even create a right-angled, ball-positioning line.

$1.65 from The Golf Works.

SWING-R SWAY CONTROL

If you're either all over the fairway or seldom on it, chances are you're swaying as you swing. This handy little practice device is aimed at helping you hit 'em straight down the middle by checking any excess head or body movement. Simply adjust the Swing-R

Sway Control so that you're looking at the golf ball through a small loop on its overhanging arm; if the ball moves out of the loop as you swing, no doubt about it—you're swaying. You also can use Swing-R Sway Control on the practice putting green to make sure that your eyes are directly over the ball at address (if they're not, you won't be able to see the target line correctly).

$6.50 from Everything for Golf.

Swing-Guide

If your golf shots seem to go every which way but where you want them to, the Swing-Guide practice mat may help straighten everything out. This three-by-four-foot piece of artificial turf illustrates the proper alignment, stance, ball position, and swing path for woods as well as for long, medium, and short irons.

$42.95 (includes three practice tees and a practice ball) from Golf Day Products.

Top-Tips

Nothing is surer to upset your concentration at address than lingering doubts about the correct hand, foot, and ball positions for the club you've chosen. Top-Tips are a convenient memory-jogger. The simple diagrams printed on these round vinyl stickers, which permanently adhere and conform to the tops of your grips, show how to address the ball with each club—from driver through wedge.

$2.75 from The Golf Works; also from Golf Day Products.

SHARPENING YOUR SHORT GAME

BLAST MASTER

To help perfect those fearsome explosion shots from greenside sand traps, try practicing with the Blast Master: a doughnut-shaped vinyl disk that's placed under the ball to create a larger target for the sand wedge. Simply hit down and through its outer edge and "splash" both the Blast Master and the ball out of the sand. While it's not for use during actual play, some diligent practice with the Blast Master may get rid of your sand-trap shakes once and for all.

A package of three is $3 from The Golf Works or Practice House Golf.

THE BUNKERBOARD

Here's another clever practice device aimed at upping your percentage of "sand saves." Made of sturdy, treated oak, the Bunkerboard is contoured to control the path and depth of your sand wedge as it cuts through sand. Permanent guidelines show where the ball should be placed and where the clubhead should enter and exit from the sand. If your sand game leaves something to be desired, practicing with the Bunkerboard might be a real confidence-builder.

$29.95 from The Golf Works; also from Banff Golf.

Blast Master

The Bunkerboard

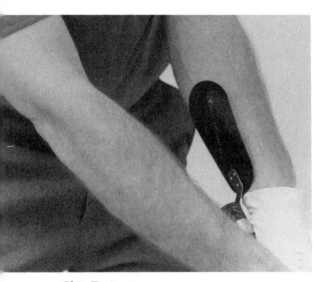

Chip Trainer

CHIP TRAINER

If "wristiness" is wreaking havoc with your short game, this simple little training aid may help straighten things out. The Chip Trainer consists of a plastic flange that's easily attached and removed from any club by means of a metal clip. If the flange remains against your forearm as you hit chips or short pitch shots, your arm and wrist motion is correct. But if it separates from your forearm during the stroke, your technique is too "wristy."

$7.95 from The Golf Works.

THE KOSTIS KRUTCH

This simple but effective practice device was designed by and named for Peter Kostis, one of golf's top teaching professionals. The Kostis Krutch— an adjustable aluminum brace that's positioned on the forearms just below the elbows— encourages your arms, wrists, and

Chip Trainer

hands to move as a unit in chipping and putting.

$22.50 from Banff Golf.

The Separator

If you've lost that all-important "feel" in your short game, here's an ingenious little device that can help you regain it. Simply attach the Separator to any club you use for shots that don't require full breaking of the wrists— pitches, chips, and putts. Then grip the club with your left hand and the Separator with your right hand. By keeping your hands apart, the unit encourages smooth acceleration through the ball and all but eliminates "wristiness" and other bad short-game habits.

$34.95 from The Golf Works; also from Banff Golf.

Wrist Lock

Many professionals teach that a firm left wrist provides maximum control for pitching, chipping, or putting. If you don't believe it, try practicing these shots while wearing Wrist Lock. This plastic guide is positioned inside a golf glove, to just above the knuckles, and secured at the top end by an elastic strap. You won't be able to bend your wrist, which should mean greater control of the clubface and straighter, more solid, shots.

$4.50 from The Golf Works or Practice House Golf; also from J. White Industries.

CHAPTER TWO
THE ART AND SCIENCE OF PUTTING

Clyde Guide and Arm Guide

When Hal Sutton's putter went ice cold back in 1985, he turned to the late teaching pro Davis Love, Jr., one day and asked: "Do you have time to watch me hit a few putts? I can't seem to get the ball started on line." Love soon noticed that Sutton's forearms weren't squarely aligned with the target, and to prove his point Love reached for the flagstick. When he held it across Sutton's forearms, it pointed 20 degrees left of the cup.

The rest, as they say, is history. Sutton started knocking 'em in and three weeks later won the Memphis Classic by shooting a final-round 65 and sinking a long putt on the first hole of a sudden-death playoff.

You may not have Sutton's stroke or Love's eye, but these two metal units may help. The V-shaped rods of the Clyde Guide rest against your forearms and maintain their correct position through the swing or putting stroke (too much wrist action will cause the rods to waggle). The adjustable Arm Guide maintains the correct angle formed between your shoulders, elbows, and hands.

$14.95 from The Golf Works.

Clyde Guide and Arm Guide

The Edge Putter

Are you sure that you're lining yourself up properly on the putting green? If your answer to that question is anything but yes, The Edge may be able to set you straight once and for all. The secret behind this putter— and we're speaking literally here— is a mirror that attaches in seconds to the back of the clubhead. It allows you to sight your ball, its intended path, and the cup without lifting your eyes from the putter itself. By practicing with the mirror in place, you can make sure that the face of the putter is always aligned with your intended target line. When the mirror is replaced with a brass insert (counterbalanced for the same feel), The Edge meets all USGA specifications.

$35 from Snyder Golf Creations.

ELECTRIC PUTTING PARTNER

So you haven't yet trained Fido to retrieve those practice putts? Then maybe you need the Electric Putting Partner, which faithfully returns them to your feet and never needs to be taken for a walk. Its regulation-size target is divided into three zones so that you practice putting to the left side, right side, or center of the cup. You can adjust the ball-return mechanism for long, short, or in-between putts, and it'll even send them back in any direction you'd like.

$14.95 from Las Vegas Discount Golf; also from Golf Day Products, Nevada Bob's Discount Golf, Northern Golf Ball Company, and Polar Golf.

FORCE II PUTTER GRIP

Next time you step on the putting green, may the force be with you. By adding some extra ounces above your hands, the backweight that's built into the butt end of the Force II Putter Grip may turn the shortest stick in your bag into a better-balanced weapon. Feel is everything in putting, the theory goes, and the more you control the clubhead the more putts you'll sink.

$4.75 from Austad's.

GOLF GREEN SPEED-METER

Back in the mid-1930s Edward Stimpson, an amateur golfer and USGA Committeeman from Massachusetts, invented what since has become known as the "Stimpmeter"—a grooved, 36-inch-long aluminum track that's used to measure the speed of putting greens. When a golf ball is placed in a slot at one end of the Stimpmeter and the track is raised to a level at which the ball will roll freely down the groove and onto the green, the distance it travels determines the speed of the putting surface. (In official practice, the speed of a green represents the average of four rolls of the ball in different directions.) A Stimpmeter speed of 10 feet is considered fast, and most professionals on the PGA Tour think of any speed greater than 12 feet as something on the order of greased lightning.

The USGA, which began manufacturing Stimpmeters in 1979, receives orders for a couple of hundred or so every year. There's just one catch: The USGA won't sell you a Stimpmeter unless you represent a golf club. Fortunately, however, golfers who want to reduce the art of putting into more of a science do have an alternative. This Golf Green Speed-Meter is a close cousin to the Stimpmeter, and anybody can buy one.

$25.50 from Golfsmith.

GOLF PUTT STROKE GUIDE

If your putts seem to go every which way but in the hole, either you need an eye examination or your putter needs some straightening out. While this portable practice track won't do anything for your eyesight, it will train your putter to behave properly whenever you let it out of the bag. Simply place the wayward weapon between the unit's parallel rails and it will have no choice but to move straight back and through the ball. There's also a calibrated scale on the outer rail to help you fine-tune your feel for distance. You can use the Golf Putt Stroke Guide at home, in the office, or on the practice green, and if it doesn't soon have you sinking more putts you'd better make an appointment with the ophthalmologist.

$24.95 from Everything for Golf.

GOLFSMITH XL DESIGN PUTTER GRIP

Take a tip from Phil Rodgers, the former PGA touring pro who's been something of a short-game guru to Jack Nicklaus and others. In his highly regarded how-to book, *Play Lower Handicap Golf*, Rodgers writes: "An orthopedic surgeon once told me that there are about four times as many nerves in your hands and wrists than in your shoulders and arms. Which is to say, if you're in a pressure-putt situation you don't want to— can't— depend on so vast and complicated a collection of physical parts. You're better off hitting the ball with your arms and shoulders. There should be no wrist motion. There are fine putters who have some, but the less the better."

If you want to practice what Rodgers preaches— "no wrist motion"— why not try the Golfsmith XL Design Putter Grip on for size? It's designed to help you achieve a smooth, pendulum-style putting stroke by taking your wrists out of the picture once and for all. The XL stands for extra large, which this com-

position grip unquestionably is. Its flat front surface, in fact, is more than an inch wide (nearly twice as wide as conventional paddle-style grips), which stabilizes your wrists and helps keep your putter square to the intended target line. Think of it this way: The fewer moving parts in your putting stroke, the less likely it is to break down.

$2.75 from Golfsmith; also from Florida Golf Warehouse.

INDOOR PRACTICE GREEN

If putting is about all you practice during those long winter months indoors, here's a jumbo, kidney-shaped green that will help you sharpen up your short-iron work at the same time. Its four-by-nine-foot polypropylene surface is designed to mimic the distinctive speed and feel of Bermuda grass, and a matching 18-by-24-inch mat lets you gently pitch or chip balls up to the hole. Or, more accurately, *holes*: The five cups cut into the slightly inclined surface of this green are positioned to let you practice from a variety of angles, and they're just four inches in diameter (a quarter-inch smaller than regulation) to sharpen your accuracy. There's also a set of five turf-topped plugs that fit flush with the surface to smoothly cover any cups you don't want to use, and a fenced border around the green's target area to snag any errant or speeding shots. The Indoor Putting Green is backed with urethane foam to prevent slipping and rolls up for easy storage.

$146.50 from Hammacher Schlemmer.

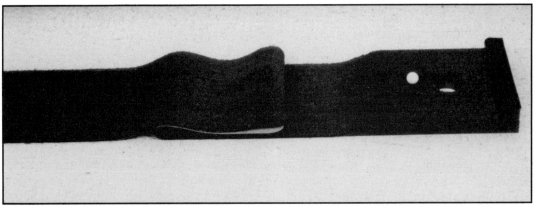

Indoor Putting Mat

INDOOR PUTTING MAT

This 12-foot-long mat, used in your home or office, simulates a real putting green. Roll it out and putt into an elevated, standard-diameter cup; when you're done, simply roll it up for storage. The putting surface is 18 inches wide and rolls out flat for a smooth, even surface.

$34.95 from The Golf Works.

THE KLANGER

The idea here is to point The Klanger's parallel aluminum rails to the target, with the toe and heel of your putter barely clearing them; then practice putting without allowing the clubhead to "klang" against either rail. The Klanger includes a special marking pen that you can use, among other things, to draw a series of dots around the center seam of your ball; when the

The Klanger

dotted ring is lined up with the intended path of your putt, each perfect stroke will make it roll right toward the target.

$21.95 from Las Vegas Discount Golf; also from Practice House Golf.

MacGregor Putting Green

"Six feet, straight in," you think to yourself. "Easy." Then you step up to the ball. Suddenly, inexplicably, you think of all those six-footers you've missed before, and the fear of missing this one creeps into a corner of your consciousness. You try to block it out by promising yourself that you're not going to leave another birdie putt short. Never up, never in, they say. But now you must actually move the putter, and somewhere along the line, without even realizing it, you begin trying to stab or steer the ball into the hole. As your eyes turn toward the cup, you already know that you've missed the putt. It's weak again, and wide enough to make even the application of a little body english look foolish. You mutter a four-letter word under your breath and say to your partner, as you have so many times in the past, "Sorry."

Sound familiar? If so, the MacGregor Putting Green may help you stop sweating and start sinking those heretofore elusive six-footers. Its foam-backed putting surface, which measures six and a half feet long, approximates the speed and feel of an actual green; a molded plastic ramp at the far end not only elevates the regulation-size cup but automatically sends every putt back to your feet (even if you miss). A white line down the middle helps you make sure that you start— and keep— your putts on line to the hole.

$39.99 from Nevada Bob's Discount Golf.

Miya Computer Putting Checker

If those nerves of steel vanish the minute you step onto the putting green, meet the Miya Computer Putting Checker. This portable practice unit weighs in at only three pounds and features a series of light-beam sensors that track both the angle of your putter face and the position of its sweet spot as you stroke the ball. A computerized screen instantly displays the exact path your putter traveled over the sensors; it shows whether your putter face was turned in, turned out, or was square at each of three critical positions— downstroke, impact, and follow-through— and also illustrates the relative positions of your putter's sweet spot.

If your putting stroke leaves something to be desired, the machine emits a short beep. But achieve perfection and you'll hear a long beep of congratulations. The device works indoors or out, with any putter, and with or without a ball. Several accessories are available, including a Correcting Guide ($24.95) that helps you keep the face of your putter square as it passes over the sensors.

$198 from Miya Epoch; also from J. White Industries.

Miya Putting Trainer

Unless your floorboards at home are incurably warped, you'll find it all but impossible to practice breaking putts on the living-room carpet. That's where the Miya Putting Trainer comes in. Its inclined, grasslike putting surface is nearly six feet long, and by adjusting a leveling device behind the cup you can create a left-to-right break or vice versa. A built-in gutter automatically returns balls to the foot of the unit. You can putt to a regulation-size cup or practice with one of two skill-sharpening inserts. By rotating an oval-shaped insert in various ways, you can refine your feel for direction and distance. By inserting a smaller-than-regulation round cup, you can hone accuracy. The Miya Putting Trainer easily folds up into a 39-inch-long carrying case.

$169 from Miya Epoch; also from J. White Industries.

THE 19TH HOLE PAR ELECTRIC PUTTING CUP

This one takes all the work out of putting practice. After you putt into a target the exact size of a regulation cup, an adjustable-speed return mechanism sends the ball right back to you. (If you miss wide, though, you're on your own.)

$12.95 from The Golf Works; also from Golfsmith.

THE 19TH HOLE PUTTING GREEN

Why let a hardwood floor, linoleum tile, or sculptured carpeting stand in the way of a little indoor putting practice? The 19th Hole Putting Green can cover a multitude of sinful surfaces— in your home or office. The spongy foam-rubber mat measures one foot wide by nine feet long, rolls up for easy storage, and comes with a handy plastic putting guide (to help you check your ball placement and alignment).

$6.25 from Austad's; also from Golfsmith.

THE 19TH HOLE ULTIMATE ELECTRIC PUTTING CUP

This electric putting cup, unlike most others on the market, treats you to one of the sweetest sensations in all of golf: the sight and sound of your ball actually dropping into the hole. You aim for a regulation-size cup (4.25-inch-diameter) in the middle of the unit, but if you hit your putt too hard a set of speed deflection pins will keep it from entering the hole. And should you wish to engage in a little friendly competition, you'll find the 19th Hole Ultimate Electric Putting Cup to be an accommodating— and even forgiving— golfing companion. The ramp leading up to the hole is divided into several numbered scoring zones, and the unit's automatic-return mechanism dutifully sends both hits and misses back from whence they came.

$17.95 from Austad's.

NoRamp

Sinking practice putts doesn't have to be an uphill battle— or at least that's the idea behind the NoRamp adjustable putting cup. It's not really a cup, in fact, but an open-mouthed, corral-like device that's placed flat on the putting surface. Once you've mastered running putts into NoRamp's 4.25-inch opening (the size of a regulation cup), narrow its width and you'll be working toward even deadlier accuracy.

$3.95 from Everything for Golf.

Oak Putter Stand

Out of sight, out of mind, the saying goes, so why keep the paraphernalia you need to practice putting tucked away in the closet? This handsome, solid-oak stand holds two weapons of your choice at the ready (along with a couple of golf balls), and a regulation-size putting cup is built into the felt-covered practice ramp that doubles as its base. The Oak Putter Stand is 38 inches high, finished in a natural stain, and occupies only a square foot on the floor. And thanks to the brass finial on top, it's a snap to move around your office, den, or other practice haven.

$59.95 from The Golf Works.

Oversize Putting Green

If those snaking 10-footers give you the shakes, practicing on this extra-large putting green may help you get rid of them. Its foam-backed, polypropylene surface is two feet wide and 12 feet long, and two regulation-size cups at each end let you spend more time sinking putts and less time retrieving them. And because both ends of the Oversize Putting Green are inclined, each cup has a different break.

$49.95 from Golf Day Products.

Dave Pelz Putting Track

Dave Pelz entered college on a golf scholarship and graduated with a degree in physics. But after 14 years as a research scientist at NASA's Goddard Space Flight Center, he decided to take a one-year leave of absence to manufacture and market the Dave Pelz Teacher Putter (see below). Inspired by its success, Pelz resigned from NASA in 1976 and went into the golf business full-time. His silent partner in the venture was "Perfy," a mechanical putting robot he'd invented several year earlier. The robot's flawless putting stroke and permanent immunity from the yips paved Pelz's way to several other inventions, among them the Dave Pelz Putting Track, which he developed with PGA touring pro Jim Simons. Here's how it works: Adjust this arched, railroad-track-like device to slightly more than the width of your putter, position it on the floor or practice green, and try to smoothly stroke the ball down the middle without letting your putter touch either rail. When practice makes perfect, you're well on your way to deadly accuracy.

$35 from Adams Golf.

Dave Pelz Teacher Putter

Even if you know the precise location of your putter's sweet spot (and many golfers don't), how can you be sure that you're actually striking the ball on the spot? One way is to dust some chalk or talcum powder on the face of your putter before you hit the ball, a practice technique that grows more tedious with each passing stroke. A better way is to use the Dave Pelz Teacher Putter, which utilizes two ingenious inserts— one for practice and one for play— to help you "memorize" the feeling of a sweetly stroked putt.

The practice insert, when fitted to the face of the putter, "traps" the sweet spot between two protruding prongs. Hit the ball dead on the sweet spot and the prongs won't get in your way. Miss on either side, however, and the prongs will let you know in no uncertain terms. When you're ready to head out onto the course, simply switch inserts (the other one is fitted to the back of the clubhead) and you'll have a putter than conforms to USGA regulations.

$25 from Adams Golf.

PLUMB BOB TRAINING TOOL

When it comes to reading greens, are you illiterate? If so, maybe you need a little remedial education in the art of plumb bobbing, an arcane skill that can help you discern which way your ball is likely to break on the putting surface. While plumb bobbing isn't for everyone— Ben Crenshaw, Hale Irwin, and Bob Tway do it, but Jack Nicklaus, Greg Norman, and Tom Watson don't— it can come in handy on greens with particularly hard-to-read breaks.

Plumb bobbing helps you see how the ground slopes under your feet. Here's how it works. Stand directly behind the ball, using one eye to sight a straight line through the ball and to the cup; then, still sighting through the same eye, hold the putter lightly between your thumb and forefinger, let it hang at arm's length in front of you, and position it so that the lowest portion of the shaft bisects the ball. Without moving your head, look up at the cup. If the cup is to the left of the shaft, the putt should break right to left; if the cup is to the right, the putt should break left to right.

If all this leaves you plumb confused, take heart. Fortunately, there's a way to get the hang of plumb bobbing faster than you can say Fuzzy Zoeller (one of its top practitioners on the PGA Tour). The Plumb Bob Training Tool— a plastic gizmo that snaps to the shaft of your putter— will help you master this tricky technique in no time, and the accompanying booklet by golf instructor Dean Reinmuth, "Speed Reading For Golf Greens," will help you develop a soft touch and a sharp eye for slope, speed, grain, and grass type.

$19.95 from Par-Phernalia Golf Products.

THE PRECISION PUTTING SYSTEM

Satchel Paige, one of baseball's all-time great pitchers, had a favorite practice technique for sharpening his accuracy from the mound: He'd place a chewing-gum wrapper on one corner of the plate and aim to a spot directly above it. Many of golf's greatest putters have applied the same principle on the practice green, and for good reason. In addition to sharpening your aim and accuracy, repeatedly rolling practice putts up to a tee, coin, or some other small object can give you an important psychological edge. It can make the real target seem as big as a bushel basket.

The Precision Putting System has the same objective in mind, but takes exactly the opposite tack to help get you there. It's the brainchild of PGA Professional Rob Bradley, who observed that most poor putters tend to strike— not stroke— the ball, a problem that has little if anything to do with the size of their target. So Bradley simply built a bigger ball— a hollow-cored plastic sphere that's specifically intended for putting practice. Although his PPS ball is nearly as big as a tennis ball, it

The Precision Putting System

weighs about the same as a regulation golf ball, requires about the same amount of effort to move, and is otherwise designed— right down to the dimples— to roll and break like the real thing. And because it has roughly the same surface-resiliency characteristics as a regulation golf ball, it bounces off the face of a putter with pretty much the same feel.

The Precision Putting System includes a canister of three oversized balls and a booklet that shows you how to make the most of practicing with them. Follow the instructions to the tee— er, to the green— and you should develop a smooth, pendulum-style putting stroke. After a little bit of practice you may even begin to stare down your putts in a whole new light. The PPS balls will make that Titleist of yours seem downright tiny, and as for the hole itself, how could you possibly miss something that huge?

$29.95 from Precision Putting Systems.

PROFESSIONAL GOLF PUTTING CUP
Looking for a practice putting cup with few frills and a price to match? Look no

further. The Professional Golf Putting Cup is made of unbreakable green plastic and provides a regulation-size target with a gentle incline in front and a removable yellow flagstick in back.

Professional Golf Putting Cup

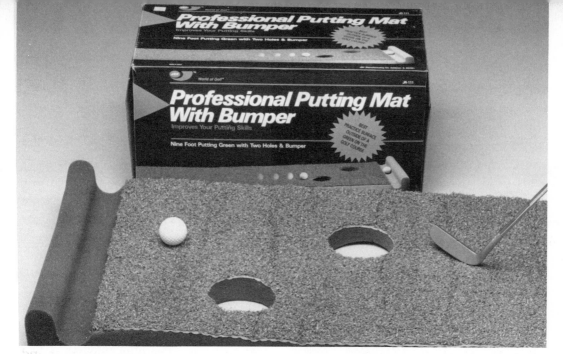

Pro Practice Putting Green

Pack one of these in your golf bag and you'll never again have to worry about competing for an open cup on a crowded practice green.

$2 from Snyder Golf Creations; also from Northern Golf Ball Company.

Pro Practice Putting Green

Never up, never in, they say, but if your living-room putts frequently wind up under the dining-room table, you may have some use for the Pro Practice Putting Green. Its 18-inch-wide, 9-foot-long surface is made of "slow roll" artificial grass, and a built-in backstop snags those high-velocity putts. Two regulation-size cups have been cut into the green's inclined target area, but a matching plug lets you tackle them one at a time.

$29.60 from Golfsmith; also from Las Vegas Discount Golf.

Pro-Green

"Drive for show," the saying goes, "and putt for dough." Yessiree, and here's a way to practice those big-money putts in the privacy of your own home (or office). Pro-Green's foam-backed, "Turf-Strand" surface closely simulates the speed and roll of the real thing, and adjustable legs beneath its inclined target area let you practice the tricky breaking putts that are so easy to miss when it really counts. Pro-Green's putting surface is 18 inches wide and 11 feet long; a 15-foot-long Tour Edition, which allows you to practice short chips, also is available.

$49.95 (or $65 for the Tour Edition) from Herrington.

Putt-a-Bout Auto Return Putting Green

Here's a putting green that sends the ball back to your feet— even if you miss

Puttband-Swingband

the cup. Putt-a-Bout's foam-backed, grasslike putting surface is a foot wide and nine feet long, and a molded plastic ramp not only elevates the cup but automatically returns every putt (gravity, not electricity, does the trick).

$35.95 from Golf Day Products.

PUTTBAND-SWINGBAND
This training aid won't turn you into a George Low or a Ben Crenshaw, but it's bound to improve— and maybe even groove— your putting stroke. Just ask Calvin Peete or any of the other 100-plus PGA touring pros who practice with the Puttband-Swingband. Invented by two PGA teaching pros, Jimmy Self and Charlie Schnaubel, the unit consists of an adjustable metal track and a set of special rubber bands that can be slipped over the head of a putter (or

other club) and fastened to pegs on both ends of the track. Lengthening the track— it's 36 inches long when retracted and 69 inches long when fully extended— increases the tension on the rubber bands.

When you slip the looped midsection of the red rubber band— the "Puttband"— over your putter, the unit will not only keep the clubface square to the target but control the length and acceleration of your putting stroke. As you practice, you'll also be strengthening key muscle groups in your hands, wrists, and arms and developing the kind of muscle memory that builds consistency and confidence on the putting green. (The blue "Swingband," with greater tension than its red counterpart, is used for full-swing drills. Because it keeps your clubhead on the correct path through the hitting zone, it's an especially effective way to cure a chronic outside-in swing.)

The Puttband-Swingband can be used indoors or out and includes a vinyl carrying case.

$42.95 from The Golf Works; also from Banff Golf and Herrington.

Putt-Caster

Putt-Caster

Putt-Caster

Combine a putter and a fishing reel and you've got the Putt-Caster. When clamped to the shaft of your putter (or, for chipping and pitching practice, to a short iron), this gizmo enables you to "reel in" a tethered practice ball just like a fish—without chasing, stooping, or even moving your feet. A swivel mounted in the monofilament nylon line prevents it from twisting and allows the ball to roll or fly freely on a true path. And, perhaps best of all, you'll never lose the ball.

$29.50 from Ban Products.

Putt-in-Cup

If you think of your wall-to-wall carpet- ing as one big putting green, here's a nifty way to simulate a regulation cup without drilling a hole into the floor. Simply fit the Putt-in-Cup into any standard heating vent in a carpeted area and you've got a realistic target that's level with the surface. Best of all, you don't even need to take it out when you turn on the heat or air-condition- ing; vents at both ends of the Putt-in- Cup allow air to flow freely from the duct below.

$19.95 from J. White Industries.

Putt Master Putting Carpet

Roll it out and roll 'em in. The synthetic surface of the Putt Master Putting Carpet is designed to mimic the look, speed, and feel of a real putting green. It's two feet wide and nine feet long, and a pair of elevated, regulation-size holes at one end let you practice putting from a variety of angles.

$29 from Competitive Edge Golf.

Putt-R-Buddy

PUTT-R-BUDDY

If you have trouble concentrating over putts, the Putt-R-Buddy just might help. Imagine a putter with a golf ball for a clubhead— that's the Putt-R-Buddy— and then imagine the control it takes to actually putt with it. After you've practiced with this unconventional (and, by the way, illegal) putter, the sweet spot on your real putter will seem downright gigantic.

$25 from The Golf Works or Matzie Golf; also from J. White Industries.

PUTT SQUARE

Putting doesn't require a great deal of physical strength, flexibility, or coordination. But it does require accurate alignment and the right "feel" for speed and distance. That's where Putt Square comes in handy. Placed on a carpet or practice green, it helps ensure that you and the face of your putter are properly aligned and helps you adjust the length of your backswing and follow-through for specific putting distances.

$18.50 from The Golf Works.

PUTT WIZZ

This practice putting mat has an elevated, regulation-size cup, but you'll never have to bend over to retrieve a ball from the hole; gravity gently rolls it out the left side of the unit. Putt Wizz's foam-backed, synthetic turf is 12 feet long and nondirectional, allowing your ball to roll smoothly up the 2.5-inch ramp without breaking left or right.

$84.95 from Enticements.

PUTTING TRAINER

Is the face of your putter square to the target line at impact? The Putting Trainer, which consists of two golf balls connected by a small plastic cylinder, will tell you as you practice. If the face of your putter is open at impact, the Putting Trainer will roll sharply to the right; if the face of your putter is closed, it will roll sharply to the left. Simple, huh?

$6.95 from Golf Day Products; also from Northern Golf Ball Company.

PUTTING TUTOR

Practicing with nearly any putting cup— even a tumbler turned sidelong on the living-room carpet— can help you with the straight-in, slightly uphill putt. It's the easiest shot in golf. But if you want to practice putts that break slightly or sharply to the left or right, you need something a little more treacherous— something, say, like the Putting Tutor.

A rotating wheel under the Putting

Putt Square

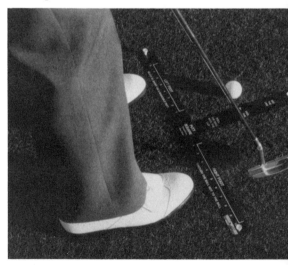

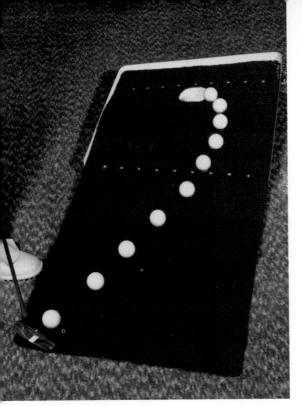

Putting Tutor

Tutor allows you to adjust the slope of its four-foot-long surface—which is designed to simulate a fast, well-groomed green—and to create breaks of varying severity. Parallel rows of white marks below and behind the hole, much like the dots and arrows on a bowling lane, help you "spot" the path of a breaking putt and aim for a target between the ball and the hole rather than the cup itself.

$29.95 from Indoor Golf (a matching green that extends the Putting Tutor's surface to eight feet is $4 extra).

THE REEL PUTTER

Amy Seiden was just eight years old when she decided to spend less time in the living room retrieving her father's missed practice putts and more time in front of the drawing board. Ms. Seiden, it turns out, is an inventor, and her decision seems to have paid off in spades: She no longer shags for her dad and is "Exec-U-Tive Vice President in charge of new ideas" at Exec-U-Putt, Inc., a family-owned company that distributes her Reel Putter. With this fishing-reel-on-a-putter gizmo, you—like Mr. Seiden—can retrieve any putt, made or missed, with a few twists of the wrist. The reel's lightweight monofilament line is attached to a gold-colored golf ball on a swivel, allowing it to roll drag-free on a true path. The brass-plated putter telescopes from 36 inches down to 17 inches, and, along with the golf ball, can be mounted on a wooden base that doubles as a putting cup.

$59.95 from Exec-U-Putt; also from A2Z/ The Best of Everything, Austad's, and Las Vegas Discount Golf.

The Reel Putter

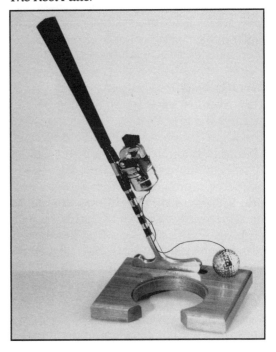

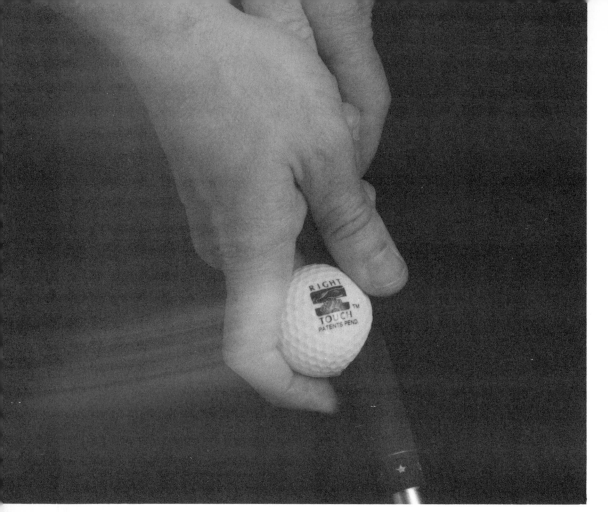

Right Touch

RIGHT TOUCH

Have you lost your touch on and around the green? If so, practicing with the Right Touch putting and chipping trainer just might help you find it again. It's a regulation golf ball with a U-shaped channel drilled through one side and a Velcro strip that allows the ball to be temporarily fitted to the grip of a golf club. As you practice putting or chipping, the thumb and first two fingers of your right hand are on the Right Touch trainer, not the grip. By focusing your attention on the feeling of rolling a golf ball to the hole with your hands— a sensation similar to pitching pennies—

Right Touch refines your control over both distance and speed. When held in your left hand, Right Touch inhibits the left wrist from breaking down and enhances the feeling of moving the club toward the target.

$8.98 from Golf Sports Engineering.

TIGER SHARK P-SQUARED PUTTER GRIP

If you believe that putting shouldn't be a wristy business— and you're by no means alone in that respect— why not equip your putter with a grip that forces

Tiger Shark P-Squared Putter Grip

you to practice what you preach? The Tiger Shark P-Squared Putter Grip, which combines the best features of pistol- and paddle-style grips, is more than an inch larger in diameter than its conventional cousins. The jumbo size promotes a steadier, wrist-free putting stroke and virtually guarantees the proper alignment of the hands (the palms should be positioned in direct opposition to each other). You can even install this composition grip yourself; it comes with two-way tape, solvent, and easy-to-follow instructions. Keep in mind, however, that the P-Squared Putter Grip won't fit in a round golf tube.

$9 from Austad's; also from Las Vegas Discount Golf and Vintage Golf.

TOP SIGHT PUTTING AID

Your putter may already have a sight line, but Top Sight carries things to an effective extreme. Simply snap this practice device onto the shaft of your putter several inches above the ball and position its ultrathin crossbar along your target line. Not only will you find it easier to sight the proper line between your ball and the hole, but by maintaining the crossbar in the same position relative to the ball you'll keep the face of your putter square and your entire putting stroke perfectly on line.

$7.95 from Top Sight Putting Aid.

THE TRACK

If you need to get your putting game back on track, this may be the way to start. The Track's parallel aluminum rails make your putter stay on the intended target line—whether it wants to or not.

$21.50 from Golfsmith; also from Florida Golf Warehouse.

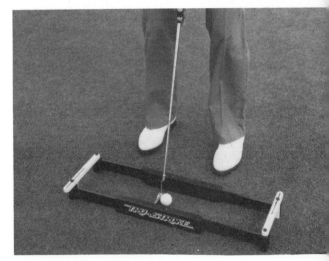

Tru-Stroke Putting Guide

TRU-STROKE PUTTING GUIDE

The Tru-Stroke Putting Guide may help you find—and keep—a smoother, straighter putting stroke. As you practice, its adjustable, parallel guide rails not only train you to take the putter straight back and straight through the impact zone but also make you keep the club low to the ground throughout. The Tru-Stroke Putting Guide is made of

THE ART AND SCIENCE OF PUTTING 59

lightweight plastic components and folds to fit in your golf bag or closet.

$32.95 from The Golf Works; also from Competitive Edge Golf.

Two-Way Indoor Putting Green

Here's an indoor putting green with a time-saving twist: Each end has two holes, which lets you putt back and forth without stopping to retrieve balls. Its 2-by-12-foot polypropylene surface effectively simulates Bermuda grass to give you a true-to-life feel for speed, line, and slope. The cups are four inches in diameter (a quarter-inch smaller than regulation) to sharpen your accuracy, and the surface is inclined at both ends to help you get the hang of the old putting adage, "Never up, never in." The Two-Way Indoor

Putting Green is backed with urethane foam to prevent slipping and rolls up for easy storage.

$49.95 from Hammacher Schlemmer.

Vision Putt

If you have trouble visualizing exactly how the face of your putter should meet the ball, a little practice with Vision Putt may put everything in proper perspective. This golf-ball-on-wheels gizmo trains you to stroke a practice ball at its exact center with a perfectly square putter blade and smooth follow-through. If the face of your putter doesn't meet the wheels on either side of the ball at the same time, Vision Putt rolls sharply to the left or right. Get the picture?

$9.95 from Las Vegas Discount Golf.

CHAPTER THREE
SPECIAL STICKS

SPECIAL STICKS:
WOODS, IRONS, AND PUTTERS

ADJUSTABLE SWINGWEIGHT FIVE-IRON

What's your ideal swingweight? Here's a reliable way to find out. The back of this five-iron's head has been machine-drilled and fitted with a special screw and brass nut, which enables you to easily alter the club's swingweight—from C-8 to D-5—by slipping lead discs on and off. The Adjustable Swingweight Five-Iron is assembled to men's standard length on a True Temper Lite stiff shaft.

$39.50 from The Golf Works.

THE BOMBER

If you've been looking to hit "The Big Stick," look no further. The face of this jumbo driver by Louisville Golf is a full two inches deep (that's 23 percent deeper than standard), with 11 degrees of loft for optimum carry and roll. The Bomber is made of laminated maple, finished in black walnut, and fitted with a white Cycolac insert and True Temper Dynamic shaft ("R" or "S" flex). Next time you need to "tee it high and let it fly," why not haul out the B-1 wood?

$67 from Competitive Edge Golf; also from Louisville Golf and Edwin Watts Golf Shops.

Adjustable Swingweight Five-Iron

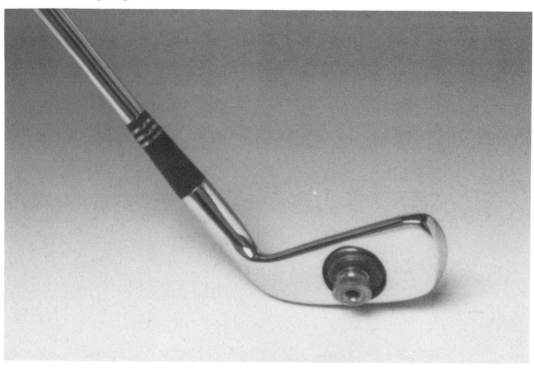

DRIVER AND A HALF

If your driver isn't only the biggest— but the scariest— stick in your bag, maybe it's time you reached for Bob Toski's Driver and a Half. Toski, a highly respected teacher and clubmaker (and currently a top name on the Senior PGA Tour), has designed a hybrid wood that gives you nearly the distance of a conventional driver but spares you the problems associated with its long length and low loft.

At 42 inches long, the Driver and a Half is an inch shorter than a standard driver and the same length as a three-wood. That makes it easier to control. It has 13.5 degrees of loft— 2.5 to 3.5 degrees more than a standard driver and about the same as the all-but-obsolete two wood. That makes it easier to get the ball airborne. Its stainless steel insert covers 85 percent of the clubface— about twice the hitting area of conventional inserts. That makes for a big sweet spot. Put it all together and you've got a club that's more forgiving off the tee than a driver and meaner than a three- or four-wood from the fairway.

The Driver and a Half is hand-crafted from U.S. Grade A persimmon in right-handed models only and fitted with a True Temper Dynamic shaft ("R" or "S" flex).

$99 from Herrington; also from Ryobi-Toski.

THE DUKE AND THE DUCHESS PUTTERS

Some folks swear the old way of doing almost anything is better than the new, and maybe they're right. To wit: The Duke and The Duchess, a pair of putters still painstakingly handcrafted from traditional materials by Scottish club-makers. Each beautifully contoured mallet head is carved from 24 lamina-tions of aged beech, weighted with lead, protected with a leading-edge insert of genuine ram's horn, and then finished by hand with a handsome oak stain and clear lacquer. A solid hickory shaft is then splined to the head and carefully wrapped with a suede grip. These men's and women's putters are faithful to the tradition of the Royal and Ancient Golf Club of St. Andrews, the home of golf— which just happens to be a stone's throw down the road from the workshop where these classics are made.

$99 each from Herrington; also from Abercrombie & Fitch and Austad's.

FORE 7-4-7 JUMBO DRIVER

After Gay Brewer started carrying one of these colossal clubs on the Senior PGA Tour, it wasn't long before 7-4-7s landed in the bags of Arnold Palmer, Lee Elder, Harold Henning, and George Lanning, among others. "Drove the ball as far and as straight as I ever have in my life," Brewer told a local sportswriter after the first round of the 1988 GTE Northwest Classic at Inglewood Country Club in Kenmore, Washington. "I almost can't make this club do anything but hit the ball straight."

The secret of the Fore 7-4-7 Jumbo Driver is mostly in its size. No matter how you measure it— from head to grip or heel to toe— this ultrabig stick makes a conventional driver seem downright puny. Its laminated-maple clubhead is 1.75 times bigger, and its clubface 1.25 times broader, than standard. The larger clubhead and longer clubface not only give you a huge hitting area and an enormous sweetspot, but increase your odds for solid impact on off-center hits. The clubhead is also perimeter-weighted (its sheer size necessitates a hollow core), which packs the 7-4-7's punch behind and around the ball at impact.

Each 7-4-7 is fitted with a solid graphite face insert and a lightweight graphite or titanium shaft, which allow it to be longer than a conventional driver without being heavier. A 44-inch graphite-shafted model, for example, weighs only about 12 ounces. Thanks to the extra length, you swing on a longer arc and thus generate greater clubhead speed through the hitting zone. The 7-4-7 is available in four standard lengths (44, 45, 46, and 47 inches) and five shaft flexes ("A," "R," "S," "X," and "XX").

This driver's only drawback may be the snickering it's likely to inspire when you pull it out of your bag. But pay no attention. Simply step up to the tee, swing away, and let the big stick speak for itself.

$219 from Oregon Golf Works.

THE GIANT NIBLICK

If sand traps give you the shakes, this jumbo-headed wedge from Pal Joey may turn you into a regular Lawrence of Arabia. Cast from a high-tensile-strength aluminum alloy, it's more than twice the size of a conventional sand iron. The Giant Niblick is 35.5 inches long, with a swingweight in the D-8 range, 60 degrees of loft, an extra-wide sole, and a low leading edge (for less bounce and more cutting action). All of which may give you the confidence you need to blast out of those nasty bunkers on the first try. Out, damn ball!

$39.95 from Las Vegas Discount Golf; also from Competitive Edge Golf.

HERO DRIVER

The easiest driver in the world to hit? That's what Ralph Maltby, a master club designer and author of numerous golf books, calls his Hero Driver. In building the ultimate "player improvement club," Maltby has changed the driver's face angle, length, swingweight, total weight, and lie to eliminate equipment-induced slicing and other problems. The Hero Driver is a half-inch shorter and a half-ounce lighter than standard, for example, to increase accuracy and to help generate clubhead speed.

The men's Hero Driver, in persimmon, is $49.50 ("R" or "S" flex); the women's model, in laminated maple, is $42.50 ("L" flex). Matching fairway woods are also available.

From The Golf Works; also from Competitive Edge Golf.

IRON DRIVER

This isn't a one-iron, but a driving iron that's specifically designed to help eliminate hooks, slices, and other undesirable by-products of the big wooden sticks. Its jumbo face— 3.2 inches wide and 2 inches deep— is three-quarters of an inch wider and deeper than a conventional two-iron and provides a bigger hitting area than the average driver. And unlike a conventional iron, you can tee it up to 1.75 inches high with the Iron Driver and still make solid contact even if you catch the ball on the upper half of the clubface. A little extra weight in the driver's stainless steel head means extra distance, making it handy for driving down narrow fairways, over the river, and through the woods. It's available in 37-, 38-, and 39-inch lengths ("R," "S," or "L" flex).

$76.95 from Practical Golfers Aid; also from Golf Day Products and J. White Industries.

JUST-RITE PUTTER

If you've been searching for a putter with just the right weight, balance, and feel, the Just-Rite Putter may let you stop shopping once and for all. It's the brainchild of PGA professional Claude Jueckstock, Jr., who wanted a single putter that could be adjusted to accom-

modate a multitude of playing conditions, putting styles, and levels of skill. Threaded ports behind both the heel and toe of the Just-Rite Putter accept up to four precision-weighted plugs apiece; by inserting them in various combinations, you can create up to 16 different variations in weight. The chrome-plated plugs range in weight from three to 15 grams and are graduated in a conventional swingweight scale (to a maximum swingweight of D-3).

With a little experimentation on the

Iron Driver

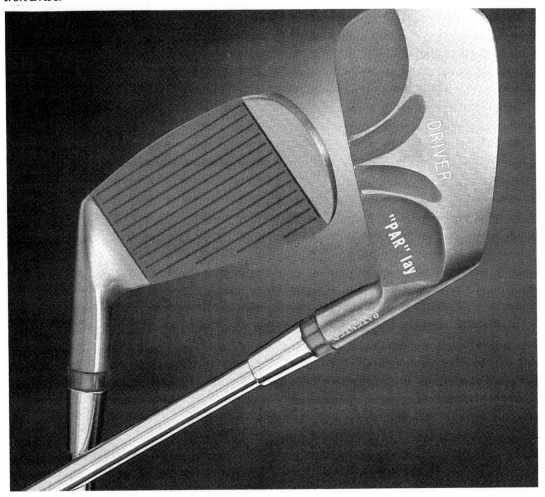

practice green or living-room carpet, you can settle on the heel-to-toe weight distribution and total weight that best suit your putting style. You also can compensate for slow greens by inserting the heavier weights, or for lightning-fast greens by leaving out the weights altogether. The idea, in short, is to adjust your putter— not your putting stroke— for various green conditions. The Just-Rite Putter is available in men's and women's models (35- or 33-inch-long shafts) and includes a storage pouch to hold the eight weights and matching wrench.

$75 from Wright Weight Corporation.

Lynx Parallax Putter with Transmitter Shaft

If feel is everything when it comes to putting, this graphite-shafted putter may give you just the right touch— delicate and deadly— every time you step on a green. It's so sensitive, the manufacturer claims, that you can almost feel the dimples on your ball. The reason? The putter's high-tech transmitter shaft has no rubber or leather grip to deaden feel— its shaft, in fact, *is* the grip. The graphite fibers that run the full length of the shaft— from clubhead to end cap— are supposed to transmit an uncanny degree of feel to your hands and fingertips during the putting stroke. Lynx's oscilloscope-monitored tests, in fact, show that the transmitter shaft conducts up to 75 percent more energy— as measured in pulse amplitude and frequency— than steel-shafted putters with rubber grips. The Lynx Parallax Putter is available in four different head designs (each with a dot that marks the sweetspot and a long

vertical topline) and four different grip sizes (.790, .850, .910, and .970).

$84.95 from Edwin Watts Golf Shops.

Mercury-Loaded Driver

Unless they take a hacksaw to that new stick in your bag, your golfing partners aren't likely to figure out why you're suddenly hitting straighter, sweeter drives. Yet the secret behind this driver is, if you will, elemental: a mercury-filled "power chamber" inside the clubhead. (While mercury weighs nearly as much as lead, it's liquid at normal temperatures.) During your downswing, centrifugal force pushes the mercury to the toe side of the chamber, balancing and squaring up the clubhead for a straight, solid hit. Studies show that most golfers consistently strike the ball forward of the center line of the clubface— in other words, toward the toe of the club and away from the heart of its sweet spot. So if you frequently push or "toe" your drives, the Mercury-Loaded Driver just might improve your distance and accuracy off the tee. It's made from laminated maple, finished in a deep burgundy stain, and fitted with a True Temper Dynamic Gold shaft ("R" or "S" flex).

$79 from Competitive Edge Golf; also from Pro-Action Golf.

Optima Driver

Is this the finest driver in the world? Maybe so (that, at least, is what its manufacturer claims), but test driving the Optima may be the only sure way to find out for yourself. Whether you take this big stick out for a spin or not, though, rest assured that the Optima

Driver has a lot going for it out of the gate.

For starters, each clubhead is crafted from the cream of the persimmon crop: a precisely weighed block of the finest Grade A+ variety. Less than 3 percent of all persimmon, in fact, meets Optima's rigorous specifications for proper density and grain (only a perfectly formed "U-grain" pattern, for example, is acceptable). And because the persimmon face itself has no grooves, it's less likely to crack or chip—even under the onslaught of two-piece golf balls.

Then there's the Optima's titanium insert. While metal inserts are nothing new—MacGregor put aluminum inserts in its Tourney woods nearly 20 years ago—the marriage of persimmon and titanium may represent something of a perfect union. Titanium is the hardest and most durable metal known to man. It's three times harder than aluminum and 45 percent lighter than steel, and it has a higher tensile and yield strength than either of the other metals. The higher yield strength means that when a titanium insert meets a golf ball, it returns to its original shape much faster than aluminum or steel—and that means a highly efficient transfer of energy from clubhead to ball.

The standard model of the Optima

Optima Driver

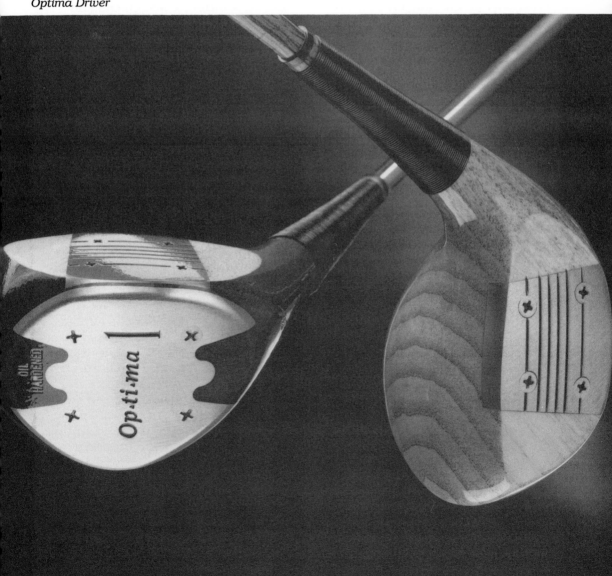

Driver is finished in black and fitted with a leather grip and True Temper Dynamic shaft. Other specifications (lie, length, and loft), shafts (titanium or graphite), stains, and grips may be custom-ordered, and matching fairway woods also are available.

$215 from Inpro Companies.

PERFLEX DRIVER

In the beginning, there was persimmon. Then came laminated maple, metal, graphite. Now comes Vexlar, a highly resilient plastic originally developed by the aerospace industry but destined, perhaps, to find its way into the world of golf. The head of the Perflex Driver is solid Vexlar— that means no insert, no screws, no soleplate. And because Vexlar has compression characteristics closely resembling those of a golf ball, the clubface is supposed to act some-thing like a shock-absorber and sling-shot rolled into one. The Perflex Driver is fitted with a lightweight graphite shaft ("R" or "S" flex), which allows you to swing faster without swinging harder. Matching fairway woods also are avail-able.

$149 from Competitive Edge Golf; also from Las Vegas Discount Golf and Perflex International,

POSITIVE PUTTER

Are two sweet spots better than one? That's the idea behind the Positive Putter, which has two striking zones to help you adjust to different green conditions. Many of the PGA Tour's top putters— including Fuzzy Zoeller, whose weapon of choice is a Ping Zing— like to shift the position of the ball relative to the face of the putter, especially on fast greens. On Augusta National's light-ning-fast greens, for example, they'll intentionally strike putts slightly toward the toe and off the sweet spot for a softer feel. Developing this kind of finesse takes plenty of practice, of course, but the Positive Putter is de-signed to take some of the guesswork out of the equation.

An orange dot on the Positive Putter's bronze head marks its primary sweet spot, which provides a crisp feel and maximum distance for slow greens and uphill putts. A green dot closer to the toe marks the putter's secondary sweet spot; it provides a softer feel and greater control for fast greens and downhill or breaking putts. What's more, the center-shafted Positive Putter is optimally balanced to stay square throughout your stroke— unlike many other putters, which twist off-line during pendulum tests, it actually maintains a perfect putting motion when freely suspended, pulled back, and released.

$69 from Herrington.

POWER POD

When push comes to slice, just pull this baby out of your bag, ignore the snick-ers, and start singing, "Yes, We Have No Banana Balls." Sure it looks strange, but so what if this maroon-faced plastic "wood" lives up to its billing as the ultimate slice-buster? For starters, the Power Pod is balanced to match the natural oblique angle of the golf swing, and its huge circular clubface— three inches in diameter— provides a hitting area 80-100 percent larger than a conventional driver. If you do manage to hit the ball inside or beyond the Power Pod's "percussion point" (otherwise known as the sweet spot), the clubface's radius-bulge design imparts gear-effect spin that makes your shot "seek" the target line. So if you're brave enough to say hello to the Power Pod, you may be able to kiss those sliced, skied, and otherwise skewed shots goodbye.

The standard men's Power Pod is 43 inches long, has 11 degrees of loft, and is fitted with a steel shaft ("R" or "S" flex); the standard women's model, in "L" flex, is an inch shorter. Both are $119.95. For right-handed men, two white-faced variations on the same scheme also are available: a Tour Model, with nine degrees of loft, at $124.95; and a "20 Extra Yards" Power Pod, with 11 degrees of loft and a fast-recovering polyethylite shaft, at $179.50.

All from Golf Day Products; also from Austad's, Las Vegas Discount Golf, and J. White Industries.

Pug-Ugly Putter

PUG-UGLY PUTTER

"It's ugly as hell," says Pug Pilcher, "but it works." Pilcher's center-shafted putter isn't all that ugly, as it turns out, but his unorthodox implement does seem at first glance to violate USGA regulations, which require the head of a putter to be longer from heel to toe than from front to back. The Pug-Ugly's margin of safety in this respect is a mere quarter of an inch, but its solid-aluminum head—anodized in black and fitted to a polished brass faceplate—is oblong enough to let you see the entire sweep of your putting stroke without the slightest lateral movement of your head or eyes. This, as Pilcher puts it, makes the Pug-Ugly "the putter that lines itself up."

$50 from The Pilcher Company.

THE SECRET WEAPON DRIVER

Add this driver to your arsenal and it's not likely to stay a secret for very long. Although the Secret Weapon has a lightweight cast aluminum head, any resemblance to conventional metal woods ends there. The driver's 13-degree loft launches tee shots on a higher trajectory than its conventional cousins, and its face is also closed two degrees as a built-in correction for outside-in swings. These two anti-slice features are coupled with a monster sweet spot— nearly 80 percent larger than a conventional driver's— to increase the odds that you'll make clean, solid contact with the ball. The Secret

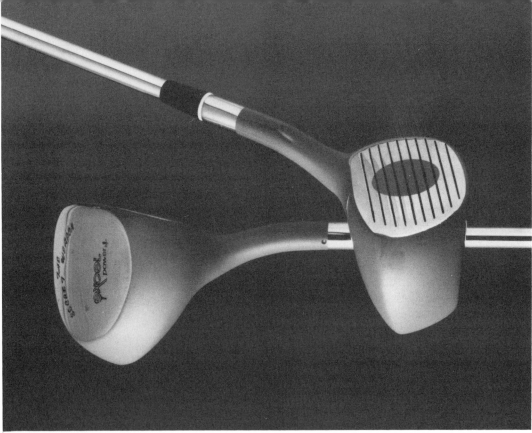

The Secret Weapon Driver

Weapon driver is fitted with a True Temper Dynamic shaft ("R" or "S" flex), although it may be custom-ordered with a graphite or titanium shaft. Matching fairway woods are also available. The standard men's model is 43 inches long; the women's is 41 inches long.

$79.95 from Golfware Originals.

Shurfire Alma Mater Putters

Next time you sink one for the Gipper, just thank that trusty Shurfire Notre Dame Putter for getting the job done. For starters, its zircon-alloy head features heel-toe weighting to widen the putter's sweet spot and forgive off-center hits, an offset hosel to keep your hands in front of the ball, and an extended sight line to help you line up your putts with pinpoint accuracy. But what really sets each Shurfire Alma Mater Putter apart is the precision paint job that lets you give every putt that old college try. First the Shurfire's entire head is bathed in an automotive-quality color coating; then your school's name and logo are screen-printed on the putter's face in the appropriate contrasting color. And, if you'd like, you can even carry your putter around in a case that's designed to resemble your college pennant.

Shurfire Alma Mater Putters and matching carrying cases are available for more than 30 different colleges and universities, including: Alabama, Arizona, Arizona State, California-Berkeley, Florida, Florida State, Georgia, Illinois, Indiana, Iowa, Iowa State, Kentucky,

Louisiana State, Miami, Michigan, Michigan State, Minnesota, Northwestern, Notre Dame, Ohio State, Oregon, Oregon State, Penn State, Pittsburgh, Purdue, Stanford, Texas A&M, UCLA, USC, Washington, Washington State, and Wisconsin.

$49 ($59 with carrying case) from Competitive Edge Golf; also from Las Vegas Discount Golf.

SIDESADDLE PUTTERS

The yips had Sam Snead in a bad way. His moment of truth came in the 1966 PGA Championship, when he double-hit one of his putts as a large gallery looked on. Snead simply couldn't keep his fingers from shaking. On the next hole, out of sheer desperation, he started experimenting with a croquet-style of putting. He straddled the ball with his legs, held the grip end of the club in his left hand and the shaft well down in his right, and fired away. The shakes disappeared. The touch returned.

Before long countless yip-afflicted golfers— professional and amateur— were mimicking Snead's unorthodox head-on style, and club manufacturers began turning out center-shafted implements especially designed for the purpose. The United States Golf Association saw something unseemly in all of this, however, and it soon moved to banish croquet-style putters— not only the newfangled weapons themselves, but those who wielded them— by enacting Rule 16-1e: "The player shall not make a stroke on the putting green from a stance astride, or with either foot touching, the line of the putt or an extension of that line behind the ball."

"I was determined not to let them or my twitch put me out of business," Snead wrote in his 1986 autobiography,

Slammin' Sam. "I kept the basics of the stance but positioned the ball to the right. I call this putting stance the 'sidesaddle.' It, too, looks like hell . . . but it works."

Plenty of folks have poked fun at sidesaddle putting— Jimmy Demaret once joked that Snead looked as if he were "basting a turkey"— but there's no denying its increasing popularity, particularly on the Senior PGA Tour. With Snead as their patron saint, sidesaddle putters say that it's far easier to sight the line to the cup straight on rather than out of the corner of an eye. As for the split-handed stroke itself, some top practitioners of the art say that it gives them the feeling of "sweeping" the ball toward the cup.

If your putting game is in need of a major overhaul, maybe one of these can put you back in the saddle again:

Dishner Concept Putter. This putter features a cast brass head, a 38-inch-long shaft, and an extra-long, foam-rubber grip (to accommodate the split-handed technique used in sidesaddle putting). Because the center-shafted Dishner Concept Putter is reversible, it can be used by either right- or left-handed golfers. And if you happen to be like Sam Snead or Ben Hogan— both natural southpaws who play golf right-handed— you can even give switch-hitting a try.

$49.95 from Austad's.

Mighty-Mite SS. The "SS" stands, of course, for sidesaddle. This model of the Mighty-Mite (there are five others in the series) has not one grip but two: a conventional grip of wrapped calfskin for the left hand, which remains in a locked position up top and provides a fulcrum for the pendulum-type stroke, and a fatter grip down below for the right hand, which controls the putting stroke. The putter's sight line is positioned on the true sweet spot for perfect alignment, and its shaft is angled into the hosel at 12 degrees to vertical for the upright stance that helps make sidesaddle putting so effective. The Mighty-Mite SS is available in men's and women's right-hand models.

$75 from Ryobi-Toski.

Side Saddle Putters. These bronze-headed putters are mostly handle; both the regular and extra-long versions have 24-inch-long Nitrile grips. They're fitted with True Temper steel shafts (offset 10.5 degrees to vertical) and two-way heads that allow them to be used either right- or left-handed.

$59.50 (39-inch shaft) or $65 (47-inch shaft) from Golf Day Products.

SLIM JIM PUTTER

If Charlie Owens managed to whip the yips with this homemade, 50-inch-long, pound-and-a-half putter, maybe you can, too. Before he designed the Slim Jim and started sinking putts on the SeniorPGA Tour, in fact, Owens's case of the yips had progressively worsened to the point where he was double-hitting putts with frightening regularity. But now he's a star, and so is his putter. In the last few years Owens and other Slim-Jim-wielding pros have scored numerous victories on the Senior Tour.

The Slim Jim's extra-long shaft allows you to stand upright on the putting green, which in addition to taming the tremors all but eliminates the back strain associated with conventional putting styles. Your left hand

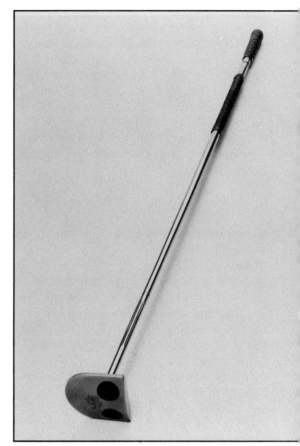

Slim Jim Putter

grips the top of the shaft and sets the pendulum, while your right hand— placed on a second grip six to eight inches below your left hand— executes the putting stroke. To accommodate golfers of different heights, the Slim Jim is available in 44-, 46-, 48-, and 50-inch lengths.

$100 from Matzie Golf; also from Competitive Edge Golf.

SUPER STICK ADJUSTABLE GOLF CLUB

No club can be all things to all golfers, but maybe this one can be all things to you. In the tradition of indoor-outdoor carpeting and the reversible suit comes Super Stick— a collapsible, 17-in-one

Super Stick Adjustable Golf Club

golf club. A simple twist of a coin turns its investment-cast, stainless steel clubhead into an entire arsenal: a driving iron with 12 degrees of loft, nine conventionally lofted irons, three different wedges, a chipping iron, and three putters. Locking teeth hold the clubhead securely in hitting position; even its swingweight is adjustable (D-6, D-4, or D-2). What's more, the club's low center of gravity and mammoth muscle-back make it easier for even the most jet-lagged golfer to get off a clean shot.

Super Stick is fitted with a telescoping True Temper shaft that easily locks for play and retracts to 24 inches for travel. It's available in right-handed versions only for men (38 inches extended) and women (36 inches extended). But use it for convenience, not competition: Super Stick doesn't meet USGA guidelines.

$47.50 from Golfsmith; also from Competitive Edge Golf, Golf Day Products, Hammacher Schlemmer, Northern Golf Ball Company, Polar Golf, and J. White Industries.

"3 IN 1" CLUB

If you can't hit a driver to save your life, this "3 in 1" Club may be just the lifesaver you've been looking for. Yes, it looks like a conventional driver, but it has the loft of a three-wood (to help get your tee shots airborne), a closed clubface (to ward off evil slices), and an extra-long— but extra-light— True Temper shaft. Its driver-sized clubhead is made of laminated maple, fitted with a black insert, and finished in walnut. In the event a test drive or two doesn't sell you on the "3 in 1" Club, the manufacturer offers this extra-yards-or-your-money-back guarantee: "After purchase and trial, if this club does not perform to your satisfaction, return the club for full refund (no questions asked)."

$64 from Ofer Custom Golf Clubs.

TOURHAWK PUTTER

In his quest for the perfect putter, Bill Gartner left little to chance. Gartner, a respected scientist and prolific inventor (with patents ranging from high-temperature insulating materials to a water-purifying straw), says that he applied "new interpretations of basic laws of physics" in developing the prototype of his TourHawk Putter. But he also turned to Fischerdesign, an internationally recognized consulting team in Scottsdale, Arizona, to refine the features of his putter through the advanced technology of computer-aided design (CAD).

First and foremost, the weight of the TourHawk's head is distributed throughout all three dimensions, which Gartner believes is superior to perimeter or heel-and-toe weighting. Its four-degree negative loft— the face of the putter is canted slightly downward— produces overspin on the ball at the moment of impact, while its centered steel shaft minimizes twisting, or "gearing." The smooth, rounded sole, which resembles a racing hull, sails over spike marks and tufts of taller grass, and elongated sight lines help square the putter to the intended target line.

If you want to be the Darth Vader of the putting green, the TourHawk may be for you. It's fitted with a black leather grip, a black scratch-resistant shaft, and a black aluminum-alloy head.

$69 from Reflex Inc; also from Austad's.

TRIPLE CROWN WEDGE

Sooner or later, somebody was bound to think of it: a three-wedge system in a single club. Three separate wedges come in handy, all right, but usually at the expense of the long irons or other clubs you must jettison to stay within the USGA's 14-club limit. Tiger Shark's Triple Crown Wedge, thanks to its specially contoured sole and multicolored alignment guides on the clubface and grip, deals with the dilemma in one fell swoop. The rounded sole enables you to open or close the clubface without raising its leading edge, which means you can hit shots of anywhere from 30 to 120 yards with the same club and the same swing. Here's how:

Right: TourHawk Putter

Square the red score line on the clubface to your target and you've got a 52-degree wedge for shots of 90 to 120 yards. Open the clubface a bit, square the white line to your target, and you've got a 56-degree wedge for shots of 50 to 90 yards. Open the clubface a bit more, square the blue line, and you've got a 60-degree wedge for those delicate sand, cut, and lob shots of 50 yards and in. (Three matching lines on the grip of the Triple Crown Wedge help make sure you've got everything right.)

$65 from Competitive Edge Golf; also from Golf Day Products.

TUNSTALL PUTTER

This may be the Rolls-Royce of mallet-head putters. Handcrafted in solid brass and laminated Canadian maple by second- and third-generation Irish clubmakers, the Tunstall is both elegant and ingenious. By selectively inserting various brass discs and barrels beneath its removable soleplate, you can adjust the putter's heel-to-toe weight distribution (as well as total weight) and create the "feel" that's just right for you. The 35-inch-long Tunstall putter comes with a leather cover and zippered pouch (which holds the brass discs and barrels, foam inserts, and hexagonal wrench) and is available only in a right-handed version.

$125 from The Golf Works.

THE WINDOW-WEDGE

Here's the ultimate teaching and practice tool for anyone who fears sand traps. The face of this wedge features a removable, transparent insert— the "window." Try bunker shots with the insert removed, and the functional role of the wedge's flange will be dramati-cally emphasized. With the insert in place, you can visualize the sole sliding through the sand, under the ball, and out again. Directional guidelines illustrate how the clubface should be opened at address. The Window-Wedge also can be used to demonstrate the importance of correct clubface-to-ball contact on conventional shots.

$86.50 from Banff Golf.

WOOD WAND

Meet the petrified putter . . . and we're not talking here about a golfer with a terminal case of the yips. We're talking about the Wood Wand, a putter fashioned almost entirely from the same chemically petrified wood that's commonly used to make knife handles. The wood is prematurely petrified by impregnating wafer-thin veneers with liquid phenolic resins and then laminating them under intense heat and tons of pressure. As a result, the Wood Wand is impervious to moisture, needs no varnish, and has a lustrous sheen that actually improves with handling. Even its distinctive "grip" is wood, too, contoured in such a way that the upper half is smaller and flatter than the lower half, with the butt end slightly fishtailed (primarily for aesthetic reasons).

Because they're made entirely by hand, no two Wood Wand putters are identical. Five designs are available, but the "Drift Wood"— with the classic styling of a blade putter, a bronze hosel-to-faceplate section, and a wood insert behind the face— is by far the most popular (although available only in right-handed models). Each Wood Wand comes with a putter cover and a bottle of Blitz Metal Polish.

$110 from Wood Wand Corporation.

CLASSIC-CLUB REPRODUCTIONS

RAY COOK ORIGINAL M-1 PUTTER

This mallet-headed classic has captured all the majors at least once: The Masters (Billy Casper, 1970); the U.S. Open (Orville Moody, 1969); the British Open (Roberto de Vicenzo, 1968); and the PGA Championship (Dave Stockton, 1970 and 1976). But its best-known devotee may be Nancy Lopez, who, since joining the LPGA Tour in 1977, has used one to rack up 39 tournament titles and more than $2.2 million in earnings. Introduced in 1963, the M-1 (for mallet) was the first putter to incorporate heel and toe weighting, a revolutionary— but now widely copied— design breakthrough. What's more, the putter's ingenious alignment system features two horizontal sightlines that are spaced 1.68 inches apart— the exact diameter of a golf ball— to guide your putting stroke and show you precisely where you should strike the ball. The Ray Cook Original M-1 Putter, which comes with a leather cover, is fitted with a steel shaft and a rubber paddle-style grip.

$45 (right-handed, 35-inch model) from Austad's.

JACK NICKLAUS TWENTY-FIFTH ANNIVERSARY COMMEMORATIVE CLUBS

In 1962, his first year on the PGA Tour, Jack Nicklaus won the U.S. Open by defeating Arnold Palmer in a playoff at Oakmont Country Club. The rest, as they say, is history. In 1987, to commemorate the 25th anniversary of Nicklaus's victory, MacGregor Golf Company faithfully reproduced the clubs he used at Oakmont— which, with one exception, it had originally manufactured to his specifications— in a limited edition of 2,500 sets. (The originals are on permanent display at Nicklaus's home course, Muirfield Village Golf Club in Dublin, Ohio.) Each of these sets is composed of two woods, 11 irons, and a putter, all with the wrapped calfskin grips that Nicklaus preferred. The driver and three-wood have backweighted persimmon heads with fiber inserts. The forged irons (one through sand wedge) feature MacGregor's classic diamond-back design, with black ceramic-fired faces and flat soles. The putter is a flanged blade reminiscent of the Bristol "Geo. Low Wizard 600" (the only non-MacGregor club Nicklaus carried), which went out of production in 1962. Each set of replicas is mounted in a handsome display case, which bears a brass plate engraved with a brief history of the clubs and the set's serial number.

$4,995 from Las Vegas Discount Golf.

SILVER SCOT COLLECTOR PUTTER

"Of all the golf clubs considered classics," writes Joe Clement in *Classic Golf Clubs* (see Chapter 9), "none have had the broad acceptance and lasting appeal of the MacGregor Tommy Armour putters." Although these putters bore Armour's name and typically one or both of his nicknames— the "Iron Master" and the "Silver Scot"— they were in fact designed by Toney Penna, the clubmaker-professional who crafted virtually all of the MacGregor clubs that today are considered classics. For years the most sought-after and coveted of Penna's putters has been the MacGregor Tommy Armour Silver Scot Model Iron Master's Putter Rec. No. 3852, commonly known as the Tommy Armour 3852. Armour introduced the flanged blade in 1935; it sold for $8.00 retail and $4.80 wholesale. But MacGregor didn't move many of the putters until 1938, when it began offering one free with the purchase of three dozen Tommy Armour golf balls. (MacGregor dropped the Tommy Armour name from its line in 1967.) These days you can't touch an original Tommy Armour 3852 for less than $200, unless you're lucky enough to find one at a garage sale or flea market. If authenticity isn't everything to you, however, the Tommy Armour Golf Company may have just what you've been looking for. Save for some of the trademarked stampings on the sole of the Tommy Armour 3852, its Silver Scot Collector Putter is a faithful replica of the old faithful— right down to the black leather-wrapped grip and green-sheathed steel shaft.

$73.50 from Tommy Armour Golf.

The Wilson 8802

Had it not been for the defection of Arnold Palmer from the advisory staff of the Wilson Sporting Goods Company back in the early 1960s, some of the world's premier putters— Ben Crenshaw and Greg Norman, to name just two— might never have wielded The Wilson 8802. This now-classic putter, introduced in January 1963, had its roots in a 1962 model that was designed and used by Arnie himself. The "Palmer" (stock number 8852) featured a flanged blade, Wilson's stepped-down "Head Speed" shaft, a wrapped calfskin grip with one flat side, and the words "De-

signed by Arnold Palmer" or "Arnold Palmer" on the sole. Soon after its debut, however, Palmer left Wilson to form his own golf-equipment company. Wilson wasted little time in unveiling a virtually identical putter: The Wilson 8802, which carried a suggested retail price of $14.50. Two years later the 8802 inexplicably disappeared from Wilson's catalog, but by 1970 it was back, this time with a black-chrome head and a fluted shaft. In 1975 Wilson switched to a satin-finish chrome head and began stamping the words "The Original 8802" on the sole of the putter.

The Wilson 8802 has long been a favorite on the PGA Tour, and many professionals say that it's one of the best-balanced putters ever made. But bona fide originals from the early 1960s command blue-chip prices in the classic-club market, and if you're lucky enough to find one it's likely to set you back several hundred dollars. If you don't mind making do with a remake, however, Wilson's modern-day version of the 8802 may leave you laughing all the way to the hole.

$29.95 from Polar Golf; also from Nevada Bob's Discount Golf and Edwin Watts Golf Shops.

The Wilson 8813

At first glance the Wilson 8813 resembles the legendary 8802 (see above), which it probably was intended to replace. Wilson introduced the putter in 1965, the same year it dropped the 8802 from its catalog. But several features set the 8813 apart from its classic cousin, including a sightline on the top, a perpendicular alignment line on the flange, a fluted shaft, and the Wilson Staff crest on the sole. (Wilson introduced black-headed versions of both putters in 1970.) Although the 8813 isn't as famous as the 8802, it's so highly coveted by collectors and top players that in recent years the classic-club market has bestowed virtual parity on the two models. So choose your weapon, but, as with the 8802, be prepared to pay several hundred dollars for the privilege of owning an original. If you want to soften the blow to your bank account, however, you can acquire Wilson's modern-day remake of the 8813 for a fraction of what you'd pay for the genuine article.

$29.95 from Polar Golf; also from Nevada Bob's Discount Golf and Edwin Watts Golf Shops.

CHAPTER FOUR
THE PRACTICE RANGE

BALL BOY

This shag-bag-in-a-tube is 38 inches long and holds up to 20 golf balls. Slip the Ball Boy into your golf bag— it's about the length of a three- or four-iron— and you'll always be ready to practice whenever you're near a shagging area or putting green. Simply press the opening of the see-through plastic tube over a golf ball and push; the ball automatically pops up into the tube. A removable plastic cap makes emptying easy.

$8.95 from Golf Day Products.

CHIP-N-PITCH NET

"When anyone who has played golf for any time scores much above 90," the legendary Bobby Jones once wrote, "the reason can be found in his work around the greens." So now that your problem has been diagnosed, what's the cure? Same as with any other part of your game: practice. Fortunately, you can sharpen up your short game in your own backyard with the Chip-N-Pitch Net, which offers a 17-inch-diameter target hoop. The vinyl-dipped steel frame resists rust and scratches, the net is nylon, and a ground anchor holds the unit in place as your practice. Practice enough, in fact, and your playing partners won't think it's an accident next time you're up and down in two.

$16.50 from Austad's.

CHIP SHOT TARGET

Here's a golf net that you hit balls onto, not into. Lay down the Chip Shot Target on the grass in your backyard and you're ready to sharpen up your short game. The center of this eight-foot-square net is marked off with a four-

Chip-N-Pitch Net

Chip Shot Target

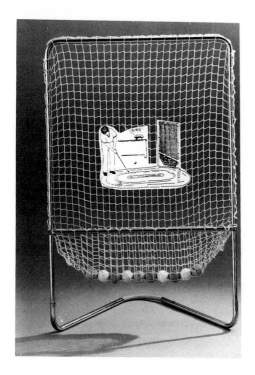

Chip 2 Par Practice Net

trajectory chip shots (it's something like trying to thread a needle) or for any kind of indoor practice (if you miss the hoop, your golf balls are likely to go bouncing around your basement). The Chip 2 Par Practice Net is designed to solve both of these problems. Because the unit stands upright and offers a 32-inch-square target area, it should be able to accommodate virtually all of the shots in your short-game arsenal. Its 42-inch-high frame is made of polished steel tubing, and its durable nylon net safely snags chip and pitch shots in mid-flight. (On impact they gently drop into a bag-like trough below, which holds up to several dozen golf balls at a time.) The easy-to-assemble unit weighs under five pounds and includes a special stake for anchoring it to the ground outdoors.

$19.95 from Triple Tee.

foot-square target area; for alignment purposes, there's also a white target line through the middle. The Chip Shot Target includes corner anchors for the net itself as well as a six-foot flagstick. And if you've ever tried to fit a flagstick into the trunk of your car, you'll be pleased to know that this one breaks into two pieces.

$24.95 from Northern Golf Ball Company.

CHIP 2 PAR PRACTICE NET

Most of the chipping and pitching nets on the market resemble oversize basketball hoops, which is fine for practicing those lofted wedge shots you'd like to land softly on the green. But just try using one of them for longer, lower-

CHIPPER NET

If the yips have crept into your chips, this nifty little practice net may help you get rid of them for good. You can

Chipper Net

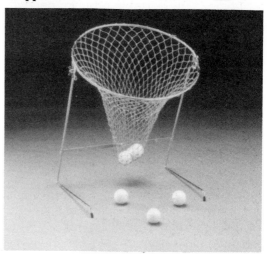

use the Chipper Net just about any-where, indoors or out, and its 16-inch-diameter hoop can be tilted to accommodate virtually any kind of shot in your short-game arsenal— from low-flying chips to high-flying pitches. The frame and hoop are made of chrome-plated steel, the net is nylon, and two wing nuts let you assemble and adjust everything with a few twists of the wrist.

$24.95 from Markline.

THE CLIKKA BAG
As shag bags go, the Clikka is clearly a breed apart: no zippers to jam, fabric to tear, or metal parts to rust. Made in England from high-impact plastic, the bag is lightweight yet durable and holds up to 80 golf balls, which pour out easily through a hatch in the top.

$24 from Competitive Edge Golf; also from Austad's.

GULL-WING PRACTICE NET
If you never quite feel at home on the range, why not set up your own range at home? This portable practice net will let you hit buckets of golf balls when-ever— and virtually wherever— you want. What's more, you needn't worry about being sued for malpractice: The Gull-Wing Practice Net's extended sides and high "ceiling" are designed to snare any shanked or skied shots that otherwise might sail through the neighbor's picture window. Best of all, once you've assembled the unit (with a screwdriver and a pair of pliers), you'll never need to worry about taking it apart or putting it back together; the steel-tubing frame and nylon net can be collapsed in seconds for convenient storage in your garage, basement, or utility room. When open for business the Gull-Wing Practice Net measures eight to nine feet high (depending on how you adjust it), 12 feet wide at the mouth, six feet wide at the back, and 6.5 feet deep; when folded up it measures just four inches deep.

$169.95 from Austad's.

HITTING MAT
If you're tired of the worn-out or torn-up hitting mats at your local driving range, why not take your own? The astroturf surface of this 18-by-24-inch mat may be the next best thing to a well-groomed golf course, and its extra-heavy construction allows it to be used even on concrete. Two rubber tees are included.

$19.95 from The Golf Works.

INDOOR GOLF NET AND FRAME
Want to turn your basement or garage into a full-fledged private driving range? If so, fear not: The Indoor Golf Net and Frame will do the trick and eliminate all risk of ricochet at the same time. The frame is made of high-strength alumi-num tubing and measures nine feet high, nine feet wide, and 12 feet deep when assembled; the net is extra-strong nylon in a three-quarter-inch mesh. The netting, which covers everything but the open end of the cage, is secured to the frame with hooks (in shower-curtain fashion); rubber floor mounts keep the unit from shifting. The Indoor Golf Net and Frame also includes a baffle, a 30-square-inch bull's-eye target, and a rubber hitting mat with replaceable tee.

$395 from Northern Golf Ball Company.

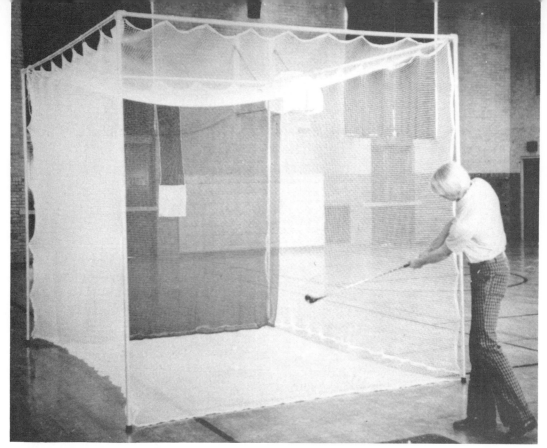

Indoor Golf Net and Frame

INDOOR/OUTDOOR PRACTICE NET

Just a minute . . . that's all it takes to set up this portable practice range in your backyard, basement, or garage. Since the Indoor/Outdoor Practice Net is completely self-supporting, you don't have to worry about securing it with guy wires or ground stakes, and you can rest assured that it will withstand even the heaviest artillery in your golf-bag arsenal. Its telescoping aluminum frame measures seven feet high, seven feet wide at the top, and 10 to 12 feet wide at the base, and its all-weather nylon net won't mildew or rot. As an added attraction, the unit comes with the Par-Buster Target and Chart (see below).

$109.95 from Golf Day Products; also from Par-Buster.

MACGREGOR CHIP AND DRIVE MAT

If you like the idea of hitting golf balls in your backyard but don't like the idea of hiring a full-time groundskeeper, the MacGregor Chip and Drive Mat may be the answer. Beyond protecting your lawn from all those unsightly divots, it features a detachable golf-ball-on-a-swiveling-arm gizmo that lets you swing to your heart's content without shagging. The durable rubber mat is completely weather-resistant, and its non-skid bottom prevents it from sliding or slipping— even on smooth concrete. You can hit shots either from a replaceable rubber tee or from a built-in strip of heavy-duty polypropylene turf, which has a white line down the middle to help you check your alignment. And just in case you'd like to take your own mat to the driving range for a change, there's even a handle cut into one end.

$34.99 from Nevada Bob's Discount Golf.

The 19th Hole Chip & Putt

The perfectly executed chip-and-run is one of golf's deadliest scoring shots. (How many times have you found yourself cursing an opponent who consistently chips the ball to within one-putt range?) Yet most high-handicap golfers rely far too much on the pitching wedge around the green and far too little on the less-lofted irons that can maximize the ball's roll on the game's smoothest surface— the putting green. If your scorecard is littered with double- and triple-bogeys, chances are you need to work on these delicate short shots, and The 19th Hole Chip & Putt can make your indoor or backyard practice sessions pay off in spades. It resembles a conventional electric putting cup— and, in fact, doubles as one— except for a high, rounded backstop that's specifically designed to snare chips on the run. The ramp leading up to the target is divided into numbered scoring zones (to help you chart your progress or engage in a little friendly competition), and the unit's automatic-return mechanism dutifully sends all but the most errant shots back from whence they came.

$24.95 from Everything for Golf.

No-Fore Practice Ball

As backyard practice goes, this may be the next best thing to a remote-controlled golf ball. It's a sturdy elastic-and-nylon-cord assembly with a ground stake attached to one end and a regulation golf ball secured to the other. Simply anchor the stake in the ground, hit away, and watch as the No-Fore Practice Ball flies, bounces, reverses course, and returns for more.

$6.95 from Golfsmith.

The Original Bag Shag

The Bag Shag's business is picking up— picking up golf balls, that is— and this one is the original article. Since it first took the dirty work out of shagging golf balls, there have been plenty of imitations but few real improvements. Its zippered, heavy-duty canvas bag holds up to 90 golf balls, and its aluminum pick-up tube is the next best thing to a well-trained Golden Retriever. What's more, the folks who manufacture The Original Bag Shag guarantee its faithfulness for five years.

$39 from Golf Day Products; also from Golfsmith and J. White Industries.

Par-Buster Target and Chart

Most sharpshooters wouldn't even think of practicing without a target. (Why do you think they call it *target practice*?) Golfers, on the other hand, often seem to have something else in mind when they practice. There's no other way to explain why so many of them spend so much time wantonly whacking golf balls into targetless nets. Hard to figure, particularly when practice-net targets are such invaluable— and inexpensive— accessories. This one is a green bull's-eye, 13 inches in diameter, that hangs on adjustable cords from the top or sides of any practice net. What's more, you can really improve your net results by using the chart that comes with the Par-Buster Target; simply raise or lower the bull's-eye to the precise height settings listed for each club. (And just in case you didn't realize it, the behavior of the ball as it hits the net will also tell you whether you've hooked or sliced a shot.)

$19 from Par-Buster.

The "Par"-Fect Golf Net

If you've always thought of golf nets as more trouble than they're worth— ever try dismantling one before the neighbors arrive for your backyard barbecue?— this retractable version may be the answer. The "Par"-Fect Golf Net works in window-shade fashion; you can let it down or put it away in just five seconds. The 12-foot-wide net can be used outdoors (installed over the opening to a garage, for example) or indoors (in a large basement or game room). The "Par-Fect" Golf Net is available in three ceiling heights, each with a bull's-eye target that pulls down independently.

$199.50 (eight-foot ceiling), $219.50 (nine-foot ceiling), and $229.50 (10-foot ceiling) from The Golf Works.

"Perfect Stroke" Golf Practice Net

If you happen to have a couple of big trees in your backyard, consider the alternatives: You can string up a hammock and go to sleep, in which case you don't need to bother reading on, or you can string up a golf net and go to work. The Perfect Stroke Golf Practice Net is 10 feet high, eight feet wide, and weighs just three and a half pounds. All four sides of its extra-strong, all-weather nylon netting are heavily bound to prevent unraveling, and the top edge is grommeted to hold the 30-foot cords that let you hang the net just about anywhere you please. (If your backyard is still in the sapling stage, you can set it up in the opening to your garage.)

$39.95 from Austad's or Northern Golf Ball Company.

Pitching Net

Need to tune up your short game? This anodized aluminum hoop with synthetic netting may be the answer. The net is 24 inches in diameter and sets up easily for indoor or outdoor use.

$14.50 from The Golf Works.

Practice Golf Cage

When you think of all the money you spend on those weekly trips to the local driving range— not to mention the time you waste in transit— the idea of forking out several hundred dollars for a home hitting cage may not seem so extravagant. At the end of the year you'll at least have something to show for your investment, and once you've recouped the initial outlay you can plow your savings into something else (a new set of clubs, perhaps?). The Practice Golf Cage's galvanized steel frame measures nine feet all around and is fitted with no-mar rubber feet for freestanding use indoors; guy lines and ground stakes are included for outdoor use. Its heavy-duty nylon net, which has a green baffle and scarlet target on the hitting surface, is completely bound and grommeted.

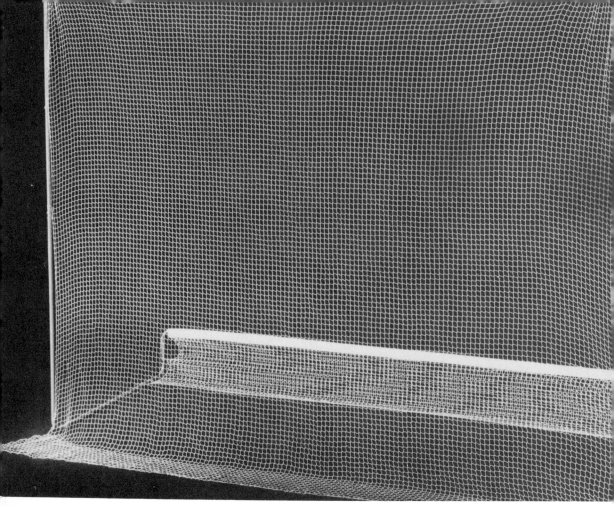

Practice Golf Range

And if you find this cage confining, the folks at Goal! will manufacture an even bigger one to your specifications. (One of the company's custom-built models sits atop a building in New York City.)

$399 from Goal!

PRACTICE GOLF RANGE

True, you can find a golf net that's taller or wider than this one. But what's the use if you then find yourself spending more time stringing up guidelines than teeing up golf balls? Therein lies the beauty of the Practice Golf Range. No guidelines, trees, or telephone poles are needed; a tubular steel frame lets the unit stand on its own at seven feet high and nine feet wide. You can set the thing up in just 10 minutes (it also folds laterally for convenient storage), yet it's durable enough to leave outdoors year-round. And thanks to its rear safety trap and "ride up" netting, the Practice Golf Range prevents bounce-backs as it snares golf balls, making it an ideal partner for practicing in the backyard, garage, or even— if you've got the nerve— the den.

$57.50 from Golfsmith; also from Competitive Edge Golf.

Putt-Caster

While this reel-and-retrieve gizmo is designed primarily for putting practice (see page 55), it also can take some of the tedium out of chipping and pitching practice. Simply clamp the Putt-Caster to the shaft of a short iron and you'll be able to "reel in" a tethered practice ball just like a fish—without chasing, stooping, or even moving your feet. A swivel mounted in the monofilament line prevents tangling or twisting and allows the ball to fly and roll just as if it were unattached. Perhaps best of all, this is one ball you'll never lose.

$29.50 from Ban Products.

Sand Trap Practice Net

Although trying to "baby" a ball out of a sand trap seldom works, that's exactly what most higher-handicap golfers do. Their sand-timid swings generally stem from the fear that they'll skull the ball and send it careening way past the pin—or, even worse yet, over the green. Practice is the only cure, and this may be the only net that's specifically designed to help you perfect those fearsome explosion shots from greenside traps. Its 18-by-24 inch target area can be rotated and locked into position at any angle. The net itself is made of durable knotless nylon, and the unit's legs are welded from one-inch-diameter steel tubing and coated with a white enamel finish. Spend enough time with this portable practice net and you'll soon be able to step into traps without thinking that they're filled with quicksand.

$29.45 from J. White Industries.

Shag King

If you're lucky enough to have a big backyard—the size, say, of a small driving range—you may already have realized that it's something of a mixed blessing. The good news is that you can hit hundreds of practice balls at a time; the bad news is that, sooner or later, you have to pick them up. Even if you let a shag bag do the dirty work, retrieving all those balls is golf's version of cruel and unusual punishment. Several options are available: (a) You can drive yourself into debt at the range; (b) You can buy used balls by the gross, find an open field somewhere, and leave 'em where they lie; or (c) You can acquire some oceanfront property, hit "floaters" (see page 196) into the water, and wait for them to come back in with the tide.

Or, if none of these alternatives seems particularly appealing, you can buy the Shag King, a compact manual version of those tractor-pulled picker-uppers that driving ranges use. This 35-pound, all-aluminum unit retrieves up to 300 balls at a time, can be easily maneuvered in and out of tight spots, and is virtually maintenance-free. And if don't let your nosy neighbors in on the secret, they may just think you're pushing a lawn mower around the backyard.

$365 from Hollrock Engineering; also from Northern Golf Ball Company.

Short Flyte Golf Balls

If using a golf net is out of the question, these foam-rubber golf balls may be the answer. It's virtually impossible to hit one more than 30 yards, in fact, making the Short Flyte ideal for backyard or indoor practice. And thanks to its solid

Short Flyte Golf Balls

core, the Short Flyte sounds like the real thing when hit and will even hook or slice. The soft foam rubber makes for minimum rebound and maximum safety.

$3.99 for a package of four from The Golf Works.

TARGET GREEN KIT

With a little space in your backyard and a garden trowel, you can easily create a realistic target area to practice your chipping and pitching. The Target Green Kit includes a regulation fiberglass flag-stick with an aluminum ferrule tip, a 13-by-17-inch red nylon flag (the number "19" is sewn on), and a regulation-size cycolac cup that sits six inches in the ground. Just remember, though, that those holes-in-one at home don't count.

$33.75 from The Golf Works.

TEE WIZZ

Tired of teeing up all those balls on the practice range? Let the Tee Wizz do it for you. Just tap its control switch with your clubhead and a mechanical arm automatically places the next golf ball in hitting position— either on a rubber tee or on the putting surface. You don't even need to bend over or break your stance between shots. The unit's dis-penser holds up to 50 golf balls at a time, and four "D"-cell batteries will keep it ticking for more than 50,000 swings. And because Tee Wizz is both cordless and lightweight (just under seven pounds), you can use it just about anywhere— indoors or out, at home or at the driving range.

$84.95 (includes an 11-by-24-inch practice mat and rubber tee) from Golf Day Products; also from Austad's, En-ticements, and Markline.

Tee Wizz

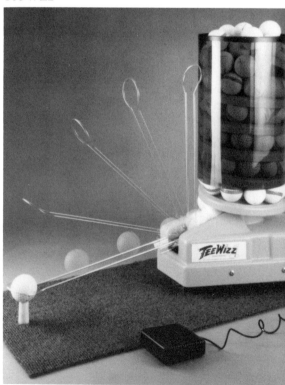

T-Mats

These look like ordinary driving-range mats, but the resemblance ends once you probe beneath the surface. Just try, for example, to insert one of those wooden tees into your run-of-the-mill range mat; chances are you'll wind up with bruised knuckles and a broken tee. Twist a tee into a T-Mat, however, and it simply stands at attention—at least until you strike the ball. The pile is three-quarters of an inch deep, which lets fairway woods and irons sweep right through, and the backing is a half-inch thick, which guards against slipping. T-Mats are available in three sizes: one foot by three feet ($25), three feet by four feet ($82), and four feet by five feet ($140).

From Par-Buster.

Wiffle Golf Balls

The one, the only, the original. If your backyard doubles as your practice range, you'll be pleased to know that the folks at Wiffle, who still make the best plastic baseballs money can buy, haven't forgotten golfers. (Your next-door neighbors won't really care, after all, whether you yelled "Fore!" just before your golf ball crashed through their plate-glass window.) You can whack away at Wiffle Golf Balls just about anywhere, indoors or out, without worrying about what errant hits might do to the premiums on your home-owner's insurance policy. These hollow, regulation-size balls are made of white plastic and have holes instead of dimples.

$6.95 for a bag of 36 from Sportime.

CHAPTER FIVE
KEEPING FIT FOR GOLF

KEEPING FIT FOR GOLF

THE AIRCAST PNEUMATIC ARMBAND

If you suffer from "golfer's elbow," the Aircast Pneumatic Armband may provide some welcome relief. By compressing the extensor muscle-tendon complex on the upper side of the upper forearm, the armband focuses pressure where it counts and constrains the normal expansion that occurs with contraction. Its air-cell unit conforms to the contour of your arm (one size fits most adults), cushioning the injured muscle and tendon.

$11.50 from Golfsmith; also from The Golf Works.

JERRY BARBER PRACTICE SWING DRIVER

As Bob Toski, one of the game's top teaching professionals and a regular on the Senior PGA Tour, wrote not long ago in *Golf Digest:* "There's no way around it. To increase distance you've got to increase strength and flexibility. And the best method I know for stretching and strengthening the golf muscles is to swing a weighted club, probably an extra-heavy driver."

For starters, practicing with a weighted club not only strengthens your shoulder, back, and leg muscles, but builds up the speed-generating power of your hands, wrists, and upper forearms. It also lengthens your arc— from takeaway to follow-through— and forces you to slow down your backswing so that you can properly "set" the club at the top. And because you must use a firmer grip, you'll maintain better control of the club throughout the entire swing.

As you add strength to your swing you'll also be improving your tempo and hand-eye coordination. You'll develop a better sense of how fast the clubhead is moving and find it easier to time your release through the impact zone. That means greater clubhead speed and greater accuracy.

The Jerry Barber Practice Swing Driver may not give you a powerful, repeating golf swing overnight, but it will give a thorough workout to the muscles you need to develop such a swing. It has a built-in swinging balance and is available in three different weights: light (for women, juniors, and seniors), medium (for most men), and heavy (for big hitters). Because it's only 40 inches long (slightly shorter than a standard driver), you can use it just about anywhere— in your home, at the office, or outside.

$56 for the 30-ounce model, $60 for the 40-ounce model, and $64 for the 50-ounce model (add $8 if you'd like it fitted with an optional training grip) from Barber-Goldentouch Golf; also from Las Vegas Discount Golf.

BIOCURVE HAND DEVELOPER

This may be news to you, but playing with a tennis ball actually can help improve your golf game. Don't hit it, though, just squeeze it— firmly and frequently enough to give your gripping muscles a good workout. Or go one step better and put your hands on a Bio-

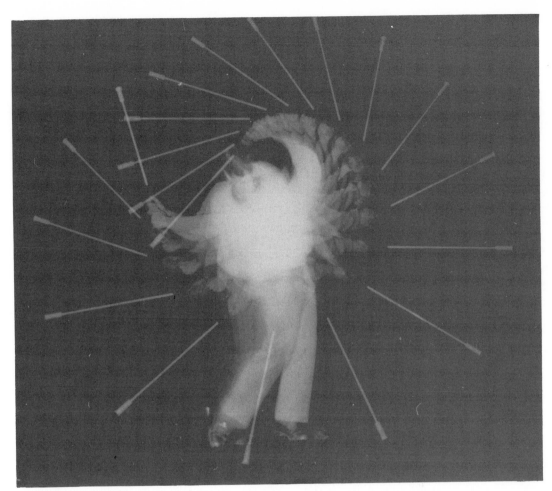

The Distance Builder

Curve Hand Developer. Unlike a tennis ball, its 19-degree curved shape lets your fingers fall naturally into place and your wrist remain straight. For maximum benefit to your hands, wrists, and forearms, squeeze and release this device at least 10 times in succession several times a day. The biggest payoff, believe it or not, may come on and around the green, not off the tee. "The players who have the best short games," Sam Snead once observed, "usually are the ones with strong hands."

$5.50 from Golf Day Products.

THE DISTANCE BUILDER

No pain, no gain? Well, here's a relatively painless way to gain distance in your golf game by developing the muscle groups used in a sound swing. The Distance Builder is a variable-weight training club that's designed to let you gradually build strength and suppleness. The base club itself is 37 inches long— about the length of a five- or six-iron— and weighs 37 ounces. But by adding five progressively heavier disks to the club in various combinations, you can work your way up to 68 ounces in a series of one-ounce increments. The

Distance Builder is accompanied by an instruction booklet and suggested training program.

$54.95 from The Golf Works; also from Banff Golf, Golf Day Products, and Gary Wiren's "Golf Around the World."

The Golferciser

Most warm-up weights add their ounces near the bottom of a club; this device—a heavy handle that fits over the grip— does its stuff at the other end. But the Golferciser, which was designed by Joe Spoonster of the Golf School for the Blind, is really a three-in-one training tool: In addition to letting you limber up before play or practice, it can strengthen some of your key golf muscles and improve your feel around the green. (Its large diameter, which makes for a grip about the size of a baseball-bat handle, helps take your wrists out of the action in chipping and pitching.) Ken Venturi's instructions take you through the paces of practicing with the Golferciser, but be forewarned that you shouldn't hit full shots while it's clamped to a club (such malpractice can crimp the shaft). Best of all, as you help yourself you'll also be helping others: All proceeds go to help blind people learn to play golf.

$59.50 from Everything for Golf.

GolfGym

Here's an ingenious exercise device designed specifically for fitness-conscious golfers. While it's based on the same principles of dynamic tension that body-builders have used for years, GolfGym's secret is a special golf train-ing grip that makes it possible to isolate and strengthen the muscles you need the most for maximum distance, control, and performance. The unit automatically adjusts to any swing and provides 16 physiologically correct exercises— from chest pulls to torso stretches— that build and condition golf-specific muscles. Best of all, the GolfGym can be used virtually anywhere: at home, in the office, while traveling, or for warming up on the course. The Regular GolfGym provides a moderate workout for men, women, seniors, and youth; the Advanced GolfGym provides a heavy workout for men.

$24.95 from Austad's; also from Competitive Edge Golf, The Golf Works, and Las Vegas Discount Golf.

Heavy Weighted Practice Club

Here's another entry in the swing-a-heavy-club sweepstakes. (If you're not yet sold on the benefits of practicing with a weighted club, see the entry in this chapter for the Jerry Barber Practice Swing Driver). The Heavy Weighted Practice Club looks like most any laminated driver, except that the face of its walnut-finished head has no insert. And for good reason: You should never, ever attempt to hit a real golf ball with this extra-heavy stick. There's more than a pound of weight in the clubhead alone, and it's fitted with a 40-inch, heavy-duty steel shaft.

$37.50 from Golfsmith.

"Limber-Up" Golf Mitt

This may be the heaviest headcover you can buy, but that, after all, is the idea . . . it's specially weighted for warm-up

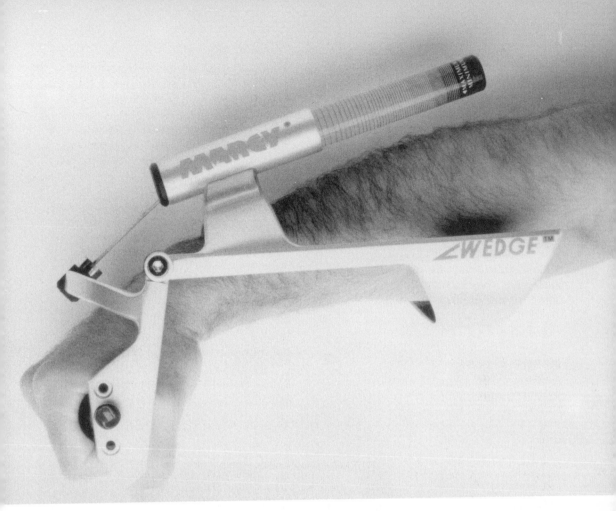

The Marcy Wedge

purposes. Place the vinyl "Limber-Up" golf mitt over any wood in your bag, zip it up, and slowly swing away.

$3.95 from Northern Golf Ball Company; also from Golfsmith, Las Vegas Discount Golf, and J. White Industries.

THE MARCY WEDGE

Although you can carry it in your golf bag and it might help you blast out of bunkers, this wedge is not— repeat, not— a golf club. Developed by Marcy Fitness Products, it's the first exercise device specifically designed to isolate and strengthen the flexor and extensor muscles of the hands, wrists, and forearms— muscles that can mean power, speed, and control in your golf swing. Unless your daily training regimen includes wrist curls with small dumbbells, however, chances are you've been neglecting them.

With the lightweight Marcy Wedge in your bag, briefcase, or desk drawer, you need neglect them no longer. Simply slip your forearm between its cushioned aluminum struts and grab the adjustable, foam-padded grip. As you bend your wrist back and forth, your muscles extend and flex— at first with little opposition. But twist the spring-loaded "variable tension cylinder" and you can gradually increase the resistance as you get stronger— up to the equivalent of a 15-pound dumbbell. Daily workouts with the Marcy Wedge (five or more sets of 15 to 20 repetitions per arm) should strengthen your grip, lengthen your drives, and let you dispose of any wise guys in the gallery with a mere flick of the wrist in lieu of a late lunch of persimmon.

$49.95 from Prism Marketing; also from Austad's, The Golf Works, Markline, and The Sharper Image.

POWER BUILDER

Nothing exotic here: The 38-ounce Power Builder is simply a sawed-off golf shaft (it's just 24 inches long) with a steel weight epoxied and pinned to the end. But swing it just 25 times a day and you'll begin to feel added strength and flexibility in the muscles you need most for golf. With the optional training grip, your hands will be correctly positioned at the same time.

$21.95 ($24.95 with training grip) from The Golf Works.

POWER FLEXOR

You don't need arms the size of sequoia saplings to hit the ball a country mile, but you do need, among other things, a good grip and sufficient strength in your wrists and forearms. Just a minute or two a day with the Power Flexor— an adjustable-tension, rotary-action exer-

Power Flexor

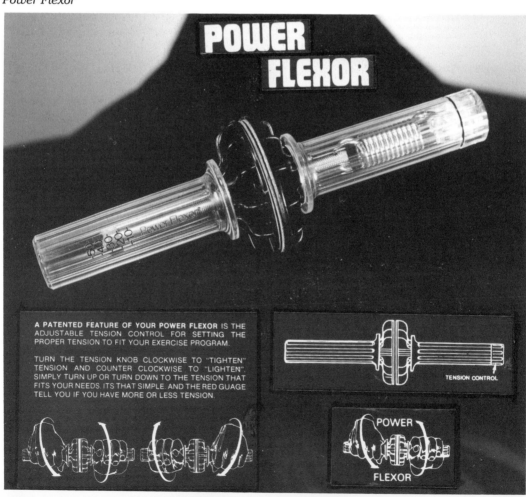

ciser—will build up the muscles in your wrists and forearms and maybe even add some of those yearned-for yards to your golf game. Just grab hold of the cylindrical unit with both hands, begin twisting its clear plastic grips in opposite directions, and you're on the way.

$14.95 from Rebound Systems.

POWERSTROKE

You don't need the strength of a gorilla to hit a long ball, but once you've built a sound golf swing there's little doubt that stronger means longer. Powerstroke, a simple exercise device based on the principle of increasing elastic resistance, is designed to strengthen the muscles you need the most in the impact zone—those precious moments preceding and following the clubface's contact with the ball. Attach one end of Powerstroke's elastic tubing to a secure anchor point (a doorknob, handrail, or table leg, for example), and loop the other end around the shaft of any golf club just below the grip. Then, with one or both hands, swing the club back and forth through the impact zone—an arc of no more than four feet or so—in the desired number of repetitions. Powerstroke's basic exercise motion builds muscles in the hands, wrists, arms, shoulders, and legs, and as your strength increases you can gradually move the elastic tubing down the club shaft for greater resistance.

$12 from Powerstroke.

POWER SWING

A smoother, more powerful golf swing out of thin air? That's the idea behind Power Swing, a warm-up and exercise device based on the principle of progressive air resistance. Although the upper half of Power Swing resembles a conventional golf club, the lower half—with four large airfoils at right angles to each other—looks more like a rocket's tail fins. Simply swing the device as you would any golf club, and air resistance will give your golfing muscles—in the hands, wrists, arms, shoulders, and back—a good workout. The faster you swing, the greater the resistance (with maximum effect at peak velocity). That means you don't need to add weights or step up repetitions to build an increasingly powerful swing . . . air, and air alone, does the trick.

$40 from Sunland Marketing; also from Polar Golf.

POWER TONE EXERCISER

"You don't need to be a scientist to figure out that the faster the clubhead moves the more strength it takes to control it," Sam Snead, one of the game's genuine legends, wrote a while back in *Golf Digest.* "For that reason, I recommend exercises to build up the strength in your hands, wrists, and forearms. Your biceps aren't all that important. If you look at a person like Gary Player you'll see what I mean. He's got forearms like Popeye."

The Power Tone Exerciser may not have you swinging like Player on the course or Popeye off, but it will help increase the strength of your hands, wrists, forearms, and shoulders. Just grab hold of this cylindrical gizmo as you would a baseball bat and begin twisting your hands in opposite directions; then work your way through any or all of the 11 other strength-building exercises outlined in an accompanying booklet. By spending only 10 minutes a

Powerstroke

day with the Power Tone Exerciser, says the retired PGA professional who developed it, you'll dramatically strengthen the muscles that put power—and precision—in your golf swing.

$19.95 from Competitive Edge Golf.

SWING DEVELOPER
The perfect golf swing is a thing of power and grace. If you've got plenty of the latter but little of the former, work out for a while with this weight-and-pulley exercise device and you just might be able to see more of Arnold

Schwarzenegger in your swing. The Swing Developer consists of a 12-inch wall-mounting bracket, a pulley, and a length of rope connected to a handle that resembles a sawed-off golf club. Simply secure standard gym weights (they're not included) to the other end of the rope, take hold of the grip, and swing oh-so-slowly away from the wall. Once you've sufficiently built up the golf-specific muscles in your back, shoulders, and forearms, you won't need to think of a 300-yard drive as the impossible dream. And best of all, those wedge-wielding bullies on the golf course won't splash sand in your face anymore.

$27.75 from Golfsmith; also from J. White Industries.

TOUR BELT

It's as simple as this: You can't play good golf with a bad back. If hours of hunched-over putting at the practice green, endless buckets of balls at the driving range, or simple stress and fatigue have left aches, pains, or strains in your lower back, maybe you should try on the Tour Belt. It's designed to banish golf-induced backaches for good by relieving tight, sore, and injured muscle tissues in the lower back or oblique abdominals— during and after play or practice.

Simply center the Tour Belt around the small of your back, fasten it in place with a Velcro strap, and "pressure up" by pumping air into the belt through the nozzle of a squeeze bulb. As the belt's air cells expand, they contour

around your back and force tight, knotted muscles to return to their natural resting length. (The air-acti-vated belt, in fact, acts as a mechanical muscle relaxer.) Soreness, stiffness, and spasms usually disappear within a few minutes.

So if you can't afford to spend the golf season in your recliner, you might be wise to invest in a Tour Belt. Unlike corsets or braces, it doesn't restrict movement. And while it's designed to be worn over regular clothing— on or off the golf course— it also can be hidden underneath. The Tour Belt is available in four belt sizes: small (23-29), medium (30-38), large (39-46), and extra-large (47-52).

$59.95 from The Golf Works.

WARM-UP PRACTICE WEIGHT

After Elston Howard introduced profes-sional baseball to the "swing dough-nut"— a circular, plastic-coated weight with a hole in the middle— most major-league sluggers stopped using two bats to warm up in the on-deck circle. This smaller version lets you loosen up your golfing muscles before you reach the first tee— or strengthen them as you swing in your backyard— without the worry of clacking clubheads. Just slip the "doughnut" on the shaft of any wood— it won't slide off— and swing away.

$3.95 from Las Vegas Discount Golf; also from Austad's, Golf Day Products, The Golf Works, Golfsmith, Northern Golf Ball Company, and J. White Industries.

CHAPTER SIX

GAMES, TOYS, AND SOFTWARE

GAMES, TOYS, AND SOFTWARE

APBA PROFESSIONAL GOLF GAME

A warning of sorts is in order before you take up this game: Play a few rounds of APBA Professional Golf and odds are you'll be addicted—helplessly, hopelessly, and happily hooked. Unlike most other golf games, this one lets you step into the shoes of the greatest players in history—Tommy Armour, Jimmy Demaret, Walter Hagen, Ben Hogan, Bobby Jones, Byron Nelson, Gene Sarazen, and Sam Snead, among others—and hit every shot just as they might have in real life. You get 32 player cards that capture the legends at the peak of their games and faithfully replicate their performance with every club in the bag (three woods, 10 irons, and a putter). Hagen, for example, is somewhat erratic off the tee but brilliant in recovering with his mid- and short-irons. Jones, with his renowned "Calamity Jane," fears no green; in this game he's downright deadly from within 12 feet and occasionally sinks putts from more than 100 feet away.

APBA's par-71 championship course is a challenging composite layout drawn from 18 of the most difficult and famous golf holes in America. The 17th hole, for example, is the breathtaking but treacherous par-3 16th at the Cypress Point Club on California's Monterey Peninsula. From the tee you look out over the pounding surf of the Pacific Ocean to a smallish green, guarded by five sand traps, some 220 yards away. Big-hitters may be able to reach it with a two-iron, but most players will have to use a three-wood. APBA's 378-yard par-4 finishing hole is the celebrated 11th of the East Course

at Merion Golf Club in Ardmore, Pennsylvania, where in 1930 Bobby Jones played his last shot in formal competition—and completed his historic Grand Slam—by clinching the U.S. Amateur Championship in match play, eight and seven. As with the player cards, each of APBA's 18 holes is a realistic reproduction of its real-life counterpart—right down to the trees, sand traps, and water hazards. A five-yard-square grid system allows you to track the golf ball's movement on a hole in any and all directions.

The APBA Professional Golf Game accommodates from one to four players at a time. (Even if you choose to make it a solitary pursuit, you can call all the shots for up to four golfers.) Every shot in the game is activated by APBA's double-digit dice principle: A large red die creates the first digit and a smaller white die the second, providing 36 numerical possibilities in all (from 11 to 66). After assessing your player's lie (tee/fairway, rough, or sand) and shot-making abilities (a distance key on each card provides some guidance), you select a club and roll the dice. You then consult the player card and game board to determine the result. The game board breaks each tee and approach shot into carry and roll, and some rolls of the dice can produce hooks and slices of varying severity. Each green has six possible pin locations, and once on the putting surface you can either charge the cup or lag up for a likely tap-in.

The APBA Professional Golf Game includes a folding game board that opens to a size of 16.5 by 29.5 inches; the APBA course, which is printed in

CHAMPIONSHIP GOLF— THE GREAT COURSES OF THE WORLD (VOLUME ONE: PEBBLE BEACH)

"The finest meeting of land and sea in the world." That's how Robert Louis Stevenson described the Pacific coastline around Carmel Bay, the spectacular setting of California's Pebble Beach Golf Links. Each year hundreds of thousands of golfers make the pilgrimage to Pebble Beach, where for $150 they can play the only public golf course ever to have hosted the U.S. Open championship. (Jack Nicklaus won his third of four U.S. Opens there in 1972, and Tom Watson won his only U.S. Open title at Pebble Beach in 1982.) Its 548-yard par-5 finishing hole, which is widely considered to be the greatest 18th in the world, may alone be worth the steep price of admission. Depending on your point of view (and perhaps your handicap), the crashing waves of the Pacific Ocean, which flank the left side of the hole from tee to green, make for either a breathtaking piece of beachfront property or a heart-stopping, ball-swallowing hazard.

Championship Golf, a computerized golf-simulation game from Gamestar, lets you and up to three other players experience many of the thrills— and chills— of a real-life round at Pebble Beach. Its full-color animated graphics are eye-popping, but that's just for openers. The software's 32-page instruction booklet bears the byline of Michael McTeigue, a leading PGA professional and the author of *The Keys to the Effortless Golf Swing*. McTeigue is perfectly on target when

color on nine 16.75-by-14.75-inch boards; the set of 32 player cards; four metal golf-ball markers; two dice and a shaker; and, of course, the rules of the game. If you're like most APBA golf addicts, however, you'll soon come to think of this game as merely a starter set. The company also offers five additional golf courses (Merion; Pebble Beach; Firestone Country Club's South Course in Akron, Ohio; Pinehurst Country Club's Course No. 2 in North Carolina; and Pine Valley Golf Club in Clementon, New Jersey) and two sets of contemporary player cards (one issued in 1981 and the other in 1985).

$18.25 from APBA Game Company. Additional golf courses are $8 each and additional sets of player cards are $3.50 each.

he writes: "These instructions are called 'Fools Rush In . . .' because, like real golf, Championship Golf is easy to play but not so easy to play well. You have been warned."

Each player begins by choosing a set of tees (forward, middle, or back) and pin placements (preliminary or final round), as well as a set of 14 clubs (from six woods, nine irons, two wedges, and a putter). A punch of a key then whisks your group to the first tee, where you'll see a split-screen depiction of Pebble Beach's opening par-4. The left side of the screen gives you a direct overhead view of the hole from tee to green (including trees, rough, water, and sand) and keeps track of all the vital statistics (including the prevailing speed and direction of the wind); a "zoom-lens" option also lets you close in on the area around your ball. The right side of the screen gives you a ground-level view of the hole, just as if you were standing behind your ball. Now for the really nifty part: Championship Golf gives you complete freedom to move and look around as you play each hole. Can't see around the dogleg? Just walk to the left until the green comes into view. Big tree blocking your shot? Hit a key and you're 100 feet up, looking right over it. If you need to, you can even widen the right-side view for a full-screen perspective on your shot. What's more, the entire course is overlaid with an ingenious grid system to help you reckon which way your ball is likely to bounce on the fairway or break on the green.

Shot-making in this game has all the elements of real golf; you select the club, aim the shot, and control the tempo and timing of your swing. You can open or close your stance to fade or draw a shot, and you even put some extra spin on the ball by opening or closing the clubface. But you ain't got a

thing if you ain't got the swing, they say, and this can be either the easiest—or the trickiest—part of Championship Golf. You can take all of the guesswork out of your golf swing by pressing F10, which kicks the computer into cruise control and delivers consistent, average shotmaking at about 60 percent of full power. With judicious club selection you can play a competent round of golf by using the "easy-swing" key for every shot. But if you want to play Pebble Beach like a Nicklaus or a Watson, you'll have to work the computer's keyboard like a Paderewski. Various keys control your body turn, arm speed, and wrist action, and you must strike them in just the right combination and with just the right timing to produce maximum distance and accuracy. (The trick is to let your fingers do their talking in the downswing's "power zone.") Uncoil your body or release your wrists too early and you'll lose lots of power at impact; wait too long and you'll top your shot or even miss the ball altogether. (If you whiff, don't despair—the game lets you take as many mulligans as you need.)

Championship Golf takes care of everything else as you play Pebble Beach—from recommending the right club to filling out the scorecard—and you can even tune up your game at the practice range and putting green. The software also keeps a running chart of all-time low scores and allows you to halt play in the middle of a round, store the game in progress, and pick up later wherever you left off. (The last feature can come in handy at the office, particularly if you can't squeeze all 18 holes into your lunch break.) Championship Golf is available for Amiga (512K) as well as IBM/compatible (128K) computers.

$14.95 from Activision.

COMPU-GOLF

Suffering from a chronic case of flying elbow? Have the outside-in blues got you down? Then maybe it's time for a house call from Don Trahan, a.k.a. "The Swing Surgeon." Trahan, a PGA professional and teaching editor of *Golf Magazine*, has developed the first computer software program that diagnoses ailments of the golf swing and then prescribes corrective action. After you answer a series of questions about your stance, alignment, posture, grip, ball-striking ability, and the like, Compu-Golf draws color-graphic illustrations of your swing at various stages. It then analyzes more than 30,000 possible set-up and swing combinations, explains why you hit the ball the way you do, and prescribes the cure. The software (for IBM PCs/compatibles) stores personalized data for up to 10 golfers.

$59.95 from Golf Day Products, GolfSmart, and Las Vegas Discount Golf.

CONDO GOLF

The best thing about Condo Golf may be this: When you command your approach shots to "bite," they do. Because the lightweight golf balls used in this indoor game are covered with Velcro, they obediently adhere to Condo Golf's fabric target— the 19th hole at "Club Zanzibar"— the instant they hit it. You'll have to watch out for the various hazards that have been silk-screened onto the layout— water on the left, trees on the right, and two sand traps tucked behind the green— but otherwise you have a clear shot to the stick. Condo Golf includes an artificial-grass hitting mat (to protect your carpet or floor); four Velcro-covered balls; the green-and-white target, which is easily as-

sembled and adjusted on a tubular frame; and, of course, a scorecard. You supply the chipping or pitching irons. The game is safe to use around the house or in the office, and the folks next door won't ever complain about the loud thwack of golf balls against the wall.

$29.95 from Las Vegas Discount Golf; also from Haverhills.

GOLF ATTACHÉ

Want to sneak in nine holes on your lunch hour? Now, thanks to the Golf Attaché, you can do just that— without even leaving the office. This miniature-golf-course-in-a-briefcase goes anywhere you do, and the layout is a lot more formidable than it seems at first glance. The built-in ramps, sharp doglegs, and assorted obstacles (there's no windmill, but there are simulated sand traps and water hazards), make any hole-in-one a real cause for celebration. Everthing you need to play is packed right inside the Golf Attaché, including a pair of teeny-weeny putters, golf balls, and, of course, a scorecard.

$119.95 from The Price of His Toys.

GOLF CLASSIC

If you'd rather be playing golf than helping your kids with their math homework, here's a computer game that should make everyone happy. This challenging 18-hole golf course— complete with trees, water hazards, and sand traps— teaches youngsters how to estimate angles and distances. It also demonstrates the untoward mathematical consequences of hitting a ball out of bounds. Golf Classic accommodates up

to four players (ages nine and up recommended) and is available in Apple II
(64K and 128K) and IBM PC/compatible
(128K) versions.

$34.95 from Milliken Publishing.

GOLF DOCTOR

Something ailing your golf game? Maybe
it's time to make an appointment with
John Jacobs, a.k.a. "Dr. Golf," whose
common-sense approach to teaching
has made him one of the world's leading
golf instructors. This is basically a
software version of Jacobs's hard-
bound book by the same name (which,
if you don't happen to have an IBM
PC or compatible computer, will have
to suffice). In the first two "chapters"
Jacobs outlines the fundamental tenets
of his teaching philosophy, namely: The
golf ball doesn't care about anything but
what the clubhead does to it, and how
the ball flies tells a lot about how you
swing. Then, after the basics are out of
the way, the software presents you with
a menu of 15 full-swing and five short-
game faults. Pick one, punch a key, and
presto— Golf Doctor prescribes the cure.
If you'd like, you can also print out the
prescriptions and take them with you to
the practice range.

$59.95 from 1 Step Software.

THE GOLF GAME PAR EXCELLENCE

Whether you're grounded by acropho-
bia, a lean bank account, or just plain
awful weather, this ingenious board
game will let you play 18 of the world's
greatest golf holes— from England, Ire-
land, Japan, Portugal, Scotland, Spain,
and the United States— without leaving
home.
After teeing off at
the legendary Ailsa Course of
Turnberry Golf Club in Scotland, you'll
decide which pin to shoot for on the
double-greened sixth hole at Kasumi-
gaseki Golf Club in Saitama, Japan;
risk an evil encounter with "Hell's Half
Acre" on the 7th hole at Pine Valley Golf
Club in Clementon, New Jersey; choose
whether to play it safe or go for broke
on the par-3 12th at Augusta National
Golf Club in Georgia (which Jack Nicklaus once aptly called "the most demanding tournament hole in the
world"); and finish on the heart-stop-
ping 18th at Pebble Beach Golf Links in
California.

The composite course on which
you travel around the world in 18 holes
is beautifully laid out on a set of nine,
full-color, 14-by-23-inch laminated
sheets. Each side features a stunning,
aerial-view illustration by artist Barry
Mitchell, complemented by one or more
color photographs of the hole and an
incisive review by Robert Green, whose

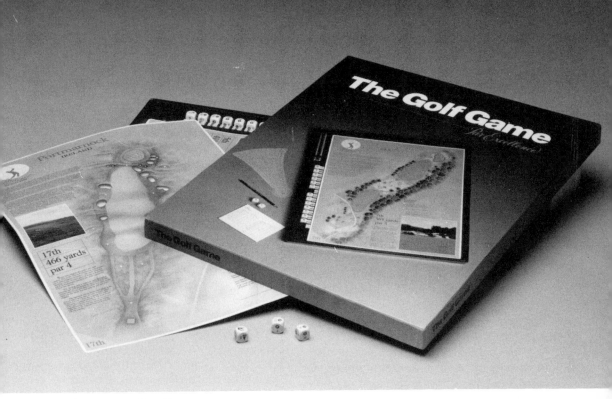

The Golf Game Par Excellence

commentary is rich with anecdotes and tactical advice. The game is played with a set of 15 dice— 13 for the various clubs, one for direction, and another for hazards— and a transparent template that lets each player plot and mark his shots. The Golf Game Par Excellence is easy to learn (5 or 10 minutes should do the trick), accommodates up to four players, and, thanks to Mitchell and Green, is as much fun to look at and read as it is to play.

$65 from Abercrombie & Fitch.

Golf Handicapper

If you happen to own a Commodore 64 computer, you probably haven't had much trouble finding golf games designed with your machine in mind. As for the serious business of tracking scores and calculating handicaps,

however, virtually all of the software on the market is aimed at Apple and IBM-compatible computers. So here's a little bit of good news: Golf Handicapper, which was written specifically for the Commodore 64, will let you maintain and update data for up to 149 golfers at a time, including each player's name, 20 most recent scores (and differentials), best score, total number of rounds, and handicap (based on anything from the single best round of the most recent five to the 10 best rounds of the most recent 20). As new scores are added beyond the 20th, the oldest scores are automatically dropped from the database. If you have a Commodore 1525 or compatible printer, this easy-to-use software will even generate handicap sheets.

$39.95 from Dynacomp.

GOLF PARTNER

Golf, for better or for worse, is a game of numbers, and this menu-driven handicapping and trend-analysis system should help you improve the bottom line. Golf Partner is designed for individuals or small groups of players who wish not only to maintain accurate and up-to-date handicaps but to analyze and learn more about their games. For starters, this easy-to-use software calculates traditional and Slope handicaps in accordance with the rules set down by the United States Golf Association (or, if you choose, the Royal Canadian Golf Association). It can also can store up to 75 course definitions, maintain handicaps and performance statistics for up to 15 different players, and generate several types of on-screen and printed reports. Once you've stored a course definition, you need only enter a player's score and number of putts on each hole. Golf Partner does the rest. It can display various statistics and indexes derived from those figures (greens in regulation, for example) round by round and break them down into par 3s, 4s, and 5s. It also can analyze the same statistics for an entire season, comparing a player's most recent round, last five rounds, and overall performance. Each feature is selected by pressing the appropriate function key (F1 through F10). Golf Partner is accompanied by a comprehensive user manual and is available for IBM PCs/XTs/ATs or compatibles (256K) with PC- or MS-DOS 2.0 or higher.

$49.95 (specify USGA or RCGA version) from Traders Marketing.

GOLFER'S CRIBBAGE

A word of caution at the outset: If you lose your tee in this game, you're out of luck. This 9-by-24-inch hardwood cribbage board has been disguised as a nine-hole golf course— complete with trees, water hazards, and sand traps— and uses real tees in lieu of pegs. You'll need at least a twosome to play Golfer's Cribbage, along with a standard deck of playing cards (not included). And when you've finished, you can just hang it up . . . on the wall.

$45.95 from Golf Day Products.

GOLF'S BEST—PINEHURST No. 2

Tommy Armour said it best: "The man who doesn't feel emotionally stirred when he golfs at Pinehurst beneath those clear blue skies and with the pine fragrance in his nostrils is one who should be ruled out of golf for life." Amen, for the Number 2 course at Pinehurst Country Club may— with the possible exception of the Seminole Golf Club in North Palm Beach, Florida— be the most beautiful and challenging layout ever designed by the legendary Donald Ross.

Today Ross is considered the patron saint of the American Society of Golf Course Architects (whose official jacket is in the Ross plaid), and justly so. From 1912 until his death in 1948, he was the nation's most prominent and prolific golf course architect, with hundreds of courses— from Cuba to California— to his credit.

At the turn of the century Ross had been persuaded by soda-fountain tycoon James Tufts to sign on as winter golf professional at the resort he was developing in Pinehurst, North Carolina. Ross immediately rebuilt and expanded the primitive nine-hole layout that Tufts had installed, and in 1901 he set about

tion of Ross's signature course can bring some of its treasures— and treacherousness— right into your home. Each hole is represented in monochrome and color and simulated exactly to scale. The electronic layout is absolutely faithful to the real one, with rough, trees and bushes, out-of-bounds areas, water hazards, and sand traps. Even the undulations in the terrain and the vagaries of the wind affect how well you'll play Golf's Best— Pinehurst No. 2.

Before you tee off, you specify how many are in your group (one to four can play), their names, and whether you wish to play from the regular or championship tees. Pin placements vary from game to game. While you can request on-screen instructions before you begin, playing a few holes is all it takes to pick up the basics. You'll see bird's-eye views of each shot until you get close to the green; from there, the screen zeroes in on the putting surface itself. After the computer determines who's away and displays the remaining distance to the pin, the player chooses a club (from any of 14 you put in your bag at the beginning of the game), the force of the swing, the intended line of flight, and the type of shot (if you'd like, you can try to draw or fade the ball). A club selection chart helps you pick the right stick, and you can preview and adjust the direction of your shot, which is measured in clock hours and minutes, as much as you'd like before you hit. Be forewarned, however, that if you fail to take into account the wind's direction and speed, which can range from five to 25 miles per hour, you're asking for trouble. With each shot the ball flies, bounces, and rolls just as it would on the actual golf course. The computer keeps score, of course, and displays the scorecard at any point during a round.

The software has some other nice touches, including a save-a-game

designing and building a second 18 from scratch. Pinehurst's Course Number 2 opened for play six years later, but Ross really never considered his pet project finished. He extensively remodeled the course twice, once in 1925 and again in 1935, when he converted its old sand greens to Bermuda grass, rebunkered nearly every hole, and added strategic mounds and hollows. Over the years Ross built three more courses at Pinehurst, although two of them— his original Number 4 and Number 5 courses— were abandoned during World War II as an austerity measure. Despite his far-flung activities as a course architect, Ross maintained his position as golf manager at the Pinehurst complex until his death. He considered the Number 2 course, with all its masterful subtleties, to be his finest achievement.

If you've never made the pilgrimage to Pinehurst, this computerized simula-

feature (just in case the boss walks in before your group has completed its appointed rounds), a running chart of all-time low scores, and special key options to speed up play. Golf's Best— Pinehurst No. 2 contains disks for Apple II series (48K), Commodore 64/128, and IBM/compatible (128K) computers.

$24.95 from 1 Step Software.

Golf's Best—St. Andrews

Mother Nature knew best. She carved the Old Course at St. Andrews out of the low, sandy ground along the Fifeshire coast of Eastern Scotland and added bunkers by forcing her flocks of sheep to scratch out shelters from the fierce winds of the North Sea. By 1754, when 22 gentlemen banded together to establish the Society of St. Andrews Golfers, the course was already more than three centuries old. Some 80 years afterward King William IV was induced to recognize it as "royal and ancient," and ever since then the Royal and Ancient Golf Club at St. Andrews has faithfully maintained the game's heritage and honor. Even though "The Home of Golf" is actually home to four courses in all, the name St. Andrews is synonymous for just one of them: the Old Course.

Since 1900 the Old Course has served as the site of 15 British Open championships, and until recently the only way you could hit these historic links yourself involved some transatlantic travel. No more. If you're willing to settle for a software-based substitute, Golf's Best— St. Andrews will, for a one-time greens fee, let you play the Old Course as often as you'd like. All of its obstacles and hazards— trees, bushes, sand and pot bunkers, stone bridges, and so forth— are realistically replicated

on the screen, and you'll even have to cope with gusting winds of up to 25 miles per hour. Otherwise the game is played just like its computerized cousin, Golf's Best— Pinehurst No. 2 (see above).

Unlike most modern layouts, the Old Course has only two par-3s and two par-5s. Nonetheless, St. Andrews is responsible for fixing the standard round of golf at 18 holes. No one knows exactly why, but legend has it that back in the 1700s golfers customarily drank a jigger of Scotch on each hole. The fellows of St. Andrews, the story goes, decided to end their appointed rounds when their bottles, which held 18 jiggers of whisky, were empty. Anyone who plays this addictive electronic version of the Old Course, however, would be well-advised to forget the royal and ancient tradition. Golf's Best— St. Andrews contains disks for Apple II series (48K), Commodore 64/128, and IBM/compatible (128K) computers.

$24.95 from 1 Step Software.

Golf Tournament Scoring Program

Running a golf tournament can involve all kinds of logistical and statistical headaches— from assigning tee times and otherwise managing the field to figuring out the final results and awarding all the prizes. It's a tedious, time-consuming, and often thankless job— just the kind of job, in fact, that should be turned over to a personal computer. That's where Sportsware's easy-to-use Golf Tournament Scoring Program enters the picture. If you're in charge of a tournament, outing, or other event, this menu-driven software, which tracks up to 300 players over one to four rounds, may be the next best thing

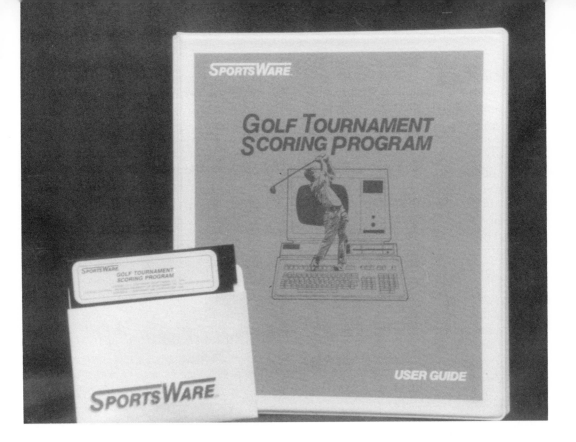

since cruise control. For starters, you can use it to create and update player and prize lists, to print fully stroked scorecards, and to assign all tee times, carts, and tee numbers (for shotgun starts). The program offers nearly a dozen different individual and team scoring formats, including gross, USGA net, Callaway net, quota points, points, Stableford, scramble, and various best-ball combinations. It even lets you run skins games on the side. As play proceeds the software will generate leader boards and other scoring reports, and when all the scores have been posted it will verify them, automatically break any ties, match prizes to winners, and present the final results. (If you'd like, it also will generate a complete statistical analysis of the tournament scores.) You'll be able to go directly from the scoring table to the awards ceremony in a matter of minutes and with complete

confidence that everything's right. And if there's still light, you'll even be able to head for the first tee and get in a round yourself. The Golf Tournament Scoring Program is available for IBM PCs/compatibles (256K) with PC- or MS-DOS 3.1 or higher.

$350 from SportsWare.

HANDICAP MANAGER

If you think that organizing a golf league is lots of fun, just try running one. Aside from maintaining accurate and up-to-date handicaps for dozens— maybe even hundreds— of players, you'll have to promptly post individual scores and tournament results, constantly compile all kinds of rankings and statistics, and otherwise immerse yourself in the nightmarish nitty-gritty of managing a golf league. If you don't have a computer at home or at work, here's what you should do: resign right now.

If you happen to have an IBM PC, XT, AT, or compatible computer, however, you're in luck. Handicap Manager, a menu-driven handicapping and reporting system for leagues of up to 3,000 players, can ease most of the logistical and statistical headaches. For starters, this easy-to-use software calculates traditional and Slope handicaps in accordance with the rules set down by the United States Golf Association (or, if you choose, the Royal Canadian Golf Association). It can also can store up to 75 course definitions, maintain lists of players in up to 15 different flights, and generate a wide variety of printed reports, including handicap cards, player lists (by name, number, or rank within flight), tournament results (by gross or net scores), and course lists. Each feature is selected by pressing the appropriate function key (F1 through F10). Handicap Manager is accompanied by a comprehensive user manual and requires 256K with PC- or MS-DOS 2.0 or higher.

$49.95 (specify USGA or RCGA version) from Traders Marketing.

Bob Hope Golfer

He doesn't sing "Thanks For the Memories," but this radio-controlled, robotic replica of Bob Hope does play a mean— if somewhat miniaturized— game of golf. He's just 10 inches tall, and he moves around any layout you design (indoors or out) by means of a motorized golf cart to which his legs are permanently affixed. After inserting one of three different golf clubs in Hope's hands, you control his set-up and swing with a hand-held transmitter. In this way up to four players can drive, chip, and putt toward the hole; each of the three flagsticks provided has a magnetic "cup" that catches the metallic golf balls. A wise crack of the ball can even get you a hole-in-one. The Bob Hope Golfer uses one 9-volt and 11 "AA" batteries.

$99.95 from The Price of His Toys; also from A2Z/The Best of Everything and Austad's.

"In Pursuit of Par" Par 72 Edition

Harold Trimble is a golfaholic. So when he developed tendonitis in his left elbow several years ago, his doctor's orders— give up the game for three months— only added insult to injury. "I'd thought of designing a golf game before," Trimble later recalled. "And with time on my hands I got serious about it."

Serious indeed. Several months and $80,000 later, Trimble had invented "In Pursuit of Par," a board game that's as challenging from tee to green as a real round of golf. (Trimble's personal best after playing 70 rounds on his fictitious 6,966-yard layout was a four-over-par 76.) Up to four players execute their shots by choosing a club, rolling the dice, consulting a chart to determine the outcome, and advancing the ball with a calibrated shot locator. A six-sided die determines distance, a 12-sided die determines accuracy, and another six-sided die is used for trouble shots (players need to watch out for rough, trees, sand traps, and water hazards). With only a 50-50 chance that any shot will be straight and 42 different places for the ball to land, high-handicappers are bound to feel right at

home. And while luck is important, the game rewards good judgment in club selection and course management. *Games* magazine ranked "In Pursuit of Par" among the top board games of 1987, and *Golf Illustrated* followed by rating it "the best of the bunch" (four stars for fun and realism) in a survey of a dozen different golf games.

The game includes three folding, full-color playing boards (with three holes to a side), the three special dice, club-selection and shotmaking charts, a set of Stabilo wipe-off marking pencils, and enough scorecards to while away a whole winter.

$24.95 from Austad's; also from Pursuit of Par Enterprises.

"In Pursuit of Par"—TPC at Sawgrass Edition

It may be the most diabolical, most famous, and most photographed hole in all of golf: the par-3, island-green 17th at the Stadium Course of the Tournament Players Club at Sawgrass in Ponte Vedra, Florida. ("The only way to improve it," Dale Hayes once joked, "would be to put the green on a barge and have it float around the lagoon.") If you've ever dreamed of playing this nightmare of a hole, here's your chance— and you won't even have to leave your home to do it.

The TPC at Sawgrass Edition of "In Pursuit of Par" faithfully replicates all 18 holes of the challenging course that's earned architect Pete Dye both bravos and brickbats. ("It's *Star Wars* golf," Ben Crenshaw told *Sports Illustrated*. "The place was designed by Darth Vader.") While this board game plays just like the original version (see above), it's been improved in several significant ways. Instead of simple schematic outlines of generic holes, the TPC at Sawgrass Edition features detailed aerial diagrams drawn precisely to scale and beautiful full-color photographs by Golfoto, the PGA Tour's official photographer. The course is laid out on four double-sided folding playing boards instead of three, and each hole can be played from any of four color-coded tee boxes— championship, blue, white, and red. And although both editions let you bet just as you would on a real golf course— skins, sandies, greenies, presses, and so forth— maybe you should think twice before pressing on this one's No. 17.

$40 from Competitive Edge Golf; also from Pursuit of Par Enterprises.

MacGolf Classic

Rain, snow, or slipped disk keeping you off the links? Well, if you happen to have a Macintosh with at least 512K of memory, simply boot up this computer-generated substitute and you'll be in the swing again within a matter of minutes. MacGolf Classic, a delightfully realistic tour de force of programming wizardry, lets you and up to three other players make the rounds at six different courses, all from the comfort of home— or, boss willing, at the office.

This challenging and captivating computer game, which represents a merger of two previous releases (MacGolf and MacCourses), makes the most of the Macintosh's mouse, high-resolution animated graphics, and user-friendly interface. Once you type in the names of the players, in fact, everything is managed with the mouse. You have complete control of your stance (square, open, or closed), aim, ball position, and swing speed, and after you get the hang

MacGolf Classic

of it you'll be able to hit any shot in the book (straight, fade, or draw— high or low) with any club in the bag (three woods, eight irons, two wedges, and a putter). Along the way, however, you'll have to watch out for rough, trees, fairway bunkers, greenside sand traps, water hazards, and out-of-bounds areas. Club selection and course management are half the game: Choose an eight-iron when you need a seven, for example, and your shot will drop short of the green or even in the sand; fail to take the wind into account and you may find yourself roaming through the rough in search of your ball.

The left side of the screen provides a player's-eye view of each shot (in any direction desired); the right side provides an aerial diagram of the entire hole. After each player hits, the software redraws the images on the screen and updates all of the vital statistics. A box at the bottom tracks the hole number and par; the remaining distance to the pin; the player's club selection, stroke, and running score for the round; and the prevailing speed and direction of the wind.

The game's three-dimensional graphics are as good as black-and-white can be, and its digitized sound effects are remarkably realistic. (If you're swinging on the sly, the sound can be switched off.) You'll hear a thwack as you strike the ball, an "Oops!" if you hit out-of-bounds, a splash or splat when a shot drops in the water or sand, occasional oohs and aahs from the invisible gallery, and, sweetest of all, the "ker-plunk" of a putt dropping into the cup when you hole out.

The software also allows each player to choose from three levels of difficulty, which does for this game what handicaps do in real golf. You can play the "in" 9, "out" 9, or all 18 holes on 6 different and demanding par-72

layouts: the original "Augustina National" and "Shinook Hills" of MacGolf (which were designed by Jay Wohlrabe, a professional golfer and course architect) or the tougher gang of four— Cedar Creek, Golden Sands, Thunder Ridge, and PCAI International— from Mac-Courses. If you'd like to warm up before you head to the first tee, a practice range and putting green are provided. And no matter which course you decide to play, there's enough built-in adventure and excitement to keep you busy all day long . . . and, if you're not careful, well into the night.

$94.90 from XOR Corporation.

Mini Golf

Neither rain, sleet, nor snow can keep you from your appointed rounds of miniature golf . . . if you've got this portable, nine-hole course in your home or office. Mini Golf, made in France exclusively for Abercrombie & Fitch, features nine charmingly hand-painted obstacles (ramps, bridges, and the like) and nine movable "cups." Arrange them on the carpet in any which way and you've designed your own miniature golf course. The set also includes two wood-shafted putters with leather grips and a handsome hardwood storage chest.

$395 from Abercrombie & Fitch.

Mini-Putt

That's "Mini-Putt Pete" scowling at you from the cover of Accolade's miniature-golf software, and once you boot up this game his computerized clone is with you, like it or not, for the duration: 18 of the wildest and whackiest holes in the history of miniature golfdom. You, Pete, and up to three other players must navigate assorted obstacles and hazards— including walls, water, bridges, and the slipperiest slopes imaginable— on the way to each hole, but be forewarned that the easiest-looking route is often the most danger-ous. You'll also have to putt your way through various gauntlets— among them a windmill, a loop-de-loop tunnel, and a killer castle complete with moat— all with high-tech twists designed to test your skill (and maybe even your sanity). Mini-Putt is available for Commodore 64/128s and IBM PCs/compatibles (256K).

The IBM version is $39.95 from Austad's or Golf Day Products; the Commodore version is $29.95 from Golf Day Prod-ucts.

Nerf Indoor Golf

This indoor golf game from Nerf proves that a hole in every room is a whole lot better than a hole in one. The set includes everything you need to turn your home or office into a nine-hole miniature golf course, complete with flower-pot bunkers and doorway doglegs: nine target cups with num-bered flagsticks, two clubs, four plastic balls, and scorecards.

$26.95 from Sportime; also from Falk's.

PAR 5 Golf Handicap and Sta-tistics System

One of the worst handicaps in golf is not having one. If your course or club won't oblige, maybe it's time to take matters into your own hands by putting

them on this easy-to-use, menu-driven software. The PAR 5 Handicap and Statistics System will not only compute your handicap according to USGA rules and procedures but also will generate the kind of performance statistics that should help you lower it.

First you'll need to enter your hole-by-hole totals from recent rounds, along with some other data drawn from the scorecards of the courses you've played (ratings from the appropriate sets of tees, plus pars and handicap rankings for every hole). The software calculates your existing handicap under USGA rules and then uses it to automatically adjust— on a hole-by-hole basis— successive rounds. Your new handicap is computed, in fact, as soon as you've entered the new scores.

Then the real fun begins. Pick any course you've played and PAR 5 will compute your average score on each hole or tell you what percentage of your drives wound up in the fairway . . . and that's just the tip of the statistical iceberg. The software also will generate graphs that chart your performance over the last 20 rounds in such catego-ries as actual scores, total putts, drives in fairway, greens in regulation, and birdies, pars, bogeys, and double bogeys or worse. The PAR 5 Golf Handicap and Statistics System is available for IBM PC/compatibles (256K) with PC- or MS-DOS 2.1 or higher.

$24.95 from B L & S Enterprises.

Par T Golf—The Incredible Golf Machine

If you think you've seen everything, you probably haven't seen Par T Golf. Dubbed "The Incredible Golf Machine," it does for golf what the Astrodome did for baseball . . . it takes the game indoors.

In 1986 Robert Katzman and Irving Bookspan set out to fill what they saw as a gaping void in the market: the severe shortage of golf courses and practice facilities. The result of their quest is an ultrahigh-tech golf simulator that takes players through an entire round at Pebble Beach Golf Links in California— or a number of other top courses around the world— day or night, rain or shine, summer or winter.

The Incredible Golf Machine's computer, 35-millimeter film projector, optical cameras, and infrared lamps are programmed to provide players with the same situations and sensations they'd encounter on a real golf course— just about everything, in fact, but fresh air and sunlight. Players use their own clubs to hit real golf balls into a high-impact, 14-by-10-foot screen, which shows the same view they would see on the course. After a player hits a shot, the ball's actual flight— right down to the last bounce— is reproduced on the screen, and when the ball comes to rest, the distance it was hit and the distance remaining to the pin are shown on a digital display. (Three optical cameras track the flight path of each ball— including any hook or slice— and transmit the data to a computer, which calculates the shot's distance and destination.) A ball may land in any of more than 26,000 locations, and the simulator's 800 full-sized color pictures change automatically as the game progresses.

As in a real round of golf, it's possible to hit a shot out of bounds, into the woods or water, or into a fairway or greenside bunker (the simulator's "sand trap" is made of a soft, squashy material). And yes, it's even possible to score a hole in one.

When all the players have reached the green, the computer turns off the projector and turns on the lights, illuminating a realistically contoured artificial putting surface that's positioned directly in front of the screen. The computer tells players where to place their balls on the green— 21 different putting spots are provided— and keeps track of who's away. And when the last putt drops on the 18th hole, it displays each golfer's front-nine, back-nine, and total score.

The Incredible Golf Machine, which undoubtedly would make you a whole host of new foul-weather friends, doesn't require a lot of room (600 or so square feet). It does, however, require a hefty bank account: the basic unit is $19,500, a "ball flight simulator" is $3,500 extra, and delivery and installation adds another $6,500. Once you've mastered the original course, you can add additional layouts— California's Spyglass Hill Golf Links or Switzerland's Château de Bonmont among them— for $550 apiece. And if The Incredible Golf Machine is a bit too steep for your budget, the company hopes that a U.S. Indoor Golf Center— a 90-minute jaunt across the simulated links for about $12— may one day soon be coming to a location near you.

From U.S. Indoor Golf.

PLA-GOLF MINIATURE GOLF GAME

This may be the only miniature golf game on the market with built-in water hazards and sand traps. Arrange PLA-GOLF's elevated plastic greens in any configuration you'd like, indoors or out, and you've got a challenging three- or five-hole layout that's ready for the miniature and full-sized golfers in your

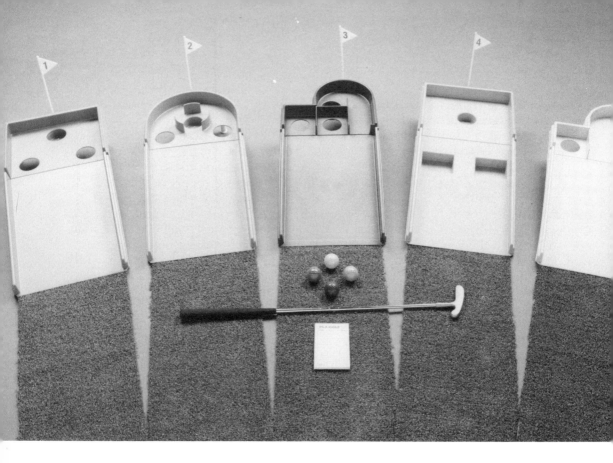

family. Every hole is different, and making or breaking par isn't as easy as it may look. On some holes your ball can make it up the plastic ramp only to drop through "lost ball" or "out-of-bounds" penalty openings. On another hole your ball can be stopped by sand or water on its way up the ramp. Each ramp-and-green section is made of high-impact plastic, measures approximately 13 inches wide by 26 inches deep, and includes a numbered flagstick.

Several versions of PLA-GOLF are available. The basic par-6 set includes three different holes, a steel-shafted (but nonregulation) putter, two colored golf balls, and a scorepad; the deluxe version of this set substitutes a regulation putter and adds three four-foot-long sections of artificial turf. The deluxe par-10 set includes five different

holes, five sections of artificial turf, a regulation putter, four colored golf balls, and a scorepad. (You supply the sand and water.)

PLA-GOLF's basic three-hole set is $44.95 from Enticements; the deluxe version is $69.95 from Golf Day Products. The deluxe five-hole set is $89.95 from Sportime; also from Golf Day Products and The Price of His Toys.

PLAY GOLF—YE OLD COURSE AND PLAY GOLF—PINEVIEW

If you don't mind doing without a few of the bells and whistles of Golf's Best—Pinehurst No. 2 or Golf's Best—St. Andrews (see above), now you can play either "Pineview" or "Ye Old Course," two similar but generic layouts, for cut-rate greens fees. These computerized golf simulations provide only two views of each hole instead of three, sacrifice some true-to-life touches (undulating terrain and gusting winds, for example), and don't let you choose your own clubs, save games-in-progress, keep a running chart of all-time low scores, or speed up play with special key options. Otherwise, however, the games are more or less the same, even if the names aren't. Play Golf— Pineview and Play Golf— Ye Old Course are available for Apple II series (48K), Commodore 64/128, and IBM/compatible (128K) computers.

$9.99 each from 1 Step Software.

PRO GOLF

This hand-held, computer-animated game simulates an 18-hole round of golf, complete with doglegs, water hazards, and sand traps. A full-color guide to Pro Golf's 6,200-yard, par-72 course shows the yardage and layout of

each hole, and a liquid crystal screen shows the view from wherever you may be on the course—tee, green, or in between. After selecting a club for each shot, you determine the force of your swing and the precise moment of impact by pressing a button below the screen. Hit too soon and you'll slice; hit too late and you'll hook. Pick the wrong club or swing too hard and you may knock the ball out of bounds. In the worst of all cases, you may even whiff.

You can tee off alone or in a two-some, and Pro Golf takes care of the scorekeeping chores for both stroke and match play. The battery-powered unit comes with a folding, 4-by-7.5-inch black vinyl case that fits easily in your coat pocket, briefcase, or desk drawer. (If you don't want anyone else in the office to know what you're up to, you can even switch off Pro Golf's realistic sound effects.)

GAMES, TOYS, AND SOFTWARE 121

$64.95 from The Sharper Image; also from A2Z/The Best of Everything, Austad's, B.N. Genius, Competitive Edge Golf, Enticements, Golf Day Products, Hammacher Schlemmer, Las Vegas Discount Golf, Louisville Golf, Nevada Bob's Discount Golf, Somerton Springs Golf Shoppes, Edwin Watts Golf Shops, and J. White Industries.

PROFESSIONAL-CLASS GOLF

William H. "Bert" Way was one of the legends. Born in 1873 in Devonshire, England, he and his two brothers grew up alongside the Royal North Devon Golf Club in Westard Ho! All three eventually emigrated to the United States to further their golf careers, but Bert was the first.

In 1896 Way landed a $100-a-month job as the resident professional at the Meadow Brook Club in New York, and by the turn of the century he'd become a successful tournament golfer (in 1899 he was joint runner-up in the U.S. Open). As Way moved around the country he began to lay out golf courses, too, principally in and around Detroit and Cleveland. In 1909 he designed the course at the Mayfield Country Club in South Euclid, Ohio, and he remained as its professional until 1952. It was there that Bert Way introduced John D. Rockefeller to golf. And it was there that he set about planning his most famous work: the original Firestone Country Club course (now the South Course) in nearby Akron.

Way's Firestone course opened in 1929. Toughened by Robert Trent Jones in the late 1950s, it was for many years home to the World Series of Golf. (The monstrous 16th, a par-5 that measures 625 yards from the championship tees, is one of the most famous holes in all of golf.) It's still a regular on *Golf Digest's* annual list of America's 100 greatest golf courses, and now, thanks to Professional-Class Golf, you can play this legendary layout on your own personal computer.

Professional-Class Golf accurately simulates each of the 18 holes at the Firestone Country Club's South Course— right down to the greens, water hazards, sand traps, and trees. Your caddy carries a complete set of clubs (four woods, nine irons, a wedge, and a putter), and you can adjust your stance, the timing of your swing, and the force with which you hit the ball. You can play an entire round, if you'd like, or simply sharpen your skills at the driving range or practice green. Professional-Class Golf, which features realistic sound effects and color graphics, displays the results of each swing— and even keeps score. Requires: Apple (64K) or IBM (128K) with MS-DOS 2.0 or higher and BASICA or GWBASIC.

$29.95 from Dynacomp.

RULES MASTER

Here's a game that will quickly force any know-it-alls among your golfing friends to put up or shut up. Each year the United States Golf Association and the Royal and Ancient Golf Club of St. Andrews, golf's two rules-making bodies, receive hundreds of questions from clubs, golf associations, tournament officials, and players— professional and amateur— about situations that, for one reason or another, don't seem to be addressed by the Rules of Golf. (What happens, for instance, if your golf ball comes to rest inside a broken bottle, in a hippopotamus's hoofprint, or next to a irascible rattlesnake?) The joint answers of the USGA and R&A become part of

Decisions on the Rules of Golf, a mammoth loose-leaf binder filled with 900 or so pages of rulings. (A snake, by the way, is considered an "outside agency," not a "loose impediment.")

Although some might consider forging through Decisions on the Rules of Golf as golfdom's surest cure for insomnia, that didn't stop Jane and Charles Van Pelt of Radnor, Pennsylvania, from turning it into a trivia game. The fruit of their labor— Rules Master, a set of question-and-answer cards in the manner of Trivial Pursuit— should sharpen your knowledge of the rules and allow you to make better-educated guesses in out-of-the ordinary situations. And if your memory's any good, playing this game might even save you a few penalty strokes down the line. And, lest there be any doubt, Rules Master carries the USGA's seal of approval.

$39.95 from Golf House.

SHAKE-A-ROUND

Arthritis forced Bill Besson to give up the game of golf back in the mid-1950s, but 30 years later he dreamed up another way to play and dubbed it Shake-a-Round. Indeed, the formula for this Yahtzee-like golf game came to Besson in his sleep. "When I got up the next morning," he says, "the first thing I did was to write down that formula." Each hole is played by rolling a white "tee-off" die in combination with two to four green "strokes" dice, depending on its par. Scoring is the same as in real golf. The game includes the five dice, a plastic shaker, and enough scoresheets for 240 rounds.

$5.95 from Creative Specialties of South Dakota.

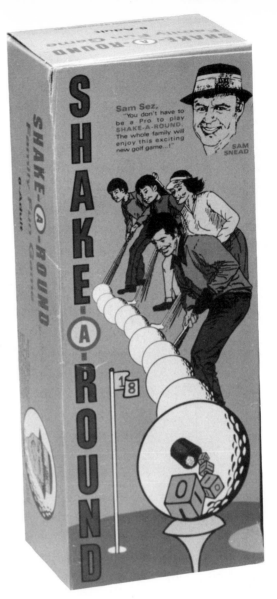

TRS-80 GOLF HANDICAPPING SYSTEM

While the TRS-80 Golf Handicapping System was originally written for the early Radio Shack computers— Models II, III, and IV— an MS-DOS version for the Tandy IBM-compatibles has recently been added to the line. The software can store, sort, and retrieve data for 300 to 1,100 golfers (depending on the computer used), filing the most recent 20 differentials for each

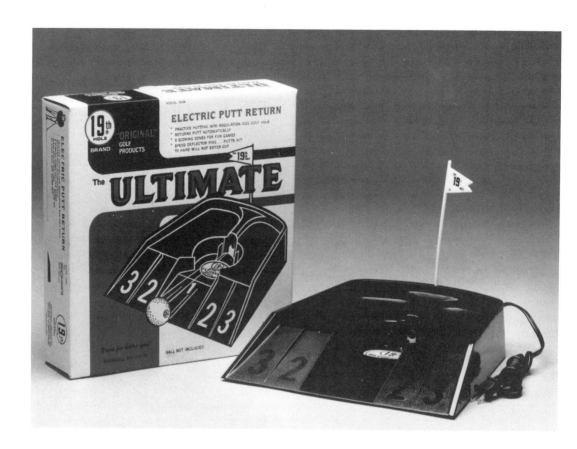

player and choosing the appropriate number of lowest scores to calculate and record the handicap. Because the program retains course ratings, original scores can be generated from the differentials at any point. This menu-driven software also can be used to generate handicap cards, a wide variety of letter-sized reports (including handicap rankings and lists of "most improved" players), and even the sheets used to post net scores.

$99.95 from Hancock Techtronics.

Ultimate Golf

This board game takes you and up to three other players through what may be golf's ultimate test: 18 challenging holes from the world's most famous courses, each of them stunningly recreated by illustrator J. Crompton. You'll tee off on the Old Course at St. Andrews, Scotland, say a little prayer as you pass "Amen Corner" at the Augusta National Golf Club in Georgia, and finish up on the spectacular 18th hole of the Pebble Beach Golf Links in California. Along the way you'll also face famous holes from the Royal St. George's Golf Club in Kent, England; the Stadium Course of the Tournament Players Club at Sawgrass in Ponte Vedra Beach, Florida; and the East Course of the Winged Foot Golf Club in Mamaroneck, New York.

Each player uses a set of 20 cards that represent all of the clubs in the bag, along with various shot-making situations. After you select a club and aim your shot (with a movable meter), you roll two dice to determine how far— and how accurately— you've hit the ball. But watch out: Ultimate Golf faithfully reproduces all of the trees, bunkers, water hazards, and other obstacles that make each hole a classic. The course is laid out in full color on nine 15-inch-square, double-sided laminated game boards, and a molded plastic base keeps everything in prime playing position. To break par you'll need skill, judgment, and a little bit of luck— kinda like real golf, huh?

$44.95 from Ultimate Golf; also from Golf Day Products and Somerton Springs Golf Shoppes.

WASTEPAPER GOLFER

Ready ... aim ... fore! Why slam-dunk those wads of wastepaper when you can let this miniature golfer sweep them gracefully off your desk and into the nearest circular file? Just place your trash on the tee, line him up, press a spring-loaded lever, and keep your fingers crossed. If you're lucky, he'll come through with an ace. The Waste-paper Golfer is nine inches tall and

Wastepaper Golfer

comes with two interchangeable clubs (a driver and a niblick), a target cup that can be attached to your wastebasket, and, of course, a flagstick.

$19.95 from Enticements.

WOODEN GOLF JIGSAW

Putting together a good round of golf requires plenty of concentration. So does putting together this Wooden Golf Jigsaw, which is hand-cut from layered Italian poplar into 100 interlocking pieces. But when you're all done you'll at least have something more than a scorecard to show for your persistence. You'll have one of six brightly colored prints by Charles Crombie, whose "Rules of Golf" series whimsically captured many of golf's most embarrassing predicaments.

$16.95 from Hurley Style.

WORLD CLASS LEADER BOARD

If you've ever wondered what it might be like to play one of the world's greatest golf courses, switch on your computer and stop wondering. World Class Leader Board lets you take on three 18-hole layouts that have challenged golf's greatest champions: the Old Course at St. Andrews, Scotland; the "Blue Monster" at the Doral Country Club in Miami; and Cypress Creek Country Club in Boynton Beach, Florida. Each is a faithful electronic recreation of the original, right down to the rough, trees, sand traps, and water hazards. And once you've mastered these three layouts, you may be ready to tackle the game's toughest test: the mythical 6,443-yard course of the "Gauntlet Country Club."

You'll need skill, concentration, and a little bit of luck to make or break par. After warming up on the game's practice range and putting green, you and up to three other players are ready to tee it up on the course of your choice. Each player can choose from two skill levels— amateur and professional (where wind comes into play and putting becomes vastly more difficult)— and there's an even easier one just for kids. The screen offers two views of each hole— one from directly behind the player and the other a tee-to-green aerial diagram— and a box on its right side keeps track of all the vital statistics. A built-in "course editor" lets you arrange the holes in any playing order, and scorecards for each round can be printed and saved for posterity.

For the aspiring golf course architect, World Class Leader Board also features a powerful program that lets you modify the existing layouts or design your own from scratch. You can even realistically recreate your home course, which should make sure that neither wind, rain, snow, nor sleet will ever again keep you from your appointed rounds.

And if all this doesn't manage to keep you happily occupied, two additional "Famous Courses of the World" disks are available. Like the main game, each disk offers faithful reproductions of three top-notch courses and one imaginary layout (plus a special "punch" shot for use around the greens and under trees). Volume I contains Harbour Town Golf Links in Hilton Head Island, South Carolina; Sunningdale Golf Club in Berkshire, England; Dorado Beach Golf Club in Puerto Rico; and the "Pine Ridge" challenge course. Volume II contains Pebble Beach Golf Links in California; Muirfield Golf Club in East Lothian, Scotland; Colonial Country Club in Fort Worth,

Texas; and the "Glenmoor Country Club" challenge course.

World Class Leader Board and its companion disks are available for Amiga, Apple II series, Commodore 64/128, Macintosh, and IBM PC/compatible computers.

$39.95 from Access Software; also from Golf Day Products. "Famous Courses of the World" disks are $19.95 each.

WORLD TOUR GOLF

From the makers of such software classics as "Chuck Yeager's Advanced Flight Trainer" and "Mail Order Monsters" comes World Tour Golf, a computerized golf game and simulator that lives up to its name. A typical day's play might have you starting in Scotland, on the windswept links of the historic Old Course at St. Andrews ("The Home of golf"); sailing across the Atlantic to the site of the 1896 and 1986 U.S. Open championships, the Shinnecock Hills Golf Club in Southampton, New York; heading south to the venue of the venerable Masters Tournament, the Augusta National Golf Club in Georgia; and finishing up on the shores of the Pacific, at the spectacularly scenic Pebble Beach Golf Links in California. World Tour Golf lets you play these and more than a dozen other computerized versions of the world's greatest courses— complete with trees, hills, water hazards, sand traps, and changing weather conditions— anytime you'd like. You can also tackle a challenging composite layout drawn from the most difficult holes in the world or play any of several goofy courses that are more game than golf.

The conditions under which you play— from the speed and direction of the wind to the pin placements and dew on the greens— vary randomly from round to round, just as in real life. You start by entering the names of up to four players, choosing either medal or match play, and assigning various attributes to each golfer in the group. You designate each player's handicap, swing strength, shot-making skills, and so forth— even whether he or she typically draws or fades the ball. (This feature enables you to create imaginary— or even legendary— opponents by modeling a player after anyone from Amy Alcott to Fuzzy Zoeller.) As each player prepares to hit, the left half of the animated split screen shows a bird's-eye view of the entire hole, the right side shows a golfer's-eye view of the terrain and target, and a box in the upper right-hand corner of the screen displays all of the vital statistics. You can use the "Range Finder" to instantly check how far you can hit any club and the "Power Meter" to adjust your backswing, downswing, and moment of impact. As play continues, an on-screen scorecard keeps track of both gross and net scores.

If you'd like, you can warm up on the driving range or practice green before heading to the first tee. Or, if you're so inclined, you can even design the course of your dreams (or nightmares) with World Tour Golf's built-in construction set. This ingenious course-architect feature puts you in charge of everything from the length and par of each hole to the shape and contour of its green. Trees, bunkers, hills, water hazards, sand traps, and so forth go exactly where you want them— for better or for worse. World Tour Golf is available, with minor variations, in three versions: Apple IIGS ($39.95), Commodore 64/128 ($34.95), and IBM/compatible ($49.95).

From Electronic Arts.

CHAPTER SEVEN
THE LIGHTER SIDE OF GOLF

THE LIGHTER SIDE OF GOLF

BABY GOLF SHOES

These all-leather, brown-on-white saddle oxfords look like an ordinary pair of baby shoes, except for one thing: they're fitted with golf spikes. They're the perfect shower, birthday, or any-day gift for a putting papoose.

$12.85 from Golfsmith.

THE BENT ONE

When an irresistible force and an immovable object collide, there are a couple of possible outcomes. You might get off the couch and clean up the garage, as your mate demanded. Or, if you happen to be the unlucky driver that just sliced one into the water for

Cloud-Flite Trick Golf Ball

the third time in a row, you might find your shaft taking on the outline of the nearest tree trunk. The Bent One resembles a double-dogleg relic of the latter encounter.

This gag driver, twisted shaft and all, looks as if it's been abused within an inch of its slim life— except for its fresh black paint job. The Bent One isn't meant for actual use, but it does make a great psychological weapon, conversation piece, or booby prize for the worst golfer in your outing or tournament. Or just put it in your golf bag and it'll keep those other wiseguy clubs in line.

$29.95 from Everything for Golf.

CLOUD-FLITE TRICK GOLF BALL

There seems to be one in every foursome: the hacker who swears that his stroke is mighty enough to actually crush a golf ball. Well, here's a little number that will give the big hitter a chance to make good on his claim. When your golfing buddy isn't looking, simply replace his ball on the fairway with one of these; then challenge him to reach the green. When he lays into his shot he'll be in for something of a surprise: the ball disintegrates on impact, blowing up in a spectacular cloud of billowing, smokelike powder. The Cloud-Flite Trick Golf Ball, which was invented by Jack Boundy of Australia (who's shown here hitting one), looks like the real McCoy— right down to the last dimple.

$3 for a sleeve of three from Austad's;

also from The Duck Press, Las Vegas Discount Golf, Somerton Springs Golf Shoppes, and J. White Industries.

FISHERMAN'S PAR-TEE PAK

You've heard about the one that got away, but what about the one that came home and stayed for a week in your golf bag? Hooo-wee! What's that smell in the garage?

Telling the biggest fish story you can muster may well be worth a round or two at the clubhouse some afternoon. It goes something like this: "Well, it all started when I hit my approach shot into the pond and remembered the Fisherman's Par-Tee Pack you guys gave me on my birthday. It was a great gag gift. But I never thought I'd actually catch anything with it . . ."

Sure, pal.

The Fisherman's Par-Tee Pack, a pocket-size tackle box with four golf-gimmick lures, can turn a simple round of golf into a full-fledged fishing expedition. The kit also includes "The Golfer's Fishing Guide," a tongue-in-cheek rule book that admonishes golfers who live by the hook to "Never keep a fish under a club's length," and to be careful when soaking their night crawlers. Now that's advice to live by.

$12.95 from Everything for Golf.

FOOT WEDGE

If the game of golf is getting a bit too rough for you, this little do-it-yourself groundskeeper may be just the answer. Slip the Foot Wedge on your golf shoe before you head for the high grass; a few swift kicks with this blade should be enough to get you out of the rough.

$3.95 from Leister Game Company.

THE GOLFAHOLICS ANONYMOUS OFFICIAL DRIVING KIT

Honk if you're hooked. The official driving kit of Golfaholics Anonymous should bring any golf fanatic a little bit of attention, both on the road and on the course. It consists of a standard-mount license-plate frame (one size fits all cars) with the message KEEP SWINGING on top and the name of its sponsor— GOLFAHOLICS ANONY-MOUS— down below, plus 10 of the organization's official golf tees.

$8.95 from Competitive Edge Golf.

GOLFER'S CROTCH HOOK

There may be safer ways of teaching yourself to keep your head down and your eye on the ball, but none quite so effective. This inexpensive training aid consists of two red straps that are connected at one end to an adjustable elastic headpiece and at the other to a giant metal hook. Before you hit away, put on the headpiece and place the hook— gently, of course— in your crotch. Keep your head down and everything is hunky-dory. But lift up your head as you swing and the hook is pulled up into your crotch, which undoubtedly will put a damper on your day. Look up too much— Did you see that plane overhead?— and you'll be the talk of the clubhouse. One size fits all.

$4 from Leister Game Company.

GOOFY GOLF BALLS

It's hard enough trying to figure out which way the greens break, but the unsuspecting victims of this prank also are going to find themselves trying to

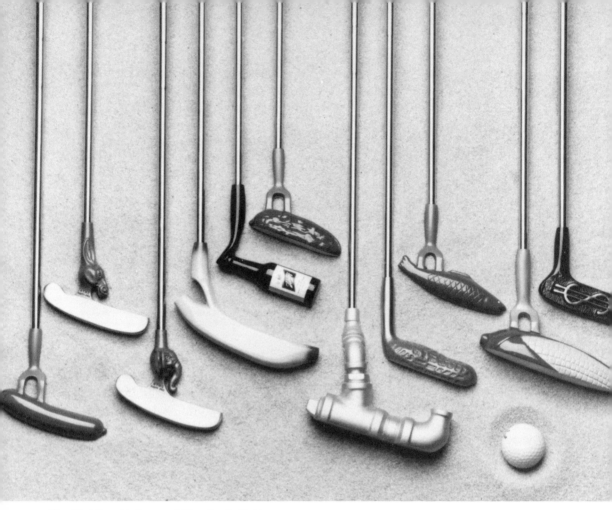

The Hot Dog Putter and Plumber's Putter

calculate the break on their ball. Goofy Golf Balls look like the real thing, feel like the real thing, and weigh about as much as those trusty Titleists. But the similarities end there. Because they're weighted off-center, it's simply not possible— try as you might— to putt them in a straight line.

$4.95 for a sleeve of three from Leister Game Company.

HOT DOG PUTTER

Next time you get your buns in a sling by bragging about your putting prow-

ess, don't let your golfing partners grill you or rake you over the coals. Don't let them say that you just can't cut the mustard anymore. Simply be frank and admit, "Yes, guys, we're in a pickle, but I know how we can catchup." Then pull out this red-hot putter and prove once and for all that you really belong in the weiner's circle.

The brass head of the Hot Dog Putter is painted sizzling red, joined to a forked hosel, and individually balanced to accommodate its unorthodox shape. And believe it or not, it actually conforms to USGA rules.

Matzie Golf Company markets more than a dozen other oddball putters— among them beer-bottle, corn-on-the-cob, fish, and banana models. But when you pull out the Hot Dog Putter, you can relish the fact that never before has anyone on the links sausage a sight.

$34 from Matzie Golf.

INTERNATIONAL DUFFERS ASSOCIATION

If the PGA won't have you, don't despair; the International Duffers Association just may be your kind of club. Join this not-so-prestigious organization and you'll get you a membership card that offers invaluable advice on such subtle aspects of the game as "handicap deception" and "slip-of-the-pencil scorekeeping," as well as useful pointers on how to effectively irritate others by criticizing their swings and putting strokes. Membership in the association is complimentary when you purchase either the one-size-fits-all IDA Legends Cap ($6) or the 11-by-18-inch IDA Golf Towel ($3.50). Both are white, with the IDA logo imprinted in green.

From Maryco Products.

JUMBO GOLF TEES

Next time you say, "Tee it high and let it fly," why not show that you really mean it? These Jumbo Golf Tees are 4.5 inches long and loaded with laugh-provoking possibilities. ("How can you possibly hope to hit the big ball," you ask, "with one of those little tees?") And when one of these extra-large tees goes flying, you won't have any trouble finding it . . . just listen for the thud.

$.99 for a package of five from Every-

thing for Golf; also from Northern Golf Ball Company.*

KNEEL 'N' PRAY PUTTER

Drop down on your knees, sink that all-important birdie putt, and say "Amen." A little divine intervention, after all, may be all you need to rid yourself of the yips once and for all. As crazy as it looks, the ultra-short Kneel 'n' Pray Putter— it's nothing more than a handle attached to a putter head— actually works, especially on those would-be gimmes. If nothing else, it beats begging for mercy from your less-than-charitable opponents. The Kneel 'n' Pray Putter doesn't conform to USGA rules, but who cares if you're appealing to a higher authority?

$2.95 from Leister Game Company; also from Northern Golf Ball Company.

LAID BACK GOLFER'S ASSOCIATION

"How many strokes?" they ask. "Who cares?" you answer with a shrug. That, at least, is what you're supposed to say if you're a card-carrying member of the Laid Back Golfer's Association, which is dedicated to the proposition that you don't have to be a good golfer to have a good time— on or off the course. The association's official membership kit ($19.95) includes a Hogan-style golf cap imprinted with the LBGA logo and motto, golf thongs (a pair of "flip-flops" fitted with spikes), and a membership card and rulebook. And for an extra $9.95, you can wake up and smell the coffee in the LBGA's own golf-bag-shaped mug.

From Las Vegas Discount Golf; also from Austad's and Somerton Springs Golf Shoppes.

19th Hole Toilet Seat

The less said about this one, perhaps, the better. This cushioned vinyl toilet seat bears a cartoon of an exasperated golfer breaking a putter over his knee; lift it up and you see the "19th Hole" legend and flagstick. The 19th Hole Toilet Seat can be easily installed in any standard-size fixture.

$25.95 from Golf Day Products; also from Somerton Springs Golf Shoppes.

Persimmon Seeds ("Grow Your Own Golf Clubs")

The persimmon tree (Diospyros Virginiana), the northernmost member of the ebony family, derives its name from an Algonquian word meaning "dried fruit." It thrives best on wet, flat lands, reaching a height of up to 60 feet and a diameter of 12 to 24 inches. In terms of hardness, strength, and resiliency, top-quality persimmon is without peer in the world of wood; it withstands extreme amounts of stress without chipping or cracking, absorbs very little energy from shock, and after impact rebounds quickly to its original shape. Even with the advent of metal woods (the loveliest oxymoron in golf), persimmon has lost little of its mystique. Most of the world's top golfers continue to prefer persimmon woods (including eight of the PGA Tour's 10 most accurate tee-off artists in 1987), and some of the most coveted classics from the 1950s today sell for upwards of $2,000 a set.

Now, thanks to the persimmon-loving folks at the Louisville Golf Club Company, you can begin growing golf clubs right in your own backyard. (Mature, just-cut persimmon trees sell for as much as $750 apiece these days and, if all goes well, yield nearly 500 clubheads.) Just plant one of these packets of persimmon seeds and let Mother Nature do the rest. In seven or eight years you'll have trees that bear a delicious orange, plum-like fruit. Then, in another 40 years or so, you'll be ready to harvest your home-grown clubheads.

$1.25 from Louisville Golf.

Plumber's Putter

We've heard of plumbing for the right line, especially on breaking putts, but this is ridiculous. The Plumber's Putter won't give you nerves of steel, but the tinny noise it produces with every stroke is sure to rattle even your most iron-willed opponent. This pipefitter's dream, the manufacturer says, has a "surprisingly good feeling."

$29.95 from Las Vegas Discount Golf; also from Matzie Golf.

Putter Power

What can you do to help a golfer whose putting stroke resembles a misfiring piston? When all else has failed, you may wish to reach for the last resort: a can of Putter Power, an aerosol-spray product that's applied directly to the wayward weapon. A few properly aimed blasts should be enough to cure your partner's terminal case of the yips, or any of a whole host of other chronic putting problems. From then on, God willing, he'll approach those knee-knocking three-footers as if they were gimmes. (Just hope, however, that your partner doesn't bother to read the ultra-fine print on the back of the can: "Contains air freshener and is intended for humor only.")

$4.95 from Austad's; also from The Duck Press and Somerton Springs Golf Shoppes.

SLICE REPELLENT

At last: A product that does to slices what Raid does to roaches. If swing-training gadgets (see Chapter One), special clubs (see Chapter Three), and a shelf full of instruction books haven't gotten rid of your banana ball, why not try a can of Slice Repellent? It purports to prevent and cure the "out-of-bounds blues," "iron-poor swing," and other slice-related sicknesses. Just follow the directions on the label: "Hold the atomizer two feet or more from the offending ball and spray for one second. If slice continues, try the triple mist (three short blasts). If problems persist, consult your local golf professional."

Although Slice Repellent is nothing more than a banana-scented aerosol spray, who's to say it won't work?

$4.95 from Austad's; also from The Duck Press and Somerton Springs Golf Shoppes.

STREAMIN' MIMI JOKE GOLF BALL

Pity the poor soul who knows that the only thing he can drive down the middle of the fairway is a golf cart. This golf ball won't solve the problem, but it may get him to spend some more time at the practice range. Let an unsuspecting victim launch the Streamin' Mimi from the tee; it responds by sending out three feet of mylar streamers as it flies through the air. And if the ball winds up in the woods or rough, at least he'll know where to look for it.

$5.95 from The Duck Press.

THINK BIG! GOLF BALL

So you wanna hit the big ball, do you? Well, this one's about as big as they get: eight inches in diameter, nearly five times the size of a regulation golf ball. Phyllis Prinz and Bob Malkin, the proprietors of the Big Apple's "Think Big!" emporium, added this artful item to their larger-than-life repertoire some time back, and now we're just waiting for the ultra-big stick to go with it. (Warning: Don't try to hit this big ball ...

it's made of stoneware.)

$35 from Think Big!

VASSISDAT PUTTER

First the good news: This putter is, as they say in the car business, loaded. Now the bad news: It wantonly violates the Rules of Golf. Nevertheless, the Vassisdat Putter may be the ideal implement for the golfer who wants to be equipped for virtually every on-the-course eventuality. A built-in compass helps you find your way to the green, the 19th hole, or any other destination; a candle illuminates the long road home; a rabbit's foot gives you luck and wards off evil swing spirits; a level helps you read tricky greens; a 40-inch tape measure eliminates arguments over gimmes; and a horn commands silence or speeds up puttering putters. The only thing the Vassisdat Putter lacks, in fact, is a guarantee that you'll actually sink anything with it.

$29.95 from Las Vegas Discount Golf; also from Golf Day Products, Hammacher Schlemmer, Leister Game Company, and Northern Golf Ball Company.

WACKY GOLF CAP

If wearing a lampshade at parties is your idea of fun, here's the perfect golf cap for you. There's a little plastic golfer teeing off on top (picture a wedding-cake groom dressed in golfing attire and just finishing his follow-through), thickets of artificial grass, and two plastic greens with cups and flagsticks— one on top and another down below on the cap's bill. The golfer's tee

shot is on its way to the lower green. The Wacky Golf Cap adjusts to fit anyone— even fatheads.

$18 from The Cat's Pyjamas; also from Enticements.

WACKY TEES

Pack a handful of Wacky Tees in your golf bag and it'll never, ever be tee time. Just wait until someone in your foursome fumbles around for a tee; then hand your unsuspecting victim one of these and watch as he tries— and tries again— to prepare for his drive. Wacky Tees may look like standard tees, but there's one important difference: they have flat tops, making it all but impossible to tee a ball up on one of them.

$4.50 for a package of 40 from Golf Day Products; also from The Duck Press and Somerton Springs Golf Shoppes.

Vassidat Putter

CHAPTER EIGHT
GOLF GIFTS

GOLF GIFTS

"AMERICAN GOLF COURSES" PLACEMATS AND COASTERS

These placemats and coasters, which are otherwise identical to the "Famous British Golf Clubs" series (see below), depict sweeping vistas from some of America's greatest golf courses. The placemats feature Cypress Point, Edgewood Tahoe, Crooked Stick, and Jupiter Hills. The coasters feature views of the four courses shown on the placemats, as well as Olympic Club and Gainey Ranch.

$32 for the set of four placemats and $11 for the set of six coasters from Golf House; also from Potpourri.

BALLPOINT PEN WITH GOLF-CLUB CLIP

What could be a classier gift for a golfer than this elegant, gold-filled ballpoint pen from Brooks Brothers? Its clip is in the shape of a golf club, and the top of the pen's barrel is embossed with the famous Golden Fleece symbol.

$60 from Brooks Brothers.

BRASS CLUB-AND-BALL DOORKNOCKER

This decorative doorknocker no doubt says more about who's on the inside than who's on the outside. It's made from solid brass (of British Admiralty specifications, no less), measures about four inches high, and features a hinged

clubhead that descends on the dimpled surface of a golf ball. When the twain meet, someone's on your doorstep.

$32.50 from Hurley Style.

Business-Card Golfer in a Bottle

BUSINESS-CARD GOLFER IN A BOTTLE

It's not a bottle, really, but a glass dome, and underneath is a 3.5-inch-tall golfer ingeniously constructed entirely from business cards. Just send 15 business cards, scorecards, or other paper items to the folks at Crossroads International and they'll trim, fold, and glue them, origami-style, into the shape of a golfer (male or female) in proper follow-through form. Then they place a little metal driver in his or her hands, put the golfer under glass (a six-inch-high dome), and mount everything on the five-inch-square, felt-bottomed walnut base. As a finishing touch, the Business-Card Golfer in a Bottle is identified with a personalized, solid brass name plate. (If golf's not your game, you also can have your business cards made into a tennis player, quarterback, angler, skier, or any of more than 50 other designs.)

$32.99 from Crossroads International.

CARPET COASTERS

These coasters for 19th-hole toasters are made of a durable carpet material that absorbs drips from sweaty glasses and won't mildew. They're emblazoned with a teed-up golf ball against a background of Abercrombie & Fitch's own registered tartan plaid. What's more, the 3 3/4-inch-square coasters have special nonslip bottoms that will help keep them on the table even if you aren't keeping your eye on the ball.

$18 for a set of eight from Abercrombie & Fitch.

CERAMIC GOLF-BALL TEAPOT

Tea time and tee time come together in this imaginative china teapot from an old-line pottery house in Stoke-on-Trent, Staffordshire, England. The pot itself is sculpted in the dimpled shape of a golf ball, with a putter as its handle and an 18th-hole flag jutting up from its lid. The Ceramic Golf-Ball Teapot has a full six-cup capacity.

$40 from Hurley Style; also from Somerton Springs Golf Shoppes.

CRYSTAL GOLF BALL

Don't spend too much time gazing into this crystal ball— it's opaque, as glass goes, and no matter how hard you look it won't foretell your golfing future. But this Crystal Golf Ball by Royal Doulton may well be the perfect paperweight for any links-loving executive. The firm's expert craftsmen start with a sphere of heavy lead crystal, and when they're done with the dimple-cutting and polishing it's a distinctive collector's piece in the shape of a golf ball.

$57 from Golf House.

EXECUTIVE GOLF TOOL

This gold-plated gizmo is really seven tools in one: a ball-mark mender, snap-on ball marker, bottle opener (perfect for the Perrier-drinkers among us), groove cleaner, knife blade, screwdriver, and spike remover. It easily clips on to your bag or belt, measures only about 1.5-by-2.5 inches when closed, and, owing to its ingenious fold-up design, won't puncture holes in your pocket if you choose to keep it there.

$12.95 from Las Vegas Discount Golf; also from A2Z/The Best of Everything and Potpourri.

"FAMOUS BRITISH GOLF CLUBS" PLACEMATS AND COASTERS

These colorful placemats and coasters

depict the clubhouses at some of Great Britain's most historic golf courses. They're cork-backed and heat-resistant to protect furniture and topped with a laminated, wipe-clean surface for durability.

$32 for the set of four placemats and $11 for the set of six coasters from Golf House; also from Golf Arts & Imports and The Golf Shop Collection.

FLAGPIN "GREAT AMERICAN GOLF HOLES" PLAYING CARDS

This may be your best chance for an ace. There are four of them, in fact, in this deck of plastic-coated, poker-size playing cards. Each card features a colorful illustration of one of America's most famous golf holes, along with an identifying legend. And even if you draw nothing better than a pair of deuces, sizing up the likes of Pebble Beach and Southern Hills should at least make those long and unprofitable hours at the poker table a bit more tolerable.

$5.95 from The Duck Press.

GODIVA GOLF BALLS

These two-piece golf balls fully conform with official USGA (United States *Gastronomy* Association) rules and regulations. They weigh in at precisely 1.3 ounces apiece and have authentic-looking dimpled covers of solid Belgian chocolate, crunchy centers of caramel and walnut praline, and Godiva only knows how many calories.

$3.50 apiece or $9 for a sleeve of three from Godiva Chocolatier.

GOLF CADDY FIRE IRON SET

That's *fire* iron, not five-iron. The handles of these solid brass fireplace tools— a hearth brush, tongs, shovel, and poker— are shaped like club heads, and the entire foursome hangs at the ready on a rack that rests behind the brass figure of a young golf caddy. The wee lad stands just under 15 inches tall, with his cap pushed back on his head, one hand in his pocket, and a golf bag tucked under his arm.

$230 from Hurley Style.

GOLF GLASSES

These glasses won't improve your eyesight on— or off— the course, but they will add an air of elegance to any cocktail party or post-round round of drinks. Each 14-ounce "double old-fashioned" tumbler is etched with the crest of one of America's premier golf clubs, along with a brief history of the club and notable features of its golf course. The set of eight glasses includes Baltusrol Golf Club (Springfield, New Jersey), Cherry Hills Golf Club (Englewood, Colorado), Doral Country Club (Miami), Muirfield Village Golf Club (Dublin, Ohio), Oakmont Country Club (Oakmont, Pennsylvania), the Olympic Club (San Francisco), and Pebble Beach Golf Links (Pebble Beach, California).

$40 from Abercrombie & Fitch.

GOLF HOUSE BALL MARKER

This solid brass marker is embossed with the image of Golf House, the United States Golf Association's museum and library in Far Hills, New Jersey.

$2.50 from Golf House.

GOLF ORNAMENTS

These beautifully crafted Christmas-tree ornaments are made of satin-white glass and permanently imprinted with old-fashioned golf scenes (the cherub-cheeked "Golf Boy," for example, is from a turn-of-the-century color lithograph by C. Spiegle). The set of four different Golf Ornaments is packed in a gift box.

$26 from Golf House; also from The Golf Shop Collection.

GOLF QUOTES

"When I'm on a course and it starts to rain and lightning," Lee Trevino once joked, "I hold up my one-iron, 'cause I know even God can't hit a one-iron." Years later Trevino actually *was* struck by lightning on the golf course and lived to tell about it. "When God wants to play through," he said, "you let Him play through." Trevino's quips are among the many gems in this cloth-bound gift edition of *Golf Quotes*, an illustrated collection of wry, wise, and inspiring words about the game.

$12.50 from Falk's.

GOLF SUNDIAL

Words of wisdom, these: "Grow old along with me. The best is yet to be." That's the legend inscribed on this heavy-lead sundial, which also features a bas-relief portrait of a gentleman golfer in the classic follow-through position. The sundial is finished in brass and measures 11.5 inches in diameter.

$69.50 from Golf House; also from The Golf Shop Collection.

GOLF TEE TIE RACK

Which tie suits you to a tee? This dark-stained, 18-inch-long wooden tie rack will help you find just the right one. It's fitted with 24 tees (each topped with a tiny golf ball) to hold your neckwear neatly in place and two brass hooks on which to hang your belts. The Golf Tee Tie Rack includes the screws needed for mounting it to your closet door.

$14.95 from Enticements.

"THE GOLFER" CHARACTER JUG

This distinctive ceramic mug from Royal Doulton portrays a gray-haired, rosy-cheeked Scottish linksman from the shoulders up. He wears a short-brimmed cap and a kind smile, and his bag of golf clubs doubles as the mug's handle. Designed by David Biggs, "The Golfer" Character Jug is hand-painted in Royal Doulton's characteristically rich hues and is available in three different sizes: large (7 inches), $105; small (4 inches), $85; and miniature (2.75 inches), $55.

From Golf House.

GOLFER'S WELCOME MAT

Your golfing friends will feel right at home when they step over this colorful doormat, whose green and tan shades gracefully blend into any 19th-hole setting. The "Welcome" message is flanked by two old-fashioned golf clubs and teed-up balls on a tartan back-ground. The Golfer's Welcome Mat is made of durable, indoor-outdoor carpet-ing and measures 30 inches wide by 20 inches deep.

$24.95 from Golf Day Products.

GOLFERS' PEWTER HIP FLASKS

When the winter wind is bone-chilling and the clubhouse is nowhere in sight, you might wish you had one of these elegant pewter flasks tucked in your golf bag or hip pocket. The 5.5-inch-high St. Andrews Curved Pewter Flask ($50) is traditionally shaped to fit snugly and discreetly against the hip, and its polished surface features artist Edward Tovey's intricate engraving of the Royal and Ancient Club House at St. Andrews, "The Home of Golf." The 4-inch-high St. Andrews Pewter Window Hip Flask ($65) features the same engraving, but this time it's on the inside, visible through a transparent window in the facing wall. The 4.5-inch-high Golfer's Pewter Hip Flask ($79), which is also round, features a scrimshaw-style medallion titled "Cock of the Green," which portrays Andrew McKellar, "the original golf maniac," with club in hand. Each flask has a capacity of six ounces and a screw-on pewter cap.

From Hurley Style.

GOLFING COASTERS

These cork-backed coasters faithfully reproduce a series of amusing golf scenes originally painted by artist Tom Browne in the early 1900s. "A Grand Day for Golf," for instance, shows one sorry soul, club in hand and caddy in tow, slogging his way through a rainy round. The 3.5-inch-square Golfing Coasters come six to a set and have laminated, wipe-clean surfaces.

$9.90 from Hurley Style.

"GOLFING HAZARDS" TOWEL

This colorful, all-cotton towel features six old-fashioned scenes that humorously depict the game's assorted headaches. A panel titled "The Last Straw," for instance, captures a young golfer in argyles and knickers as he breaks a club over his knee; "A Charge From Behind" shows a goat approaching the backside of a similarly attired player. At 19 inches wide by 29 inches deep, the "Golfing Hazards" Towel is perfect for the bar or kitchen.

$8 from Golf House; also from Hurley Style.

HEXAGONAL GOLF TIDY BOX

This neatness-counts desk accessory, which is cast from polymer resin in antique scrimshaw style, is the perfect stash for all those tees, ball markers, and other golf paraphernalia that otherwise would find their way into your desk or dresser drawer. The mellow-beige box, which measures 4.5 inches across and 1.5 inches high, features intricately carved designs on all six sides and a portrait of Andrew McKellar, "the original golf maniac," on the lid. McKellar, who in the early 19th century played after dark and made his wife bring his meals out to the course, is shown with club in hand as the "Cock of the Green."

$55 from Hurley Style.

HOLE-IN-ONE TROPHY CASE

The perfect shot— or at least the ball you made it with— deserves the perfect showcase, and this may well be it. The Hole-In-One Trophy Case consists of a six-inch-square black acrylic base, a

Look-Alike Caricatures by Joe Jahraus

clear acrylic cover, and a brass plate that's just waiting to be engraved with all the lovely details. And if you're among the aceless, this case still could make the perfect home for another memorable golf ball (like, say, the one that made the rounds on your best round ever).

$35 from The Golf Shop Collection.

"IT'S TEE TIME!" MUG

This colorful, ceramic mug is decorated in a golf motif, but it's the built-in side pocket that sets it apart from run-of-

the-mill mugs. The pocket is packed with four wooden tees, but you'll probably use it as a handy receptacle for dripping tea bags. The "It's Tee Time" mug holds 11 ounces of coffee, tea, or whatever.

$9.50 from Golf House.

LOOK-ALIKE CARICATURES BY JOE JAHRAUS

Joe Jahraus wields a wicked, witty pen. And he's ready, willing, and able to make you— or the golfing "victim" of your choice— his next target. Simply send Jahraus a photograph and some particulars (the subject's name, hair color, clothing colors, and so forth), and for $50 he'll draw a one-of-a-kind, look-alike caricature that's colored by hand and ready for framing in a 12-by-16-inch mat. Or, for just $20, Jahraus will hand-color and personalize, per your instructions, one of his seven "generic" golf cartoons (shown here is "Par: Six Shots"). Either way, send along your club's crest or logo and he'll include it in the illustration at no extra charge.

From Joe Jahraus.

"MAJOR GREEN" CHARACTER MUG

Need a classy caddy at tea time? Meet Major Green, a mustachioed gentleman who stands four inches high from the waist up, clutches a niblick in his right hand, and is colorfully clad in a necktie, cardigan sweater, and Scottish-style golf cap. This quaint ceramic mug, designed by William Barber and hand-painted in Royal Doulton's characteristically

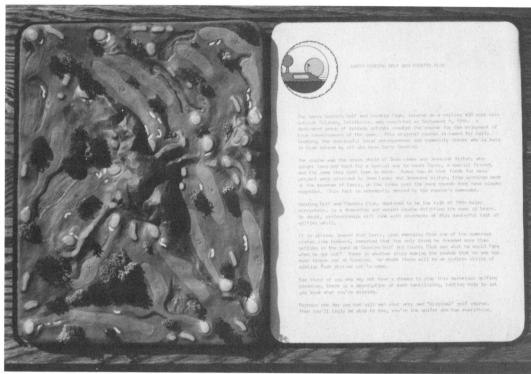

Own Your Own Golf Course

vibrant colors, is part of the Doultonville Collectors' Series.

$60 from Golf House.

OFF-THE-WALL GOLF-BALL ALARM CLOCK

Don't get mad, get even. When this golf-ball-shaped alarm clock goes off just an hour before tee time, it's time for you to swing into action and send it flying: Pluck it from its pedestal base and smack it, smash it, bounce it against the wall, or heave it across the room. The alarm will stop, but only for five minutes— forcing you to drag yourself out of bed to find it and shut it off. (For this reason, it is strongly suggested that you don't throw the thing out the window.) The Off-the-Wall Golf-Ball Alarm Clock is 3.75 inches in diameter, battery-operated, and, as you may have guessed, virtually indestructible.

$19.95 from Las Vegas Discount Golf; also from Austad's, Maryco Products, and The Price of His Toys.

THE OTEY CANE

This hickory-shafted putter is *supposed* to be used upside-down: It's a walking stick, after all, not a golf stick. The Otey Cane (so named for Otey Crisman, the legendary puttersmith) features a soft-bronze putter blade at one end and a hard-rubber tip at the other.

$49.95 from Las Vegas Discount Golf.

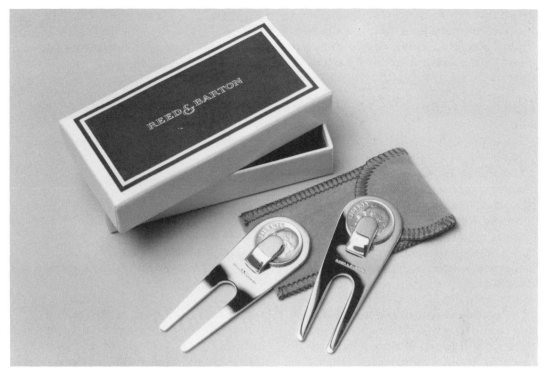

Reed & Barton Ball Mark Repair Tool

OWN YOUR OWN GOLF COURSE

Now you can buy an exact scale model of Pebble Beach Golf Links for less than you'd pay to play there. Garry Gooding's striking, three-dimensional reproductions of famous golf courses and holes are accurate in virtually every detail. From his studio in Salinas, California, Gooding crafts these miniature models by hand, mounts them on solid oak bases, and then encloses them in clear plastic covers. Any of the models may be hung on the wall or displayed on a desk or table.

If you'd like an entire course of your own, $75 will get you a faithful replica of either Pebble Beach or Spyglass Hill Golf Links; each is mounted, along with a history of the course, on an 18-by-12-inch oak base. Or for $80 you can become the proud owner of a miniature course that's uniquely your own. After you choose one of four available designs— seaside, desert, woodland, or mountain— Gooding christens the course in your honor (or the recipient's), personalizes the history of the course by liberally lacing it with information you supply, and mounts everything on an 18-by-12-inch oak base with a matching plastic cover. He also sends along colorful narrative descriptions of each hole and a batch of personalized scorecards.

If you'd prefer to stick to a single hole, Gooding also sells scale models of famous ones for $40 apiece. You can choose from the 7th and 18th holes at Pebble Beach, the 16th at Cypress Point (this breathtaking, 220-yard par-3 is one of the most photographed holes in all of golf), and the 17th at Pete Dye's

PGA West Stadium Course (that's where Lee Trevino got his ace during the 1986 "Skins Game"). Each model is mounted, along with a description and history of the hole, on a 12-by-10-inch oak base.

From Image Links.

Pure Silk Golf Ties

Only one problem with most golf ties: polyester. These handsome neckties, however, are clearly a breed apart. They're made from pure silk, with the ball-and-club designs intricately woven into— not printed on— the fabric. (Look closely and you'll even see the dimples and scoring lines.) And because these ties feature a satin-finish weave of very fine "hand," they knot easily at just the right size. You can choose from two designs: "pin dot" (two clubs crossed behind a golf ball) in burgundy, kelly, or navy; or "striped" (end-to-end golf clubs) in kelly and burgundy, navy and kelly, kelly and navy, navy and burgundy, or burgundy and navy.

$28 from Competitive Edge Golf.

Putter Tie Clip

Here's a classy clip for keeping wayward neckties in line. It's plated with 24-karat gold and resembles a miniature "Bull's-Eye" putter— right down to the wrapped grip and tapered shaft.

$24 from Competitive Edge Golf.

Reed & Barton Ball Mark Repair Tool

If you want to add a little bit of class to your greenside act, here's just the right touch: a gold- or silver-plated ball mark repair tool from Reed & Barton. Each tool includes a dime— the coin of choice for marking a golf ball— that was minted in the recipient's birth year. (If the date specified is 1922, 1932, or 1933, when no dimes were minted, a silver-plated penny is substituted). This elegant implement comes with a protective cloth pouch and gift box.

$20 (gold-plated) or $15 (silver-plated) from Practice House Golf.

CHAPTER NINE
GOLFIANA

GOLFING ART

DOUGLAS ADAMS PRINTS

In 1893 artist Douglas Adams chose the Caernarvon Course in Wales as the background for three golf scenes that since have become classics: "The Drive," "A Difficult Bunker," and "The Putting Green." These hand-colored prints, made from steel engravings of Adams's paintings, beautifully capture the brooding tones of Caernarvon as well as the mood of the game as it was played in the 19th century.

$48 each unframed (23" x 15") or $180 framed (27.5" x 18.5") from Golf House; also from The Golf Shop Collection and The Golf Works.

"The Bogey Man"

"THE BOGEY MAN" AND "ST. ANDREWS CADDIE"

These charming portraits were painted by L. Earle, a master of the character study, shortly after the turn of the century. Although at least one of the originals has disappeared, both works have been faithfully reproduced as prints. "The Bogey Man" depicts a rugged old Scotsman, tam-o'-shanter on his head and niblick cradled in his arm, dutifully marking his scorecard. "St. Andrews Caddie" catches its subject stopping for a quick smoke.

$40 unframed (11.5" x 18") or $135 framed (22" x 27") from The Golf Shop Collection.

BRITISH CIGARETTE CARDS: "FAMOUS GOLFERS 1930" AND "GOLF 1939"

For half a century, Americans and Europeans had a passion for collecting and trading the brightly colored advertising cards that were tucked into most packages of cigarettes. In the 1920s and 1930s— the heyday of cigarette cards—

more than 2,000 different sets were produced, including series that featured airplanes, automobiles, ships, trains, flora and fauna of every imaginable type, movie stars, royalty, military and sports heroes, and on and on. By the 1930s, in fact, most major tobacco companies employed teams of artists, researchers, and photographers whose only responsibility was to keep a card-hungry (and thus brand-loyal) public happy.

The paper shortages of World War II put an end to the craze, however, and the production of cigarette cards never really caught on again. Nonetheless, the hobby of "cartophily" (card collecting) is stronger than ever, with single cards selling for hundreds of dollars and complete sets bringing thousands at auction. The British cards produced in the Twenties and Thirties are particularly valued for their charming, stylized illustrations, and of these, two sought-after sets are about golf: "Famous Golfers," issued in 1930 by Wills's Cigarettes, and "Golf," issued in 1939 by Player's Cigarettes.

While the demand for these particular cigarette cards is so great that it's nearly impossible to find originals anymore, Imperial Tobacco Ltd. recently authorized the printing of reproduction sets. The new cards, 25 to a set, are virtually indistinguishable from the originals, except for the "authorized reproduction" disclaimer printed on the back of each one. The "Famous Golfers"—including Henry Cotton, Walter Hagen, Harry Vardon, and Joyce Wethered—swing gracefully on sweeping landscapes, many of them dressed to the tee in knickers and argyles; they're classic examples of pastel-and-earthtone portraiture. The cards in the second set, with their black-and-white diagrams and color illustrations of the era's leading golfers, still offer good, old-fashioned playing tips. (R.A. Whitcomb, for example, demonstrates how to properly hit a brassie from an uphill lie.)

The "Famous Golfers 1930" and "Golf 1939" British cigarette cards are available in complete sets of 25 and partial sets of 10, either framed or unframed. The frames are made of dark, furniture-finished wood, with the cards individually corner-mounted on pH-neutral mat board (20" x 24" or 16" x 20") along with an engraved brass title plate.

$85 unframed or $145 framed for complete sets and $39 unframed or $68 framed for partial sets from Westminster Graphics (a division of the British Cigarette Card Framing Company); also from The Golf Shop Collection.

"GINGER BEER HOLE" PRINT

The fourth hole of the world-famous Old Course at St. Andrews acquired its unusual nickname—"Ginger Beer"—more than a century ago, not long after profit-minded youngsters began gathering there every day to sell bottles of the stuff to thirsty golfers. The firm of G. & P. Barrie, which brewed ginger beer in nearby Dundee, soon recognized the promotional possibilities that remained untapped, and in 1894 it commissioned William Blake Lamond, a noted landscape artist, to capture the scene on canvas. From his original painting, which showed two golfers stopping at the fourth for that era's equivalent of "the pause that refreshes," Barrie made 48 show cards for advertising purposes.

Some years later 40 of these chromolithographic prints were accidentally destroyed, and the whereabouts of one of the remaining eight is still unknown. In 1987, however, Lamond's charming depiction of the "Ginger Beer Hole" was reproduced in a limited edition of 480. Each numbered print in the series is accompanied by a document that details the history of the work, including facsimiles of Barrie's stock and ledger sheets from 1894, which show the commission of .510 sterling it paid to Lamond.

$135 unframed (24" x 16") from Alexander Associates; also from The Golf Shop Collection.

"THE GOLFERS" PRINT

Painted in 1850 by Charles Lees and engraved by Charles Wagstaff, "The Golfers" captures for all time one of the most famous scenes in the game's history. This beautiful reproduction depicts the Grand Match at St. Andrews in 1841, which pitted Sir David Baird and Sir Ralph Anstruther against Major Playfair and John Campbell. In the background of this group-in-action portrait are many other golfing superstars of the time, including Allan Robertson of St. Andrews, the world's first golf professional. All of the subjects are clearly identified on a biographical key plate that accompanies each of the prints.

$49 unframed (21.5" x 14") and $174 framed (32" x 26") from The Golf Shop Collection. An extra-large rendition of "The Golfers" (37" x 25.5") is $158 unframed.

LEALAND GUSTAVSON PRINTS

The lush, evocative watercolors of Lealand Gustavson (1899-1967) often graced the pages of *McCall's, The Saturday Evening Post*, and other leading American magazines.

In this series of colorful illustrations he turned his talents on some of the greatest moments in the annals of golf, capturing each scene with a sure eye for its emotion, thrill, and historical significance. Gustavson's original watercolors have since been reproduced in a set of six prints. "The Old Apple Tree Gang, 1888" portrays the players who pioneered the game in America at St. Andrews Golf Course in Yonkers, New York. "The First Clubhouse in America, 1892," shows the original clubhouse at Shinnecock Hills Golf Club in Long Island, New York, which was designed by noted architect Stanford White. "Awarding the First USGA Trophy, 1895" commemorates the ceremony that honored Charles Macdonald as the winner of the first U.S. Amateur championship, which was held at Newport Golf Club in Rhode Island. "Francis D. Ouimet Wins United States Open Title, 1913" depicts the dramatic playoff in which the 20-year-old Ouimet, a virtually unknown American amateur, defeated British superstars Harry Vardon and Ted Ray at The Country Club in Brookline, Massachusetts. "Robert Tyre Jones, Jr., 1930" captures the legendary Bobby Jones following through in the year of his Grand Slam, with Walter Hagen, Tommy Armour, and Gene Sarazen looking on from behind the tee. "Playoff for Masters Championship, 1954" shows Sam Snead hitting the famed iron shot that gave him a slim one-stroke lead over Ben Hogan after thirteen holes and provided with his final margin of victory.

Each print is $49.50 unframed (21" x 16.5") or $189.50 framed (31" x 26") from The Golf Shop Collection.

BOBBY JONES CONCENTRATION

Robert Tyre Jones, Jr., one of the most revered figures in golf history, may well have been the game's greatest player. His brief career as a competitive golfer began when he won the Georgia Amateur at age 14. From 1923 to 1930 Jones entered 21 major championships and won 13 of them. In 1930 he became the only player in history to achieve golf's "Grand Slam" by winning the Amateur and Open Championships of the United States and Great Britain, after which he retired from competition at the age of 28.

This reproduction of a portrait by William Steene brilliantly captures the intensity in Bobby Jones's face and form as he prepares to swing. O.B. Keeler, Jones's biographer, described the photograph from which this portrait was painted as "Perhaps the best golf picture of Bobby Jones ever made. . . . It is Bobby's last look at the pin before he shoots . . . he is thinking of nothing in the world but that shot."

$40 unframed (10.5" x 15.5") or $140 framed (14 .75" x 17 .75") from Golf House; also from the Golf Shop Collection.

TERENCE LEGG GOLF SIGN

Hand-crafted by Terence Legg at his small studio in Folkestone, England, this charming wooden sign replicates a turn-of-the-century advertisement for London's B.F. Goodrich & Co., "Makers of the new Haskell No. 10." The center of the sign features the three-dimensional figure of a golfer poised at the top of his backswing; mounted below him is a replica of the company's core-wound golf ball (which, the ad proudly announces, was "Reg'd 1st. Jan. 1905"), along with its beechwood, feather, and gutta-percha predecessors. Each sign is painted entirely by hand— from the antique lettering to the old-fashioned players in the background— and measures approximately 18 inches by 30 inches.

$590 from Hurley Style; also from Golf Arts & Imports.

TOM MORRIS PRINT

In 1904, at the age of 83, Tom Morris was elected as the first honorary professional of the Royal and Ancient Golf Club of St. Andrews. Today Morris is known throughout the golfing world as "The Grand Old Man of Golf," and the 18th hole of the Old Course at St. Andrews is named in his honor. This reproduction of a portrait by W. Dendy Sadler (see below) depicts Morris with a pipe in his left hand and a golf club cradled under his right arm.

$10 unframed (4.5" x 6.5") or $55 framed (8" x 10") from Golf House; also from The Golf Shop Collection.

"OLD TOM MORRIS" TOBY JUG

Tom Morris, known to golf historians as "The Grand Old Man of Golf," is the body and soul of this hand-painted Toby jug. In 1904, at the age of 83, Morris was elected as the first honorary professional of the Royal and Ancient Golf Club of St. Andrews; the 18th hole of its Old Course was later named in his honor. This colorful ceramic mug stands 6.5 inches high and captures the gray-bearded Morris, club in hand, in a classic golfing stance.

$85 from Hurley Style.

W. Dendy Sadler Prints

As a society and sporting artist of the early 20th century, W. Dendy Sadler was as prolific as he was popular. His work celebrated the lifestyle of Britain's leisure class, and golf scenes were among his favorite subjects. Sadler's golfing art remains popular to this day, and reproductions of some of his best-known works have made their way into clubhouses around the world. Among them: "A Winter Evening," which shows a Scotsman enjoying a quiet night at home— cleaning and polishing his clubs; "A Little Practise," which looks in on a gentleman who's sharpening up his short game indoors; "The First Tee," which depicts a pair of golfers enjoying a pinch of snuff just before they tee off; and "The Stymie," Sadler's tongue-in-cheek study of greenside gamesmanship. Each of these reproductions bears Sadler's remarque— a whimsical little sketch in the margin— as well as the facsimile signatures of the artist and engraver.

The Sadler prints are available in two sizes. Miniatures are $10 unframed (4.5" x 6.5") or $55 framed (8" x 10") from Golf House ("The Stymie" hangs horizontally); also from The Golf Shop Collection. The Golf Shop Collection's large-size reproductions are $28 unframed or $123 framed; the first three prints measure 12.5" x 18" unframed or 22" x 27" framed, and "The Stymie" measures 13" x 18" unframed or 27" x 23" framed.

The Triumverate

At the turn of this century, three Britons— J.H. Taylor, James Braid, and Harry Vardon (the originator of the Vardon grip)— so thoroughly dominated the world of competitive golf that they became known as The Triumverate. At times it seemed as if the three men had a mortal lock on the game: From 1894 to 1914, for example, one or the other won the British Open 16 times and finished second in the other five. This beautiful reproduction of a work by Clement Fowler, originally done in 1913, shows Vardon teeing off as Taylor and Braid look on; the print also features facsimile signatures of the three golfing giants.

$40 unframed (11" x 14") or $115 framed (13.5" x 17.5") from Golf House; also from The Golf Shop Collection and The Golf Works.

GOLFING BOOKS

CLASSIC GOLF CLUBS: A PICTORIAL GUIDE

Joe Clement wrote the book on classic clubs. Back in 1977 he left his nine-to-five job as a cost analyst for an international engineering firm to pursue his real passion— buying and selling old golf clubs— as a full-time profession. Three years later he published Classic Golf Clubs: A Pictorial Guide, which soon became the leading reference manual on the subject. Illustrated with hundreds of close-up photographs, Clement's 198-page softbound book enables you to recognize, identify, and authenticate scores of sought-after classics, including more than 30 putters, roughly an equal number of wedges and specialty irons, nearly 20 sets of MacGregor and Spalding irons, and more than 70 different models of woods (most of them MacGregors). The book also has a useful section on the restoration of classic clubs and two handy appendixes, one that lists clubs by their model numbers and another that identifies every MacGregor Eye-O-Matic wood manufactured from 1952 to 1957. If you've ever wondered exactly what the "oil hardened" stamp on persimmon woods means or why a single putter can sell for upwards of $1,500, this is the book for you. Clement's latest price supplement ("Current Market Values of Classic Golf Clubs"), issued in 1986, is included with the book.

$15.50 from The Golf Works; also from Florida Golf Warehouse and Golfsmith.

THE CLUB MAKERS

Whether you collect old golf clubs or simply like to read up on the game's history, this 123-page reference guide from the United States Golf Association undoubtedly belongs on your bookshelf. *The Club Makers* covers woods, irons, and putters manufactured in golf's earliest era up through World War II; they're listed by maker, trademark, type of club, and method of manufacture.

$10 from Golf House.

THE GOLF CLUB IDENTIFICATION AND PRICE GUIDE

If you need to identify or appraise any golf club made from 1950 to 1988, look no further. The second edition of *The Golf Club Identification and Price Guide* has it all— from detailed descriptions of virtually every golf club manufactured during the period to their current market values. Written by Tom Wishon, revised and updated by Mark Wilson, and illustrated with more than 600 photographs, this 640-page softbound reference book lists more than 7,000 different sets of woods and irons from 46 different manufacturers, as well as hundreds of individual drivers, wedges, specialty clubs, and putters. It also contains richly detailed histories of all the major golf-equipment manufacturers, including the evolution of their product lines, shifts in marketing strategies, changes in management and ownership, notable "firsts," and other

GOLF ART AND BOOKS 155

significant innovations and achievements.

Before you sell or otherwise dispose of any old golf clubs you might have around, you'd be well-advised to consult this book, which bears the PGA's seal of approval and has come to be regarded as the industry's standard identification and trade-in guide. To anyone who deals in golf clubs it is downright indispensable; to you it might prove to be invaluable. Those MacGregor "VIP by Nicklaus" irons sitting in your garage, after all, could be worth a whole lot more than what you paid for them back in 1967.

$18.50 from The Golf Works; also from Richard E. Donovan Enterprises, Golf House, GolfSmart, and National Golf Foundation.

THE GOLF HOUSE RARE BOOK COLLECTION

Each year since 1981, the United States Golf Association has offered a limited-edition facsimile of a classic book on golf. The Golf House Rare Book Collection gives collectors and enthusiasts an opportunity to acquire early works on the game that otherwise might be all but impossible to find. These facsimile editions, enclosed in handsome slipcases, have themselves quickly become collectors' items; the volumes issued in 1981 and 1982, in fact, are no longer available. The remaining titles in the series are:

Great Golfers in the Making (1988). The world's leading golfers at the turn of the century come alive in this fascinating anthology of autobiographical essays, which was compiled by Henry Leach back in 1907. Each essay bears the autograph of its author.

Concerning Golf (1987). In 1903 John L. Low, the founder of the Oxford and Cambridge Golf Society, took a long look at how the game had progressed since its earliest times. A surprising number of Low's observations still ring true.

Golf in America (1986). This remarkable little book by James P. Lee, originally published in 1894, was the first attempt to chronicle the evolution of the game in the United States. Lee, however, didn't stop with history; he included sections on how the game should be played, what novices might expect on the course, and the prevailing rules of etiquette.

Fifty Years of Golf (1985). Horace H. Hutchinson, who won the British Amateur Championship in 1886 and 1887, later made important contributions to the game's literature (among them The Badminton Library on Golf). In this volume, originally published in 1919, he recounts how the game caught on in England in the latter half of the 19th century and then spread to North America.

Tee Shots and Others (1984). Many golf historians regard Bernard Darwin as the greatest writer the game has ever known, and this anthology of his early essays lends a good measure of support to the claim. It's laced with Darwin's wry humor and wild flights of imagination.

Rules of the Thistle Golf Club and *A Few Rambling Remarks on Golf* (1983). These books, the first written by John Cundell in 1824 and the second by Robert Chalmers in 1862, represent two of the earliest efforts to set down a history of the game. Originally published in Edinburgh, Scotland, these facsimile editions are offered as a set.

$50 each from Golf House.

HILLERICH & BRADSBY: HISTORY-CATALOGS (1922-1980)

The Hillerich & Bradsby Company may be best known for its "Louisville Slugger" baseball bats, but for nearly 70 years it's also been turning out some of the finest persimmon woods money can buy. In this softbound reference book Jim Kaplan traces the history of H&B and the evolution of its Power Bilt line of golf clubs, mostly by reproducing more than 400 pages from the company's original catalogs, complete with photographs, club specifications, and shaft descriptions. Although MacGregor woods have long dominated the classic-club market, in recent years some of the older Power Bilt clubs— chief among them the backweighted "Citation" woods made from choice persimmon turnings— have come into their own. So if you happen to have some old H&B clubs lying around, this is one book you probably can't afford to be without. And if you're interested in classic and collectible golf clubs generally, Kaplan's entire trilogy (his MacGregor and Wilson volumes are described below) probably deserves a place on your bookshelf.

$15 from Vintage Golf; also from The Golf Works, GolfSmart, Matzie Golf, and National Golf Foundation.

MACGREGOR GOLF: HISTORY-CATALOGS (1935-1970)

The MacGregor Golf Company bills itself as "The Greatest Name in Golf," and few would dispute its claim to the title. Its roots in the golf business stretch back to before the turn of the century, when the Crawford, McGregor & Canby Company of Dayton, Ohio, began to manufacture shoe lasts on a new Yankee invention called the duplicating lathe. Edward Canby, the company's owner, had become an avid golfer, and he soon realized that his lathes could turn out wooden golf clubs faster and better than the clubmakers who crafted them entirely by hand. In 1897 the company manufactured its first golf club under the MacGregor trademark (a spelling apparently intended to lend a more Scottish touch), and within a year it began making clubheads out of persimmon, then a little-known American hardwood. Soon virtually all of the world's leading golfers were playing with persimmon woods, and MacGregor's models were widely thought to be the best. Despite the rapid technological advances within the golf-equipment industry, many of today's top touring professionals— even those under contract with other companies— still carry MacGregor's classic persimmon woods.

Jack Nicklaus, who's played MacGregor clubs since he was 10 years old, signed a contract to represent the company soon after he turned professional in 1961 and eventually came to buy it. But over the years MacGregor's Advisory Staff has included plenty of other famous players, among them Tommy Armour, Jimmy Demaret, Ben Hogan, Byron Nelson, and Toney Penna. (Penna, who was the company's chief designer during the late 1940s and 1950s, crafted virtually all of the MacGregor clubs that today are considered classics.)

This softbound reference book by Jim Kaplan traces the history of the MacGregor Golf Company and reproduces more than 400 pages from its original catalogs, complete with photographs (more than 1,000 of them), and detailed club descriptions (including loft, lie, length, and shaft specifications). Add it to your golf library, and you'll be able to identify and classify virtually every club MacGregor manufactured from 1935 to

1970. And should you be lucky enough to find an old Tommy Armour 945 Eye-O-Matic driver or other MacGregor classic at a garage sale or flea market, you'll have paid for this indispensable volume many times over.

$15 from Vintage Golf; also from The Golf Works, GolfSmart, Matzie Golf, and National Golf Foundation.

A. G. SPALDING & BROS.—PRE-1930 CLUBS, TRADEMARKS, AND COLLECTIBLES

Jim Cooper of Kannapolis, North Carolina, is known as "The Spalding Man," and for good reason: He wrote the book on America's first and oldest manufacturer of golf equipment. A.G. Spalding & Bros. Company introduced the first American-made golf club— a hand-forged iron— back in 1894, and four years later it introduced the first American-made golf ball. Since then Spalding has pioneered many of the game's other innovations, including the first "dimpled" golf ball (1908), the first steel-shafted clubs (1918), the first matched sets of woods and irons (1919), the first registered sets of clubs (1926), the first heel-and-toe weighted clubs (1967), and the first two-piece golf ball (1968).

Cooper's 79-page softbound book and two slimmer addendums cover Spalding's early years as a golf-equipment manufacturer in exhaustive detail. The three volumes feature hundreds of photographs of old Spalding golf clubs— driving-irons, cleeks, mashies, niblicks, and jiggers, for example— along with Cooper's notes on trademarks, sub-marks, and other matters of interest to collectors. He shows several models of the infamous Schenectady putter, whose wooden shaft was inserted

toward the center— not the heel— of its mallet-shaped head. (The unconventional implement was named after the hometown of A.W. Knight, the obscure amateur who invented it.) In 1904 Walter J. Travis used one with deadly proficiency to capture the British Amateur Championship at Royal St. George's Golf Club in Sandwich, Kent. As one galleryite put it, "Travis could *write* with his putter if you put a nib on it." Travis, a naturalized American citizen originally from Australia, thus became the first "foreigner" to win the British Amateur. Five years later the Royal and Ancient Golf Club of St. Andrews, Scotland, finally responded to the embarrassment by banning the Schenectady putter— and its cousins— from all British tournaments. (The ruling was lifted in 1919.)

But perhaps the most fascinating bit of golfiana in Cooper's books has to do with another putter— Bobby Jones's legendary "Calamity Jane." In February 1969, two years before his death, Jones outlined its history in a letter to the late Gene Hitt of Santa Ana, California. The text of his letter, which Cooper reproduces in his book as Addendum I, reads as follows:

> Dear Mr. Hitt:
>   The original Calamity Jane was given to me by Jimmy Maiden in 1920 when he was pro at Nassau, Long Island.
>   The head bore the rose mark of a Condy iron and was probably forged sometime around the turn of the century. The head also bore the mark of W. Winton, who was probably the man who completed the club with shaft and grip.
>   In 1926, Spalding made a half dozen copies of this club, but these were for my personal use. I gave a

few to friends, but substituted one of the copies for the original in my bag because it had become too light from continued polishing.

Spalding, with my permission, first made Calamity Janes for the market in 1931.

Sincerely,

Robert Tyre Jones, Jr.

From J. M. Cooper. A.G. Spalding & Bros.—Pre-1930 Clubs, Trademarks, and Collectibles *is $10; Addendum I and Addendum II are $7.50 each. All three volumes are available as a set for $20.*

WILSON GOLF: HISTORY-CATALOGS (1931-1979)

The Wilson Sporting Goods Company has been making golf equipment—and golf history—since 1914, the same year that Henry Ford introduced the mass-production assembly line, doubled his workers' wages, and paved the way for a new era in which the average American could play what had previously been a rich man's game. Along the way Wilson has pioneered many of the industry's most significant innovations, including: "The Bomber," believed to be golf's first sand iron, in 1930 (its concave clubface was later ruled illegal); the "Reminder Grip," in 1932; Willie Ogg's toe-weighted irons, in 1933; Gene Sarazen's new-and-improved sand iron, also in 1933; the first clubs to have two different shaft flexes in the same set, in 1934; the first laminated wood clubheads, in 1941; the drilled-through, "fluid feel" hosel design, in 1956; and the first

shafts individually matched to the clubs within a set by flex, in 1961. (Here's Wilson's original catalog copy for Sarazen's invention, which retailed for $8.50 and revolutionized the game of golf: "The Sarazen Sand Iron is one of Gene's pet ideas. It's an entirely new development that is taking the fear out of traps for many players. Don't try to pick the ball clean—just hit down hard in back of it and immediately upon hitting the sand under the ball the club is forced upwards by its abrupt sole flange with the result that it gives a sharp upward lift to the ball, occasioning a much higher trajectory to the shot. The ball gets into the air fast to carry high bunkers and falls almost dead on the green.")

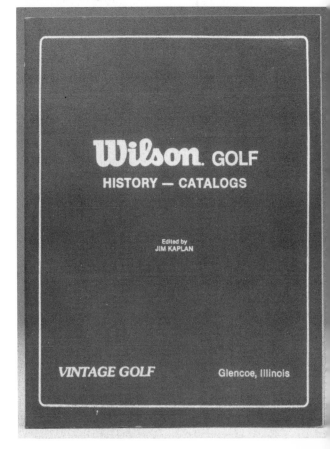

Wilson GOLF
HISTORY — CATALOGS

Edited by
JIM KAPLAN

VINTAGE GOLF   Glencoe, Illinois

Wilson also originated the concept of an "Advisory Staff" back in 1924, when it signed Sarazen not only to suggest improvements in its golf equipment but to actually test prototypes and report his findings to the company's club designers and research specialists. Over the years other members of the "Wilson Staff" have included Patty Berg, Julius Boros, Billy Casper, Walter Hagen (whose golf equipment company Wilson purchased in 1944), Betty Hicks, Helen Hicks, Lloyd Mangrum, Cary Middlecoff, Arnold Palmer, Johnny Revolta, Sam Snead, Mickey Wright, and Babe Didrickson Zaharias.

In this softbound reference volume Jim Kaplan traces Wilson's fascinating history and chronicles the evolution of its various lines of golf equipment over nearly 50 years. By reprinting more than 500 pages from the company's original catalogs— complete with photographs (more than 1,000 of them) and detailed club specifications (lofts, lies, lengths, shafts, swingweights, grip sizes, and so forth)— it lets you identify virtually every wood, iron, and putter that Wilson manufactured from 1931 to 1979. And if you're interested in any of the Wilson clubs that have become genuine classics— among them its "Dynapower" irons, R-90 sand wedges, and 8802 and 8813 putters— you should keep Kaplan's book within convenient reach.

$15 from Vintage Golf; also from The Golf Works, GolfSmart, Matzie Golf, and National Golf Foundation.

CHAPTER TEN
VIDEO AND AUDIO CASSETTES

VIDEO AND AUDIO CASSETTES

THE ART OF PUTTING WITH BEN CRENSHAW

(HPG Home Video, 44 minutes)
Ben Crenshaw, who's long been regarded by many of his colleagues on the PGA Tour as the game's best pure putter, once said: "I don't have any big secret about putting. Just hit at it. It's either going to miss or go in." In this video, however, Crenshaw proves exactly the opposite— namely, that putting is anything but a hit-or-miss proposition. With the aid of slow-motion sequences and computer graphics, Crenshaw explores every aspect of the putter's art— from the proper grip, stance, and stroke to the paramount

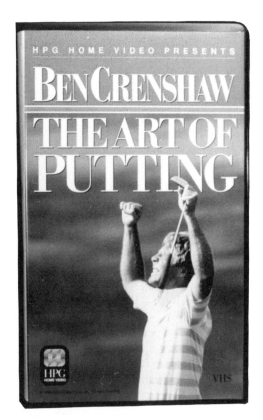

importance of "feel"— and shares the green-reading techniques and practice drills he's found to be most effective. The video also features fascinating footage of some other legendary greenside artists at work, including Bobby Jones (in highlights from his 1931 film, "How I Play Golf"), Bobby Locke (who, as Lloyd Mangrum once put it, "could hole a putt over sixty feet of peanut brittle"), Arnold Palmer, and Jack Nicklaus. So if you want to stop sweating 'em and start sinking 'em, this video should get you pointed in the right direction.

$28 from GolfSmart; also from Acorn Sports, Competitive Edge Golf, Critics' Choice Video, Richard E. Donovan Enterprises, Florida Golf Warehouse, Golf Day Products, Golf Digest, The Golf Works, Golfsmith, Las Vegas Discount Golf, Maryco Products, Matzie Golf, National Golf Foundation, Nevada Bob's Discount Golf, Sportime, and Edwin Watts Golf Shops.

AUTOMATIC GOLF WITH BOB MANN

(Video Reel, 42 minutes)
A million golfers can't all be wrong: They've made "Automatic Golf" the game's all-time best-selling video. In this hands-on workshop, Bob Mann teaches that a sound golf swing produces such key movements as "pronation" and "supination"— not the other way around— and that real strength comes from the larger muscles of the legs. Master his method, Mann says, and you'll develop a "swing you don't have to think about."

$14.95 from Video Reel; also from Acorn

Sports, *Competitive Edge Golf, Critics' Choice Video, Florida Golf Warehouse, Golf Day Products, The Golf Works, GolfSmart, Golfsmith, Matzie Golf, and Edwin Watts Golf Shops.*

THE JIMMY BALLARD GOLF CONNECTION

(JK Productions, 96 minutes)

Within the ranks of golf teachers, Jimmy Ballard is something of a renegade. You'll never hear him say "keep your head down," for example, or "keep your left arm stiff." But if you've read his book, *How To Perfect Your Golf Swing*, you already know that Ballard's idea of perfection in the golf swing has to do with the principle of "connection"— keeping the leading arm and upper body working as a unit. For some time now he's been widely regarded as one of the top swing doctors in the business, and his patient list reads like a "Who's Who" of the PGA and LPGA Tours. (Over the years he's diagnosed and treated the swing ailments of more than 130 touring professionals, including Seve Ballesteros, Bobby Clampett, Jim Colbert, Johnny Miller, Jerry Pate, Gary Player, J.C. Snead, Curtis Strange, and Hal Sutton.) In this video version of his book Ballard outlines the "seven common denominators" of the great ball-strikers— from Ben Hogan to Jack Nicklaus— and shows you, in a tee-to-green playing lesson, how to make them part of your swing.

$40 from GolfSmart; also from Acorn Sports, Austad's, Competitive Edge Golf, Richard E. Donovan Enterprises, Florida Golf Warehouse, Golf Day Products, Golf Digest, The Golf Works, Las Vegas Discount Golf, Matzie Golf, National Golf Foundation, Nevada Bob's Discount Golf, and Edwin Watts Golf Shops.

Better Golf Now! with Ken Venturi

(HPG Home Video, 40 minutes)
For years Ken Venturi was known as one of the top shotmakers on the PGA Tour, a never-say-die competitor who could repeatedly drill his long- and mid-iron shots right at the stick. And if you've seen any of his instructional tips on television, you know that he's also one of golf's most entertaining— and effective— teachers. In this video Venturi walks you through the fundamentals, from tee to green, driving his lessons home with clever drills and memory aids. He's also put together an easy-to-remember "mini-lesson" that lets you quickly review key checkpoints just before you head to the course.

$32 from GolfSmart; also from Acorn Sports, Competitive Edge Golf, Critics' Choice Video, Richard E. Donovan Enterprises, Golf Day Products, The Golf Works, Matzie Golf, National Golf Foundation, and Nevada Bob's Discount Golf.

Challenge Golf with Peter Longo

(Motivation Media, 53 minutes)
Peter Longo, a former PGA touring pro turned trick-shot artist, has been wowing audiences for years by hitting golf balls in all sorts of unconventional and amazing ways. He can hit 'em long and straight with just one arm, for example, or while blindfolded, standing on one leg, or sitting in a chair. After teaching a one-legged man to play golf, Longo realized that his trick-shot expertise could help plenty of other people with physical disabilities, including amputees, paraplegics, arthritics, stroke victims, and the blind. "Golf is the perfect game for any disabled

person," he says. "The golf swing can be adjusted to fit any need, and all the action is done from a standstill." In this video Longo relies on his repertoire of trick shots and an array of special effects to expertly prove his point: that golf is a game anyone can play.

$49.95 from Motivation Media; also from Richard E. Donovan Enterprises, The Golf Works, GolfSmart, and National Golf Foundation. (A special teaching edition for coaches and therapists at schools, hospitals, and other institutions is $79.95 from Motivation Media.)

Chipping & Putting with Charlie Schnaubel

(Morris Video, 30 minutes)
Charlie Schnaubel knows something about the short game. He's one of the two PGA teaching pros who invented the Puttband-Swingband, a short-game

training and practice device that's used by Calvin Peete and more than 100 other card-carrying members of the PGA Tour (see page 54). And in this video Schnaubel sticks to his specialty: the part of the game that's played on and around the green. Among other score-shaving tips and techniques, he shows which clubs to use for specific shots, when to gently pitch the ball onto the green versus when to use the chip-and-run, and how to sharpen your putt-sinking skills.

$12.95 from Morris Video.

Difficult Shots Made Easy with Hale Irwin

(SyberVision, 55 minutes)
Since 1968 Hale Irwin has racked up 17 victories on the PGA Tour, including the 1974 and 1979 U.S. Open championships. But he's best known among his colleagues as a player who never lets trouble get in the way of a good round. In 1984, for example, he won the Bing Crosby National Pro-Am Tournament by hitting an incredible two-iron shot out of a fairway bunker to within nine feet of the hole— and then sinking the putt to clinch the victory. In this video Irwin shows you how to master 10 of the most difficult shots in golf. You'll learn, among other things, how to hit shots from the rough with the same confidence you'd have in the fairway; how to adjust your stance, alignment, and swing for uphill, downhill, and sidehill lies; and how to cope with "fried-egg" lies in greenside sand traps. Computer-enhanced graphics, close-ups, and super-slow-motion sequences drive Irwin's points home. So if those trouble shots make you tremble, maybe this video can help you keep the wheels on your game and the triple bogeys off your scorecard.

$49.95 from SyberVision; also from Abercrombie & Fitch, Acorn Sports, Richard E. Donovan Enterprises, Golf Day Products, The Golf Works, GolfSmart, Matzie Golf, National Golf Foundation, and Somerton Springs Golf Shoppes.

18 Tips from 18 Legends of Golf

(Liberty Mutual, 120 minutes)
The title says it all, and here's the star-studded cast (in order of appearance):

Mike Souchak, Peter Thomson, Butch Baird, Doug Ford, Miller Barber, Sam Snead, Art Wall, Tommy Bolt, Gene Littler, Don January, Gardner Dickinson, Doug Sanders, Jerry Barber, Bob Goalby, Billy Casper, Gay Brewer, Charlie Sifford, and Julius Boros. The lessons are organized into five chapters— "Before You Hit," "The Full Swing," "The Fairway Shots," "Around the Green," and "Strategy and Equipment"— for easy reference, and if just one of them helps your game it might be worth the price of admission.

$59.95 from "18 Tips."

EXERCISES FOR BETTER GOLF
(PGA Productions, 73 minutes)
Move over, Jane Fonda. Here's the first scientific fitness program for golfers— a series of stretching and strengthening exercises developed by Frank Jobe, M.D., the medical director of the PGA

GET RID OF YOUR BACK PROBLEMS AND PLAY BETTER GOLF

With **Sam Snead** and **Dr. K.J. Keggi**

Tour. The exercises are designed to build up your key golfing muscles, increase your flexibility and endurance, and significantly lower your risk of injury. At the same time, they should help you achieve greater distance, control, and consistency. The program grew out of extensive research on professional golfers conducted in the Biomechanics Laboratory of the world-famous Centinela Hospital Medical Center, the official hospital of the PGA Tour, the LPGA, and almost every major-league sports team in Los Angeles. The video includes Dr. Jobe's companion book, *30 Exercises for Better Golf.*

$49.95 from Richard E. Donovan Enterprises, The Golf Works, GolfSmart, Maryco Products, or Matzie Golf; also from National Golf Foundation.

FEEL YOUR WAY TO BETTER GOLF WITH WALLY ARMSTRONG
(Gator Golf Enterprises, 52 minutes)
If you can skip a stone, mop the floor, or hold an umbrella, you may already have the makings of a good golf swing. Or at least that's the gospel according to Wally Armstrong, an 11-year veteran of the PGA tour, whose unconventional teaching methods are aimed at demystifying some of golf's most mystifying movements. Forget the mechanics of the golf swing, Armstrong preaches in this video, and focus instead on "feel." (And if it all sounds too simple, just keep your head down and say "Amen.")

$14.95 from Gator Golf Enterprises; also from Acorn Sports, Competitive Edge Golf, Critics' Choice Video, Richard E. Donovan Enterprises, Golf Day Products, The Golf Works, GolfSmart, Matzie Golf, and National Golf Foundation.

GET RID OF YOUR BACK PROBLEMS AND PLAY BETTER GOLF WITH SAM SNEAD AND DR. K.J. KEGGI

(Specialty Video Marketing, 60 minutes)
Both play golf, but that's not all that Sam Snead and Kristaps Keggi, M.D., have in common. Snead, now 75 years old ("par plus three," he likes to say), knows all about back problems; Keggi, an associate clinical professor of orthopaedic surgery at the Yale University School of Medicine, knows all about treating them. So if you're among the 25 percent of all golfers who complain of back problems, this video may be just what the doctor ordered. In it Snead and Keggi demonstrate an exercise and conditioning program that's designed to give you a healthier back, a more flexible body, and a better all-around game of golf. They're joined by Pamela Kazemekas, a registered physical therapist, who takes you through the paces of eight special back-conditioning routines. Snead, who can still swing one leg high enough to touch an eight-foot-high ceiling, may even help cure your golf and back problems at the same time; he shows how some common swing faults— spreading your legs too far apart or keeping your knees too stiff, for example— can cause chronic aches and pains.

$39.95 from Specialty Video Marketing; also from The Golf Works and National Golf Foundation.

GOLDEN GREATS OF GOLF

(Golf Digest, 60 minutes)
This veritable treasure chest, drawn from private and public film collections as well as British and American television archives, captures many of the greatest players— and greatest moments— in the history of the game. You'll see rare footage, for example, of a charity match in the Bahamas starring four true legends: Walter Hagen, Bobby Jones, Tommy Armour, and Gene Sarazen (with the Duke of Windsor tending the flagstick and the Duchess presenting the prizes). You'll see such important milestones in the evolution of the game as Harry Vardon's invention of the overlapping grip and the birth of "Arnie's Army" in 1960. You'll see highlights of dramatic head-to-head matches, including Jack Nicklaus and Tom Watson battling it out at Turnberry in 1977 for the British Open championship and at Pebble Beach in 1982 for the U.S. Open championship. Compiled by Peter Dobereiner and narrated by Peter Alliss, this video lets you watch all of the all-time greats in action— from Ben Hogan, Byron Nelson, and Sam Snead to Gary Player, Lee Trevino, and Seve Ballesteros.

$49.95 from Golf Digest; also from Acorn Sports, Competitive Edge Golf, Richard E. Donovan Enterprises, Golf Day Products, The Golf Works, GolfSmart, Golfsmith, Matzie Golf, and National Golf Foundation.

THE GOLDEN TEE

(Magnum Sports, 72 minutes)
There's a certain magic in watching these 11 legends swing a golf club. Watch them long enough, in fact, and you may begin to believe that nobody today does it any better. You'll see George Bayer hitting the longest balls anyone had ever seen, Julius Boros lofting oh-so-delicate wedge shots onto the green, and Billy Casper displaying the kind of putting wizardry that once led Gary Player to joke, "He can't putt a lick— he missed three 30-footers out

there today." You'll also see Tommy Bolt, Mac Hunter, Gene Littler, Lloyd Mangrum, Byron Nelson, Bob Rosburg, Mike Souchak, and Mickey Wright. (Watching Nelson's 24-carat swing, for that matter, may alone be worth the price of admission.)

$24 from GolfSmart; also from Acorn Sports, Competitive Edge Sports, Richard E. Donovan Enterprises, The Golf Works, Matzie Golf, and National Golf Foundation.

GOLF WITH AL GEIBERGER
(SyberVision, 60 minutes)
In 1977 Al Geiberger, the lanky pro with a picture-perfect swing, posted an unremarkable, even-par 72 in the opening round of the Danny Thomas Memphis Classic (now the Federal Express St. Jude Classic) at the Colonial Country Club in Cordova, Tennessee. But the following day, in nearly 100-degree heat, Geiberger acquired a page in the history books— and a new nickname— by shooting an eye-opening 59, the lowest score ever posted on the PGA Tour. ("I was just trying to shoot a good round, to get something going," Geiberger later recalled.) *Sports Illustrated* would recognize his record-breaking round as "one of the most significant athletic feats of the century," and over the years it has obscured even his victories in the 1966 PGA Championship and 1975 Tournament Players Championship.

Today Geiberger is one of the top stars of the Senior PGA Tour (with 15 wins since 1987), and in this video you'll see him hitting perfect shots with virtually every stick in his bag— from driver to putter. Simply watching "Mr. 59" enough, the SyberVision theory goes, will etch the image of winning

form into your mind and body, leaving you with a visual blueprint of the perfect golf swing. Thanks to super-slow-motion and other special effects, you'll be able to see and study every aspect of Geiberger's swing— and, with any luck, replicate his key movements next time you're on the golf course. The video is available either by itself or as part of a package that includes four audiocassettes (one of them an interview in which Geiberger talks about the thrill of his history-making achievement) and a 28-page personal training guide.

$69.95 (video only) or $89.95 (complete system) from SyberVision; also from Abercrombie & Fitch, Acorn Sports, Competitive Edge Golf, Richard E. Donovan Enterprises, The Golf Works, GolfSmart, Golfsmith, Herrington, Las Vegas Discount Golf, Matzie Golf, National Golf Foundation, Nevada Bob's Discount Golf, Somerton Springs Golf Shoppes, and Edwin Watts Golf Shops.

GOLF WITH PATTY SHEEHAN
(SyberVision, 60 minutes)
"It's nice to have the opportunity to play for so much money," Patty Sheehan said a few years ago, "but it's nicer to win it." Sheehan should know. Since joining the LPGA Tour in 1980 she's won more than $1.8 million and 19 tournament titles, including back-to-back victories in the 1983 and 1984 LPGA Championships. In this video you'll see Sheehan crack long drives off the tee, drill long irons down the middle of the fairway, coax beautiful shots out of her short irons, and smoothly stroke putts into the center of the cup. Simply watching her winning form, the SyberVision theory goes, will etch the image of a perfect golf swing into your mind and body. Thanks to super-slow-motion

sequences and other special effects, you'll be able to see and study Sheehan's key swing movements— and, with any luck, replay them on the golf course. The video is available either by itself or as part of a package that includes four audiocassettes (one of them an interview with Sheehan) and a 28-page personal training guide.

$69.95 (video only) or $89.95 (complete system) from SyberVision; also from Abercrombie & Fitch, Acorn Sports, Austad's, Competitive Edge Golf, Richard E. Donovan Enterprises, The Golf Works, GolfSmart, Golfsmith, Herrington, Las Vegas Discount Golf, Matzie Golf, National Golf Foundation, Nevada Bob's Discount Golf, Somerton Springs Golf Shoppes, and Edwin Watts Golf Shops.

GOLF CLUB DESIGN, SPECIFICATIONS & FITTING

(The Golf Works, 240 minutes)
If you want to learn more about the tools of the golfer's trade, you probably won't be able to find a better teacher than Ralph Maltby. Since 1973 he's conducted more than 200 seminars on the subject for PGA professionals, and his 725-page book, *Golf Club Design, Fitting, Alteration & Repair*, is widely regarded as the industry's standard reference work. In this two-volume set of videos Maltby shares his encyclopedic knowledge of how golf clubs are designed and manufactured, how their specifications affect performance, and how they should be fitted to individual players. You'll learn, for example, exactly what happens to a golf club at the moment of impact, how backspin is generated, and why a club's center of gravity is so important.

$129.95 from The Golf Works.

GOLF CLUB REPAIR—THE KNOWLEDGE & BENCH SKILLS WITH TOM WISHON AND MARK WILSON

(The Golf Works, 210 minutes)
If it ain't broke, the saying goes, don't fix it. But since when has that stopped any golfer in quest of the perfect equipment? Most of the top players on the PGA Tour, for example, constantly experiment with their golf clubs, making minor adjustments in swingweights, lies, lofts, and the like. This two-volume set of videos from The Golf Works Repair School is made to order for any do-it-yourselfers who may be so inclined. Tom Wishon and Mark Wilson, two of the school's top instructors, demonstrate how to fit and install grips, how to reshaft woods and irons, how to refinish woods (irons are better left to experts), and how to repair just about any other golf-club problem— from loose inserts to worn-out whipping.

$129.95 from The Golf Works; also from Richard E. Donovan Enterprises.

THE GOLF DIGEST SCHOOLS LEARNING LIBRARY

(Golf Digest, 26 minutes each)
If you're really serious about improving your golf game, you've probably thought at some point about attending one of the Golf Digest Instruction Schools. Since 1971 thousands of amateur and professional golfers have studied the game under the tutelage of Golf Digest's incomparable teaching staff. But if you're not quite ready to spend $3,000 or more for five days of personalized instruction at one of the nation's premier golf resorts, this 10-volume video library is an inexpensive alternative. It may help you build the swing and the confidence you need to play better golf.

Now meet the faculty. Bob Toski, who's widely recognized as one of the game's finest teachers, hosts each video as the dean of the Golf Digest Schools. Jim Flick, the director of instruction, teams up with Toski in the first two videos and teaches the short-iron course. The other instructors are John Elliott, Hank Johnson, Jack Lumpkin, Tom Ness, and the late Davis Love, Jr.

Volume 1—A Swing for a Lifetime. Bob Toski and Jim Flick teach you how to build a repeating and reliable golf swing. They'll show you how to generate greater clubhead speed with your shoulders, hips, and legs, and how to maximize your power and accuracy at the moment of impact. Toski and Flick also demonstrate a few practice drills that you can use at home or on the range.

Volume 2—Find Your Own Fundamentals. Bob Toski and Jim Flick explain and illustrate the five fundamentals of a consistent pre-swing routine: grip, aim, ball position, set-up, and alignment. They also demonstrate "The Board Drill," a practice technique you can use in your own backyard to check clubface alignment.

Volume 3—Driving for Distance. Are your tee shots shorter than you'd like them to be? Do you frequently find yourself playing your second shot from the rough— or, worse yet, from the wrong fairway? If so, this driving lesson from John Elliott may put you on the road to greater distance and accuracy off the tee. Elliott shows you his secrets for hitting 'em long and straight: how to achieve maximum clubhead speed; how to make solid, square contact with the ball; and how to synchronize all the key movements that make up a powerful and consistent golf swing.

Volume 4—Sharpen Your Short Irons. If you've lost your competitive edge with the short irons, you're proba-

bly scrambling for pars far more often than shooting for birdies. In this video Jim Flick focuses exclusively on the short irons— from mashie (five) to niblick (nine)— and shows you how to hit them crisply and accurately. Flick also offers some tips on club selection, along with a set of practice drills aimed at curing "the shanks" and other common ailments of an iron-poor swing.

Volume 5—Saving Par from the Sand. The golf ball stares at you from the sand and says, "Hit me." If you listen, however, you're asking for trouble: Most bunker shots are properly executed by swinging into the sand behind the ball and letting the sand lift it out of the trap and onto the green. In this video John Elliott shows you to cure your "bunkerphobia" and wield the sand wedge with firmness and finesse. Elliott also offers a set of practice drills that should let you significantly up your percentage of "sand saves."

Volume 6—Putting for Profit. Drive for show, the saying goes, and putt for dough. In this video Tom Ness shows you how to cash in on the greens by describing his own putting techniques in detail. In addition to explaining the mechanics of the putting stroke itself, he shows you how to control distance and direction, how to sharpen your aim, how to warm up and practice, and how to read greens.

Volume 7—When the Chips Are Down. Jack Lumpkin teaches you how to chip closer to the hole and save more pars. He covers all the basics— the grip, the stance, the set-up, and the swing itself— and then shows you how to execute various chip shots with accuracy and consistency.

Volume 8—Winning Pitch Shots. These days many golfers are packing an extra pitching wedge in their bags, and for good reason: The shots from 100 yards in are the real score-shavers and

Wally Armstrong's
Golf for Kids Of All Ages

A fun, instruction-packed golf video from PGA Tour Veteran Wally Armstrong, son Scott, and host Gabby Gator that makes the fundamentals of golf exciting and easy to remember.

Fundamentals

score-savers. In this video Davis Love, Jr., covers the three key elements of the pitch shot— trajectory, distance, and roll— and shows how to control them with the pitching and sand wedges.

Volume 9—Hitting the Long Shots. If you're not hitting many "GIRs"— greens in regulation— you're probably not scoring many pars. In this video Davis Love, Jr., shows you how to develop the kind of smooth, sweeping swing that gets the most out of your fairway woods and long irons. And by reaching more greens in regulation, you'll be able to banish some of those nasty numbers from your scorecard.

Volume 10—Trouble Shots: The Great Escapes. Hank Johnson shows you how to minimize the damage to your score— and maybe even salvage par— when your shots stray from the fairway.

$29.95 each from Golf Digest; also from Acorn Sports, Competitive Edge Golf, Richard E. Donovan Enterprises, The Golf Works, GolfSmart, Golfsmith, Las Vegas Discount Golf, Matzie Golf, National Golf Foundation, and Somerton Springs Golf Shoppes.

GOLF FOR KIDS OF ALL AGES WITH WALLY ARMSTRONG

(Gator Golf Enterprises, 50 minutes)
Who says the fundamentals aren't any fun? Here's a video geared to juniors and beginners that proves otherwise. Wally Armstrong, an 11-year veteran of the PGA Tour, teams up his 10-year-old son, Scott, and an animated narrator named "Gabby Gator" to make his lessons as entertaining and easy to remember as they are instructive. Armstrong relates the basic motions of other sports to golf and relies on some out-of-the-ordinary props to illustrate and reinforce key movements in the golf swing.

$19.95 from Gator Golf Enterprises; also from Critic's Choice Video, Richard E. Donovan Enterprises, Golf Day Products, The Golf Works, GolfSmart, Las Vegas Discount Golf, Maryco Products, Matzie Golf, National Golf Foundation.

GOLF FOR WINNERS WITH HANK HANEY AND MARK O'MEARA

(PGA Tour Productions, 42 minutes)
When PGA touring pro Mark O'Meara decided several years ago to rebuild his golf swing from the bottom up, he turned to Hank Haney, the director of golf instruction at the PGA West Golf Club in La Quinta, California, and the

GOLF LESSONS FROM **Sam Snead**
60 MINUTES IN COLOR
Presented in cooperation with GOLF Magazine

The Grand Master Shows You How

STAR VIDEO PRODUCTIONS

$48 from GolfSmart; also from Acorn Sports, Richard E. Donovan Enterprises, The Golf Works, Matzie Golf, National Golf Foundation, and Nevada Bob's Discount Golf.

GOLF LESSONS WITH SAM SNEAD

(Star Video Productions, 60 minutes)
Ah, poetry in motion. Sam Snead may well have the sweetest swing of all, and any serious golfer would be foolish to forgo this tee-to-green playing lesson with the game's Grand Master. (As sportswriter Jim Murray once put it: "Any guy who would pass up a chance to see Sam Snead play would pull the shades driving past the Taj Mahal.") If nothing else, watching this living legend at work will leave you convinced that some golf swings, like good bourbon, improve with age. As Slammin' Sam covers the entire game, from driving to putting, he shows you how to hit with every stick in the bag and every shot in his bag of tricks.

$59.95 from Star Video Productions; also from Competitive Edge Golf, Richard E. Donovan Enterprises, The Golf Works, GolfSmart, Matzie Golf , National Golf Foundation, Somerton Springs Golf Shoppes, and J. White Industries.

chief instructor of *Golf Illustrated.* Haney teaches golf in terms of absolutes and fundamentals, and chief among his absolutes is the importance of the proper swing plane. In this video Haney drives the point home with the help of O'Meara, his star pupil, who effectively demonstrates how stance, posture, and the length of different clubs affect the shape of the swing plane. But the real star of "Golf for Winners," which was filmed at the United States Golf Association's testing center in Far Hills, New Jersey, may be Iron Byron, the mechanical golfer used by the USGA in its equipment tests. While Haney and O'Meara try to replicate Iron Byron's powerful and perfectly repeating swing, they're no match for the machine. Nonetheless, your swing is bound to benefit from the plane truths they expound.

GOLF LIKE A PRO WITH BILLY CASPER

(Morris Video, 51 minutes)
Anyone who's won the Masters, two U.S. Opens, 48 other tournaments on the PGA Tour, and 60 tournaments on the Senior PGA Tour must be doing something right. In this video Billy Casper covers a lot of ground— from the fundamentals of the full swing to the

fine art of getting out of trouble— with the help of slow-motion sequences and instant replays. Casper even demonstrates his amazing water-skipping shot, which most duffers— damn the expense of practicing it— would do well to perfect.

$19.95 from Morris Video; also from Competitive Edge Golf, Critics' Choice Video, and Richard E. Donovan Enterprises.

GOLF THE MILLER WAY WITH JOHNNY MILLER

(Morris Video, 30 minutes)
"I had a stretch there for a few years where I played some golf that bordered on the Twilight Zone," Johnny Miller recalled in 1982. "I can remember that I was literally getting upset that I had to putt." (Maybe this video should have been titled "Golf the Milky Way.") In 1975, for example, Miller captured the Tucson and Phoenix Opens back to back and in the process posted the lowest eight consecutive rounds ever played on the PGA Tour: 67-61-68-64 (260), 66-69-67-61 (263). When he was hot no one could touch him; in addition to a strong game off the tee, Miller could

routinely drill his irons closer to the stick than anyone since Byron Nelson. In this video Miller shows you the swing that's won him 23 tournament titles, including the 1973 U.S. Open and the 1976 British Open, and more than $2.4 million in career earnings. Miller's on-the-course clinic covers both the fundamentals (the proper grip, stance, alignment, and so forth) and fine points (how to improve your golf swing by watching your shadow, for example). After joking with the small gallery that joins him on the tee, Miller begins by stressing the importance of warming up and hitting a few practice balls. Along the way he shares some of his own practice techniques, among them hitting shots with his left arm only (to build up his weaker left side and better control his swing plane) and with a golf ball wedged under his right foot (to make sure that he pushes off properly on the down-swing). The video also features a cameo appearance by actor Sean Connery, who joins Miller on the fairway for a mini-lesson. If Miller's tips can help James Bond— and they seem to— maybe they can help you play to a 007 handicap.

$24.95 from Morris Video; also from Acorn Sports, Competitive Edge Golf, Richard E. Donovan Enterprises, GolfSmart, Matzie Golf, and National Golf Foundation.

GOLF MY WAY WITH JACK NICKLAUS

(Worldvision Home Video, 128 minutes)
Jack Nicklaus may have been paid the ultimate compliment in the history of golf when, during the presentation ceremony for the 1965 Masters, an awe-stricken Bobby Jones said: "Jack is playing an entirely different game— a game I'm not even familiar with." And if you can't get two hours on the links with Nicklaus himself, this expertly produced video is the next best thing. In it the Golden Bear explains and ana-lyzes more than 20 segments of the game— from driving to putting— each with slow-motion sequences to illustrate key points.

$68 from GolfSmart; also from Acorn Sports, Austad's, Competitive Edge Golf, Critics' Choice Video, Richard E. Dono-van Enterprises, Golf Day Products, Golf Digest, The Golf Works, Golfsmith, Las Vegas Discount Golf, Maryco Products, Matzie Golf, National Golf Foundation, Nevada Bob's Discount Golf, Somerton Springs Golf Shoppes, Edwin Watts Golf Shops, and J. White Industries.

GOLF SECRETS WITH WALTER HAGEN

(Kensington University School of Golf, 30 minutes)
Walter Hagen once wagered $10 that he'd be able to make a hole-in-one and then left his playing partners slack-jawed by doing just that. "The trick," he explained, "is to know when that one time is about to happen." While Hagen doesn't address the art of predicting aces on this audiocassette version of a rare 1926 recording, he does disclose many of the "golf secrets" that made him one of the game's genuine legends. In this fascinating tape "The Haig" covers proper mental attitude, the grip and stance, controlled driving, fairway woods, long and short irons, sand shots, putting, and common swing faults.

$9.95 from The Golf Works.

THE GOLF SWING WITH TOM WEISKOPF

(Bilgret's Sports, 45 minutes)

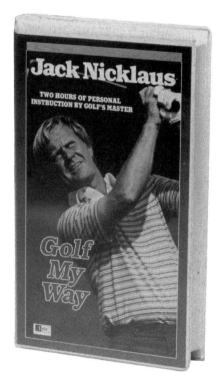

"If I had that swing," Jack Nicklaus once said, "I'd win every week." Well, even the owner of "that swing" didn't win every week. But during his years on the PGA Tour Tom Weiskopf did manage to claim 15 tournament titles, including the 1973 British Open, and more than $2 million in earnings. In this video Weiskopf covers what he calls the "necessary, key positions in the full golf swing" (eight of them in all), from take-away to follow-through. The rest of his lesson, however, isn't as spectacular as its backdrop: the Troon Golf & Country Club in Scottsdale, Arizona, which Weiskopf designed in collaboration with architect Jay Morrish and named after the site of his British Open victory.

$16 from GolfSmart; also from Acorn Sports, Richard E. Donovan Enterprises, Golf Day Products, The Golf Works, Matzie Golf, National Golf Foundation, Nevada Bob's Discount Golf, and Edwin Watts Golf Shops.

GOLF—THE WINNER'S EDGE WITH KERMIT ZARLEY
(Word Lifeware, 25 minutes)
"The pro from the moon," Bob Hope once joked. But here Zarley is decidedly down to earth as he focuses on the five fundamentals of the golf swing.

$14 from Acorn Sports; also from Richard E. Donovan Enterprises, Matzie Golf, and Sportime.

GOLF YOUR WAY WITH PHIL RITSON
(Kinemation Studio, 76 minutes)
Phil Ritson, the dean of instruction at the Kinemation Studio of Golf in Heathrow, Florida, is one of the game's

top teachers. Over the years he's tutored some 70 touring professionals and given more than 12,000 private lessons. In this easy-to-follow video, which snared a five-star rating from *Golf Magazine*, Ritson demonstrates 39 practice drills aimed at helping you build a better swing.

$22.95 from The Golf Works; also from Edwin Watts Golf Shops.

GOLF'S GREATS QUICK TIPS— VOLUMES I AND II
(Paper Back Video, 30 minutes each)
This two-volume series is packed with useful playing tips, entertaining anecdotes, and words of wisdom from a dozen of golf's greats. Volume I features Billy Casper, Bobby Nichols, Jerry Barber, Orville Moody, George Bayer, and Charlie Sifford. In Volume II Casper is joined by Tommy Bolt, Charles Owens, Jack Fleck, Doug Ford, Dow Finsterwald, and Harold Henning.

$12 each from GolfSmart; also from Richard E. Donovan Enterprises, Golf Day Products, The Golf Works, Matzie Golf, National Golf Foundation, and Edwin Watts Golf Shops.

THE GREATER GOLFER IN YOU WITH DR. GARY WIREN
(Nightingale-Conant Video)
Gary Wiren, the former director of learning and research for the PGA, is widely known as the "teacher of teachers." He's the author of the PGA's manual of golf instruction, and over the years he's taught the game's "laws, principles, and preferences" to more than 180,000 amateurs and profession-

als in 13 countries. He's currently the master teacher at the PGA National Golf Club in Palm Beach Gardens, Florida, where these videos were produced before a live audience. In Volume One (84 minutes) Wiren shows you how to build a repeating and reliable golf swing, how to achieve greater power and precision, how to practice most effectively, and how to develop a winning mental attitude. In Volume Two (87 minutes) Wiren covers the short game (pitching, chipping, bunker play, and putting), trouble shots, and course management; he also shows you how to achieve maximum performance through regular training and conditioning. The videos, which let you watch the same seminar Wiren gives PGA pros, are available either individually or as part of a comprehensive instruction package that includes three 60-minute audiocassettes (which let you listen to Wiren's lessons in your home, car, office, or wherever) and a training and exercise guide.

The complete package (two videotapes, three audiocassettes, and the training and exercise guide) is $69.95 from Gary Wiren's "Golf Around the World"; also from The Golf Works (which also offers the videos for $31.95 each and the set of three audiocassettes for $28.95), Acorn Sports, Richard E. Donovan Enterprises, GolfSmart, Matzie Golf, and National Golf Foundation.

HOW I PLAY GOLF WITH BOBBY JONES

(SyberVision, 180 minutes)
Was Robert Tyre (Bobby) Jones, Jr., the greatest golfer in the history of the game? Let the record speak: Over an eight-year period beginning in 1923, he won the U.S. Open four times, the U.S.

Amateur five times, the British Open three times, and the British Amateur once— a total of 13 victories in the 21 major championships he entered. ("Approach this record from any angle," Herbert Warren Wind once wrote, "and its mold looms more and more heroic.") In 1930, his last year of competitive golf, Jones became the first— and only— player in history to capture the game's coveted "Grand Slam" by winning the U.S. and British Open and Amateur championships in a single season. Then, having achieved the goal he'd set for himself, Jones— still an amateur at age 28— suddenly announced his retirement from tournament golf.

Although few knew it at the time, Jones was virtually broke. The enormous cost of competing in golf's

major championships, both in the United States and abroad, had taken its toll. Jones decided to devote himself to his four-year-old law practice in Atlanta, but he never lost his love for the game that had made him famous the world over. He accepted a vice-presidency from A.G. Spalding & Brothers, the sporting-goods manufacturer, and later designed the company's— and the industry's— first set of matched, steel-shafted clubs. He set about planning the Augusta National Golf Club. And in 1931 he was lured to Hollywood by Warner Brothers, which signed him to star in a series of 12 short subjects on golf that, in the fashion of the day, were to be shown before its feature films.

Jones insisted that the series be titled "How I Play Golf." He wanted theatergoers to know that they were watching his way— not the way— to play golf. While Jones wrote every word himself, Warner Brothers called on some of its biggest stars to make cameo appearances in the shorts. Yet other top celebrities secured releases from their studios and worked gratis just for the privilege of being tutored by the legendary Bobby Jones. Among those who appeared with him were James Cagney, Douglas Fairbanks, Jr. (whose father had sailed to England in 1930 just to watch Jones win the British Open at Hoylake), W.C. Fields, Walter Huston, Edward G. Robinson, and Loretta Young.

The "How I Play Golf" series turned out to be a box-office smash. The shorts were shown in 6,000 theaters to an estimated audience of 25 million— roughly one-fifth of the nation's population at the time. Jones's contract with Warner Brothers, which called for $120,000 up front plus a share of the profits if the series grossed more than $360,000, eventually netted him $600,000, which he had the foresight to put into a trust fund for his family.

By 1933 Warner Brothers was ready for more. It came back to Jones with a contract for six additional shorts, which were collectively titled "How To Break 90." George Marshall, the director who'd worked with Jones on the first series (and a low-handicap golfer himself), filmed the second set with slow-motion sequences and some other unheard-of special effects. He suspended a camera directly above Jones's head, for example, so that the audience could see his remarkably full turn. And he dramatized the principal point of each lesson by having Jones, dressed entirely in black except for the part of the body whose movement he wanted to illustrate, swing against a black background.

Three years before Jones's death in 1971, an obituary of sorts for his filmed golf lessons appeared in *Sports Illustrated*, which noted: "These movies are now unobtainable— only one copy is known to exist— and almost forgotten, although they were perhaps the best motion-picture instructionals ever made of any sport." Had it not been for Ely Callaway of Callaway Golf, in fact, the films might never have surfaced. Callaway, whose company manufactures golf clubs that bear the Bobby Jones name, began searching for them in 1986 and, through a combination of dogged persistence and pure luck, eventually hit pay dirt. He unearthed the original master prints in an old Warner Brothers storeroom in New York City, acquired them from Turner Home Entertainment (which owns the Warner film library), and arranged for them to be released in videocassette form by SyberVision Systems, Inc., of Newark, California.

SyberVision packaged Jones's 18 instructional shorts, each about 10 minutes in length, into two 90-minute videocassettes. In addition to a fascinating introduction that includes filmed highlights of Jones's career (dating back to his first appearance in 1916), the first volume contains eight lessons: The Big Irons, The Brassie, Chip Shots, The Driver, Down Swing, Fine Points, The Grip, and Hip Action. The second volume contains 10 lessons: Impact, The Mashie Niblick, The Medium Irons, The Niblick, Practice Shots, Position and Backswing, A Round of Golf, The Spoon, Trouble Shots, and The Putter. The three hours of footage are remarkable on several counts.

For starters, the production quality of the films is astonishing even by modern standards. The sound is excellent, the black-and-white images are amazingly crisp, and Marshall's special effects— some of which still seem ahead of their time— at times are downright eye-popping. Next, no golfer before or since has come close to Jones's eloquent, precise, and image-laden way of expressing himself— a talent he honed during the 1920s, when he wrote a twice-weekly golf column for a newspaper syndicate. "The right elbow is drawn away from the side of the body," he says of the backswing in one lesson, "but it remains below the club and never appears likely to begin flapping like the wings of a frightened bird." And then there's the almost-hypnotic beauty of Jones's effortless but enormously powerful swing, which alone may be worth the price of admission. Someone once said that watching Jones swing "was like watching milk being poured from a pitcher," and it is.

So if you buy only one golf-instruction video, let this veritable gold mine be it. As Ben Crenshaw put it to *Golf Digest*: "They are the most valuable films of their kind I've ever seen. Jones's explanation of the swing is a marvel of simplicity. He regarded it as a unified whole, something that flowed from point A to point B, not as a lot of complicated parts you had to mechanically fit together. People who want to know what golf's all about will be studying these cassettes 100 years from now."

The two videocassettes are accompanied by *A Golf Story*, Charles Price's 161-page hardcover book about Jones, the Augusta National Golf Club, and the Masters Tournament; a booklet by Price on the history of the films; and a numbered certificate of authenticity.

$245 from SyberVision; also from Abercrombie & Fitch, Richard E. Donovan Enterprises, Golf House, GolfSmart, Las Vegas Discount Golf, Matzie Golf, National Golf Foundation, and Edwin Watts Golf Shops.

How To Golf with Jan Stephenson

(Karl Lorimar Home Video, 50 minutes)
Since 1974 Jan Stephenson has chalked up 16 wins on the LPGA Tour, including the 1982 LPGA Championship and the 1983 U.S. Women's Open, and more than $1.7 million in career earnings. Now you can see and study the smooth, sweeping swing that's made her such a standout. In this video Stephenson covers the entire game— from practice range to putting green— in a fast-paced, easy-to-understand style. And if once isn't enough, each of the tape's teaching segments is color-coded.

$24 from GolfSmart; also from Acorn Sports, Austad's, Competitive Edge Golf, Critics' Choice Video, Richard E. Donovan Enterprises, Golf Day Products, Golf Digest, The Golf Works, Las Vegas Discount Golf, Maryco Products, Matzie Golf, National Golf Foundation, Nevada Bob's Discount Golf, Somerton Springs Golf Shoppes, and Edwin Watts Golf Shops.

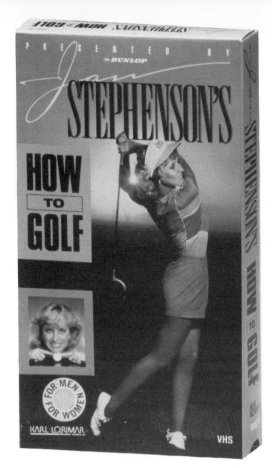

and how to manage your game on the course. And with an assist from three different playing partners, Intrieri even offers some specific advice for junior, senior, and women golfers.

$49.95 from How To Play Better Golf.

How To Play Your Best Golf All the Time with Tommy Armour

(Vintage Golf, 32 minutes)
In his time he won all the big ones: the U.S. Open in 1927, the PGA Championship in 1930, and the British Open in 1931. Even though he'd lost the sight of one eye during World War I and carried eight pieces of shrapnel in his left shoulder, Tommy Armour's iron play was so unerringly accurate that in 1926 even the legendary Bobby Jones turned to the "Iron Master" for help. (The diagnosis: Jones's right hand was overpowering his iron shots.) Armour, who later become better known as the "Silver Scot," knew how to teach. "Had Currier and Ives been around," Herbert Warren Wind wrote in *The Story of American Golf,* "they would have probably depicted Armour in his most characteristic posture— sitting in his chair beneath a large umbrella on the practice tee at Boca Raton, working on a gin buck as he rasped out his trenchant instructions to his fortunate pupils.") Armour's first instruction book, *How To Play Your Best Golf All the Time,* was published in 1953 and quickly became a best-seller. The following year the book was made into an instructional film, and more than three decades later the old black-and-white footage was unearthed and transferred to videotape. While the presentation has its share of shortcomings— the master's voice is missing

How To Play Better Golf with Bob Intrieri

(Scott Geesey Productions, 120 minutes)
Maybe you've never heard of Bob Intrieri, but he's widely known as one of the best teaching pros in the business. He's one of only 35 professionals in the 9,600-member PGA, in fact, to have earned the coveted title of Master Professional Teacher. Now, thanks to this thorough, no-nonsense video, Intrieri can be your personal teacher. For starters, he covers the proper grip, posture, and alignment, shows you how to develop a consistent pre-shot routine, and explores every facet of the full golf swing from set-up to follow-through. Then he moves on to chipping, pitching, sand shots, and putting. But the lessons don't end there. Intrieri also shows you how to choose the right equipment; how to exercise, warm up, and practice;

altogether, for example— who cares if there are a few chinks in the old Armour?

$39.99 (for the video and a 131-page paperback edition of How To Play Your Best Golf All the Time) *from Vintage Golf; also from Richard E. Donovan Enterprises, The Golf Works, GolfSmart, Matzie Golf, and National Golf Foundation.*

IMPROVE YOUR GOLF GAME WITH LARRY GARRETT

(Garrett Hypnosis Clinic, 22 minutes)
Larry Garrett isn't a golf pro, but he may be able to help you play the game with more concentration and confidence. Garrett is a clinical hypnotist, and over the last two decades he's hypnotized some 30,000 individuals in private practice and reached millions more through radio and television talk shows. This audiocassette is aimed at clearing your subconscious mind of negatives ("I'll tee up one of those old balls just in case I hit it in the water . . .") and flooding it with positives ("This putt has nowhere to go but in the hole . . ."). Simply sit back, relax, listen (preferably with stereo headphones), and let Garrett's voice gently guide you into a light level of hypnosis.

There are no subliminal messages— just soothing sound effects, hypnotic music, and Garrett's suggestions (a series of positive, goal-oriented golf thoughts). If self-hypnosis has helped others quit smoking, maybe it can help you quit slicing. "Improve Your Golf Game" is recorded in Dolby stereo and comes with an informative 25-page instruction booklet.

$9.95 from Garrett Hypnosis Clinic.

THE INNER SOLUTION WITH DR. ROBERT METZGER

(Inner Solution Clinics, 45 minutes)
"Competitive golf is played mainly on a five-and-a-half inch course . . . the space between your ears." These words of wisdom are attributed to the legendary Bobby Jones, who could so rivet his attention on the business at hand that artist William Steene's famous portrait of him (see page 153) is titled "Concentration."

For nearly 40 years Dr. Robert Metzger, a practicing hypnotherapist and avid golfer, has been helping amateurs and professionals in just about every sport to harness their powers of concentration and play "within themselves." In this audiocassette tape Metzger teaches you a simple form of self-hypnosis that's aimed at allowing you to reprogram your subsconscious mind with positive reinforcement and overcome the debilitating attitudes that stand in the way of better golf. Master his "Inner Solution Formula," the theory goes, and next time you're on the golf course you'll be able to relax, mentally visualize the shot you want, and confidently execute that visualization.

$14.95 from R.L. Kays & Associates.

AN INSIDE LOOK AT THE GAME FOR A LIFETIME WITH BOB TOSKI, JIM FLICK, PETER KOSTIS, AND JOHN ELLIOTT

(Golf Digest, 56 minutes)
Four of golf's best-known teaching professionals— Bob Toski, Jim Flick, Peter Kostis, and John Elliott— team up in this video to help you improve your game from green to tee. Their systematic approach to teaching, which is adapted from the course of study at the Golf Digest Schools, focuses mostly on the fundamentals and begins, if you will, at the end. In nine separate lessons, the members of the foursome cover putting, chipping, pitching, bunker play, the full swing, the short and middle irons, the fairway woods, and the driver— in that order.

$56 from GolfSmart; also from Acorn Sports, Richard E. Donovan Enterprises, Golf Digest, The Golf Works, Matzie Golf, National Golf Foundation, and Edwin Watts Golf Shops.

THE JOHN JACOBS SERIES— THE FULL SWING, THE SHORT GAME, AND FAULTS AND CURES

(John Jacobs Home Video Productions)
This three-volume series features John Jacobs, a.k.a. "Dr. Golf," whose common-sense approach to the game has made him one of the world's leading golf instructors. Take it from Jack Nicklaus: "John Jacobs and I share the same attitude to the golf swing— the simpler you keep it, the better it will work." In "The Full Swing" (57 minutes) Jacobs methodically moves from tee to green, using super-slow-motion sequences to dissect the correct swing from start to finish and to illustrate the importance of the proper swing plane; he also

answers a dozen of the swing questions that he's been asked most frequently over the years. In "The Short Game" (60 minutes) Jacobs offers 21 self-contained lessons on putting, pitching, chipping, and bunker play, with tips on trouble shots and tough lies. In "Faults and Cures" (58 minutes) he diagnoses 18 common swing ailments— slicing, hooking, pulling, pushing, shanking, and topping, for example— and prescribes simple cures for each one. As an added attraction, all three videos also feature cameo introductions by Sean Connery, a.k.a. "007."

$56 each from GolfSmart; also from Acorn Sports, Competitive Edge Golf, Richard E. Donovan Enterprises, Golf Day Products, Golf Digest, The Golf Works, Matzie Golf, National Golf Foundation, Somerton Springs Golf Shoppes, and Edwin Watts Golf Shops.

JUNIOR GOLF "THE EASY WAY" WITH MARK STEINBAUER
(ThetaMark Home Video, 43 minutes)
If you can't send your child to golf camp for the summer, this video may be the next best thing at a fraction of the price. In it Mark Steinbauer, the PGA professional who directs the North Texas State Junior Golf Academy, simplifies the fundamentals of the game for any would-be Palmers (Arnolds or Sandras) in your household.

$59.95 from The Golf Works.

KEYS TO CONSISTENCY WITH JACK GROUT
(Ardent Video Publishing, 43 minutes)

"Jack Grout stresses fundamentals. He keeps them to a minimum, and he keeps them simple. I can assure you that the simplicity of Jack's approach is the major reason why I've managed to play as well as I have over the years." You've been listening to Jack Nicklaus, of course, and now you can study the golf swing from the man who's been his lifelong teacher and trouble-shooter. In this video Grout focuses on the fundamentals of the golf swing, showing you how to hit the ball the same way time

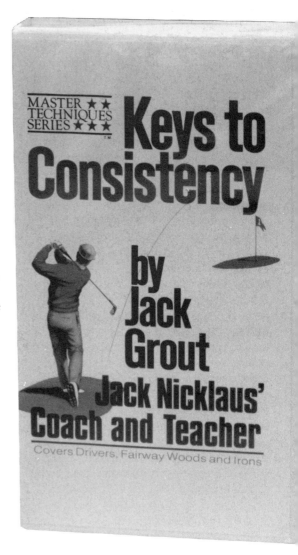

MASTER TECHNIQUES SERIES ★★★ **Keys to Consistency** by Jack Grout **Jack Nicklaus' Coach and Teacher** Covers Drivers, Fairway Woods and Irons

after time—with the driver, the fairway woods, and the irons. The package also includes Grout's Tee Square, a clever adjustable alignment aid that teaches you the correct set-up position for every shot (see Chapter One), and *On the Lesson Tee*, his 131-page paperback book.

$79.95 from Ardent Publishing; also from Richard E. Donovan Enterprises and The Golf Works.

KEYS TO GREAT GOLF WITH JOANNE CARNER

(Nova Productions, 90 minutes)
JoAnne Carner has been hitting the ball so long for so long that nearly everyone calls her "Big Momma," and the moniker is a term of both endearment and envy. Since joining the LPGA Tour in 1970, she's racked up more than 40 tournament victories, including two U.S. Women's Open titles, and more than $2.2 million in official earnings. In this top-rated video Carner packs a powerful punch as she focuses on the fundamentals and demonstrates a series of practice drills designed to help you duplicate the proper positions and moves she outlines. There's no gimmickry, no boring repetition, no pie-in-the-sky panaceas—just an hour and a half of clear, concise instruction, laced with 137 pointers for better golf, from one of the game's top players. While nearly anyone should benefit from Carner's on-the-mark lessons, men may wish to fast-forward through the section that's aimed at the Dolly Partons of the golfing world.

$64 from GolfSmart; also from Richard E. Donovan Enterprises, Maryco Products, Matzie Golf, National Golf Foundation, and Edwin Watts Golf Shops.

LEARNING GOLF WITH MIKE CALBOT

(Mike Calbot Golf Studio, 90 minutes)
This guy can really hit the big stick. Who else, after all, packs a six-and-a-half-foot-long driver in his bag? But for Mike Calbot, a PGA teaching pro who sometimes goes by the name of "Calbot the Magnificent," it's simply another rabbit in the hat, so to speak. As one of the nation's top trick-shot artists, he can hit a golf ball with just about anything or from just about any position. In this video, however, Calbot sticks mostly to the more serious business at hand: teaching you how to build a repeating golf swing through a system of "planned progressive practice." He shows you the five steps of his pre-shot routine and demonstrates a series of practice drills aimed at extending the arc of your swing and improving your strength, tempo, and timing. He also takes you through the entire short game—pitching, chipping, sand play, and putting. Calbot, who has a few green-reading tricks up his sleeve, will even show you the secret of making a golf ball disappear into the hole.

$49.95 from Mike Calbot Golf Studio.

THE MASTER SYSTEM TO BETTER GOLF: VOLUME 1 WITH CRAIG STADLER, DAVIS LOVE III, TOM PURTZER, AND GARY KOCH

(Fox Hills Video, 60 minutes)
No matter how you slice it, these four standouts of the PGA Tour should be able to improve your golf game from tee to green and in between. Through the end of 1988 Davis Love III, Tom Purtzer, Craig Stadler, and Gary Koch had collectively chalked up 18 tournament victories and more than $6 million in career earnings. This top-rate video (five

stars from *Golf* magazine) showcases their respective specialties with an assist from Peter Kostis, one of the game's top teaching professionals. So if you want to learn the methods of the modern masters, this may be an ideal way to start. "The Master System To Better Golf" (formerly titled "Fore . . . "Ways to Better Golf") is also available as four separate 20-minute videos.

Davis Love III on Driving. Love packs a one-two punch off the tee: He's one of the most powerful— and most accurate— drivers on the PGA Tour. Love swings the club at 120 miles per hour, faster than any human being ever clocked, and is so long that he consistently outdrives other pros with his one-iron. In this segment he explains exactly how he does it and then shows you how you can incorporate his key moves into your swing. Love's lesson covers the pre-swing fundamentals (grip, posture, aim, and ball position), effective ball-striking techniques with woods and long irons, and setting up for intentional draws and fades.

Tom Purtzer on Iron Accuracy. If your iron shots seem to land everywhere but on the green, at least one part of your game needs some straightening out, and Purtzer may be just the guy to do it. He owns one of the smoothest swings— and some of the deadliest irons— on the PGA Tour. In this segment he demonstrates the pre-shot routine he's perfected over the years and describes the three swing keys— posture, aim, and rhythm— that add up to "par." Purtzer also shares some of his secrets for hitting longer, crisper, and more accurate iron shots (pacing the swing, maintaining consistent pressure in the grip, and making a full turn "around the spine"); shows how to draw or fade the ball; and prescribes cures for swaying, reverse pivoting, and other common symptoms of iron-poor swing.

Craig Stadler on the Short Game. Stadler, who's known on the PGA Tour as "The Walrus," can hit the long ball; in 1988 he ranked second on the tour in driving distance (279.4 yards on average), just ahead of Greg Norman. But unlike so many of the big-hitters, Stadler also wields a wedge with a lot of finesse. In this segment he takes you step by step through the entire short game, from analyzing shots to executing them. Stadler emphasizes the importance of trajectory in pitching and chipping— it controls the distance the ball travels in the air and on the ground— and illustrates how the proper set-up and swing can maximize your accuracy and consistency around the green. He also shows you how to develop the right mindset and strategy for trouble shots.

Gary Koch on Putting. If your scorecards are littered with costly three-putts, this on-the-green clinic may be just what you need to clean up your act. In this segment Koch explains the mechanics of the putting stroke itself, demonstrates how to control both distance and direction, and offers his tips for reading greens. You'll also see how an expert aggressively approaches the short putts and confidently lags the longer ones to within tap-in range.

$32 (or $12 each as separate videos) from GolfSmart; also from Richard E. Donovan Enterprises, The Golf Works, Las Vegas Discount Golf, National Golf Foundation, and Nevada Bob's Discount Golf.

1986 MASTERS TOURNAMENT

(CBS Sports, 60 minutes)
If you saw it on television, you'll never forget it: Jack Nicklaus— winless at Augusta for 11 years, written off as "over

the hill" by many sportswriters, and three shots back with just nine holes to play— charging from behind to win his sixth Masters and his 20th major. This video captures the ecstasy of the Golden Bear's dramatic come-from-behind victory and the agony of the Great White Shark's stunning defeat. You'll also see Gary Player's hole-in-one during the par-three tournament , Nick Price's record-breaking round of 63, Seve Ballesteros's flubbed four-iron shot into the water, and, of course, the red-hot putting streak that landed Nicklaus yet another green jacket.

$19.95 from The Golf Works; also from Acorn Sports, Richard E. Donovan Enterprises, Golf Digest, GolfSmart, Matzie Golf, and National Golf Foundation.

ONE MOVE TO BETTER GOLF WITH CARL LOHREN

(Best Film & Video, 30 minutes)
If you're among the more than 50,000 golfers who've read Carl Lohren's book by the same title, you already know the move: "Start your swing with your left shoulder." But in this video you can actually see how and why it works, which adds an important new dimension to Lohren's lesson.

$16 from GolfSmart; also from Acorn Sports, Critics' Choice Video, Richard E. Donovan Enterprises, Golf Day Products, The Golf Works, Matzie Golf, National Golf Foundation, and J. White Industries.

PLAY GREAT GOLF WITH ARNOLD PALMER—MASTERING THE FUNDAMENTALS AND COURSE STRATEGY

(Vestron Video, 60 minutes each)

If you've ever wondered what it would be like to take a lesson from Arnold Palmer himself, wonder no more. This two-volume series captures Arnie in fine form at Isleworth Golf & Country Club, his home course in Windermere, Florida. In "Mastering the Fundamentals," he walks you through the basics from tee to green, with plenty of instructive stops in between. Palmer uses slow-motion and stop-action to analyze the golf swing and show you how to develop and sharpen your game.

Once you've mastered the fundamentals, you can accompany Palmer around the course— and, thanks to some nifty aerial footage, above it— for a long lesson in the finer points of the game. In "Course Strategy," he shows you how to shave strokes from your score by developing a plan of attack that makes the most of your strengths. He also tackles the typical trouble spots— bunkers and bad lies, for example— and shows you how to execute such tricky shots as the high lob and low punch. As in the companion volume, all segments are color-coded to make playback a snap.

$37.99 each from Nevada Bob's Discount Golf; also from Competitive Edge Golf, Richard E. Donovan Enterprises, Golf Day Products, Golf Digest, The Golf Works, Las Vegas Discount Golf, Maryco Products, Matzie Golf, National Golf Foundation, Somerton Springs Golf Shoppes, and Edwin Watts Golf Shops.

PLAY YOUR BEST GOLF— VOLUMES 1 AND 2

(Caravatt Communications)
This two-volume series of videos, produced in association with the National Golf Foundation, features seven outstanding golf professionals and instruc-

tors: Peggy Kirk Bell, Jim Flick, Carol Johnson, Rod Myers, Conrad Riehling, Bob Toski, and Gary Wiren. These masters of the game team up in the first volume ("The Clubs," 69 minutes) to focus on the fundamentals of shotmaking. You'll learn how to build a repeating golf swing, how to control woods and long irons, and how to achieve greater accuracy with middle and short irons. The same instructors return in the second volume ("The Strategies," 109 minutes) with 19 advanced sessions that cover everything from maximizing distance to minimizing tension. Both volumes make ample use of split-screen, slow-motion, stop-action, and other special effects (including a "video telestrator" that traces the ball's actual flight path on the screen) to augment the lessons.

$49 each from Acorn Sports; also from Richard E. Donovan Enterprises, The Golf Works, GolfSmart, Matzie Golf, National Golf Foundation, and Gary Wiren's "Golf Around the World."

Play Your Best Golf— Six Lessons

(Caravatt Communications)
This six-volume set of videos has been adapted from the two-part "Play Your Best Golf" series (see above) and features the same line-up of outstanding teachers. The individual titles and playing times are as follows: "The Golf Swing" (20 minutes); "Woods and Long Irons" (19 minutes); "Mid and Short Irons" (13 minutes); "Putting and Chipping" (20 minutes); "Approach Shot and Sand Play" (17 minutes); and "Strategies and Skills" (25 minutes).

$19.95 each from Austad's, Golf Day Products, or The Golf Works.

Power Driving with Mike Dunaway

(SyberVision, 30 minutes)
In August 1985 Mike Dunaway made the cover of *Golf* magazine with his now-famous challenge: "$10,000 Says You Can't Outhit Me." Dunaway still has his 10 grand, and now, for just a fraction of that amount, you can have his five secrets of power driving. Computer-enhanced graphics, close-ups, and super-slow-motion sequences let you study all the right moves in Dunaway's phenomenally powerful swing and make the simple adjustments needed to incorporate them into yours. Maybe you won't learn to consistently hit 300- to 350-yard drives down the middle of the fairway, as Dunaway does, but the smart money says you'd happily settle for something less.

$49.95 from SyberVision; also from Abercrombie & Fitch, Acorn Sports, Richard E. Donovan Enterprises, Golf Day Products, GolfSmart, Matzie Golf, and National Golf Foundation.

Precision Putting with Dave Stockton

(SyberVision, 30 minutes)
Dave Stockton's prowess on the putting green has helped him rack up 11 victories on the PGA Tour and more than $1 million in career earnings. In 1976, for example, he sank a tricky 15-putt on the final hole of the PGA Championship for a reprise of his 1970 victory. In this video Stockton shows you exactly how he does it. Computer-enhanced graphics, close-ups, and super-slow-motion sequences let you study every element of Stockton's smooth-as-silk putting

stroke, including his grip, stance, and alignment. Stockton also shows you how he reads greens and how he approaches putts of varying lengths (from five feet to 35 feet). If nothing else, just watching and hearing Stockton's ball drop into the cup so many times may give you a bit of newfound confidence next time you step onto the green.

$49.95 from SyberVision; also from Abercrombie & Fitch, Acorn Sports, Richard E. Donovan Enterprises, Golf Day Products, GolfSmart, Matzie Golf, National Golf Foundation, and Somerton Springs Golf Shoppes.

Putting with Confidence with Duff Lawrence and Barb Thomas

(Reflex, 28 minutes)
While this video may not teach you "all you need to know to putt like the pros," as the jacket promises, it should leave you wielding the shortest weapon in your bag with greater assurance and accuracy. Duff Lawrence (with a name like that he *must* be good), the head professional at Desert Highlands Golf Club in Scottsdale, Arizona, and Barb Thomas, the LPGA touring pro, cover the fundamentals of putting— from grip to grain— in easy-to-follow fashion. Then they head out onto the course to apply the principles in a green-to-green playing lesson that's laced with useful putting tips. The video is hosted by Bill Gartner of Reflex Inc., who manages to work in a little plug for the TourHawk Putter (see page 74), which his company manufactures.

$29 from Reflex Inc.

The Short Way to Lower Scoring with Paul Runyan—Volume I: Putting and Chipping; Volume II: Pitching and Sand Play

(Golf Digest, 35 minutes each)
Back in the 1930s and 1940s they called him "Little Poison," and little wonder: His deadly precision and delicate touch on and around the green more than made up for his lack of distance off the tee. It was Paul Runyan's lethal short game, in fact, that won him the 1934 and 1938 PGA Championships and more than a dozen other tournament titles. He's since come to be called "the man who invented the short game," and this two-volume series of videos shows why. In Volume I ("Putting and Chipping") Runyan teaches you the correct grip, set-up, and alignment, and demonstrates how to control distance and direction by minimizing your wrist motion and making a smooth, rhythmic stroke through the ball. You'll come to a new understanding of the old putting adage, "never up, never in," and learn when you should lag longer putts "to the circle." Runyan also shows you how to pick the right club for various chip shots and how to stop scooping or stubbing the ball. In Volume II ("Pitching and Sand Play") Runyan outlines his three keys to effective wedge play: properly positioning your palm on the club, keeping your weight forward, and "underreaching" as you address the ball (holding the clubhead just barely above the ground). You'll learn how to properly execute pinch, cut, and lob shots, and how to get rid of the shanks and other short-game ailments once and for all. Runyan also explains exactly how the sand wedge works and shows how to use it— from good lies or bad— to "get up and down in two." Both videos make extensive use of computer-generated

SO YOU STAND ON THE WRONG SIDE OF THE BALL TOO!

FINALLY!
A VIDEO FOR LEFT-HANDED GOLFERS!

BASIC UNDERSTANDING OF THE FUNDAMENTALS:

Grip
Stance-Alignment
Back Swing
Forward Swing
Ball Striking

felt out of place in the decidedly right-handed world of golf, at last there's an instructional video especially for you. (Ever try to mentally flip-flop what's going on in all those other videos?) Join Jay Edgar, a left-handed Class "A" PGA professional, in a one-on-one lesson with his left-handed student, Dallas businessman Noel Dickson. Edgar focuses on the fundamentals— grip, stance, alignment, backswing, down-swing, and impact— all from the "wrong side" of the ball.

$59.95 from Wrong Side Enterprises; also from Competitive Edge Golf, Richard E. Donovan Enterprises, Golf Day Products, The Golf Works, GolfSmart, Las Vegas Discount Golf, Matzie Golf, National Golf Foundation, Somerton Springs Golf Shoppes, and Edwin Watts Golf Shops.

graphics, including colorized reproductions of Tony Ravielli's masterful illustrations for Runyan's book of the same title.

$24 each from GolfSmart; also from Competitive Edge Golf, Richard E. Donovan Enterprises, Golf Day Products, Golf Digest, The Golf Works, Matzie Golf, National Golf Foundation, and Somerton Springs Golf Shoppes.

So You Stand on the Wrong Side of the Ball, Too! with Jay Edgar

(Wrong Side Enterprises, 45 minutes)
Take heart, southpaws: If you've ever

Subliminal Golf Improvement Program

(MindPower Golf, 60 minutes)
Listen to this cassette tape and you'll hear the soothing sounds of ocean waves and seagulls. Imbedded deep within these relaxing sounds, however, are some powerful subliminal messages— all of them aimed, in one way or another, at improving your golf game. They're recorded at a very low level (so low, in fact, that you can't really hear them), but over time, if all goes well, your subsconscious mind will fully absorb the positive suggestions and put them to work as you play. By repro-gramming your negative thoughts into positive thoughts, the theory goes, you'll step up to the first tee with a clear mind and carry your newfound confidence all the way through to the 18th green. You

70 minutes of personal instruction by the world-famous teacher WIDELY RECOGNIZED AS ONE OF THE FINEST INSTRUCTORS THE GAME HAS EVER KNOWN

BOB TOSKI TEACHES YOU GOLF

With Andy Nusbaum, Director of the Golf Digest Instruction Schools
A GOLF DIGEST PRODUCTION

can listen to this tape at work, at home, while watching TV or reading, but not while driving— or at least not, as the manufacturer puts it, "while operating a motor vehicle."

$24.95 from MindPower Golf.

Bob Toski Teaches You Golf

(Golf Digest, 70 minutes)
"Most golfers prepare for disaster," Bob Toski once wrote. "A good golfer prepares for success." And what better way to prepare for success than to take a golf lesson from Toski himself, who's widely recognized as one of the game's finest teachers? (Over the last 30 years he's given more than 125,000 lessons to golfers of all ages and skill levels.) Toski starts with putting and chipping, moves on to the middle and long irons, and winds up with the driver, using slow-motion sequences, close-ups, and on-

screen insets to get his points across along the way.

$40 from GolfSmart; also from Acorn Sports, Competitive Edge Golf, Richard E. Donovan Enterprises, Golf Day Products, Golf Digest, The Golf Works, Golfsmith, Maryco Products, Matzie Golf, National Golf Foundation, Nevada Bob's Discount Golf, Edwin Watts Golf Shops, and J. White Industries.

Total Golf with Bruce Crampton

(Image Video, 92 minutes)
"Golf," Bruce Crampton once said, "is a compromise of what your ego wants you to do, what experience tells you to do, and what your nerves let you do." Crampton should know. Not long ago the "Iron Man," as he's come to be called, ended a nine-year layoff from competitive golf to mount an extraordinary comeback on the Senior PGA Tour.

TOTAL GOLF

Saving Strokes with Bruce Crampton

The "Iron Man" of the Senior Pro Tour goes beyond the fundamentals with his:

↑ Specialized fitness program
↑ Golf techniques
↑ Selection of proper equipment
↑ Mental keys

1986 SENIOR Player of the Year

In this video Crampton demonstrates how an exercise program can increase your strength, stamina, and flexibility (such a fitness plan played a key role in his comeback); shows you how to select the right clubs for your game; and illustrates how the proper mental attitude can improve your play from tee to green. Finally, Crampton shares his own tips and techniques for dozens of different shots and situations.

$40 from GolfSmart; also from Richard E. Donovan Enterprises, The Golf Works, Matzie Golf, and National Golf Foundation.

The Ultimate Drive with Art Sellinger

(Morris Video, 30 minutes)
Wanna hit the ball a country mile, or at least some reasonable fraction thereof? Then meet Art Sellinger, who belts the ball far enough to have won *Golf Digest*'s National Long-Drive Championship. He'll show how he tees up the ball for maximum distance, how he generates such awesome clubhead speed, and how he modifies his stance to produce a draw or fade. He'll even show how to do it without sacrificing accuracy.

$12.95 from Morris Video.

CHAPTER ELEVEN
THE 19TH HOLE

APPAREL

"BRITISH OPEN" CAPS

So maybe you didn't buy your golf cap at the British Open (where they sell by the thousands), but why let anyone in on the secret? These classic "Hogan"-style caps are made of 100 percent wool flannel and embroidered with the names and club crests of three British Open sites: St. Andrews (navy blue), Gleneagles (kelly green) and Turnberry (navy blue). They're available in small ($6^7/_8$-7), medium ($7^1/_8$-$7^1/_2$), large ($7^3/_8$-$7^1/_2$), and extra-large ($7^5/_8$-$7^3/_4$) sizes.

$37.50 from Golf Day Products.

"CERTAINLY I LOVE HIM . . ." SWEATSHIRT AND T-SHIRT

Picture a teary-eyed blonde with a putter wistfully cradled against her right cheek. "Certainly I love him," she says. "He's a golfer." Then picture her silk-screened on the front of a sweatshirt or T-shirt in comic-strip style. Both the sweatshirt ($22.50) and T-shirt ($11.95) are U.S.-made in a 50/50 blend of cotton/polyester and available in medium, large, and extra-large sizes.

From Golf Day Products.

FAMOUS-LOGO VISORS

Nobody will pay you to wear one of these, but a visor emblazoned with a famous logo just might give you an added iota of confidence. Foot-Joy,

Hogan, Maxfli, PowerBilt, Taylor Made, Titleist, and Wilson visors are available in white and navy blue; PGA Tour visors are available in red, white, and navy blue.

$7.95 each from Las Vegas Discount Golf.

GOLF RUBBERS

No jokes, please. If you're worried about slogging through the mud and muck in those expensive leather golf shoes, why not leave them in the car trunk or clubhouse locker and wear these spiked rubber overshoes instead? Simply slip Golf Rubbers over your street shoes and you're ready for swingin' in the rain. They're fitted with standard steel spikes (for easy replacement) and available in men's sizes 7-13.

$18.95 from Austad's or Las Vegas Discount Golf; also from GolfSmith, Northern Golf Ball Company, and J. White Industries.

GOLFAHOLICS ANONYMOUS OFFICIAL SWEATSHIRT

When you're hooked, you're hooked, so why deny it? The official sweatshirt of Golfaholics Anonymous is silk-screened on the front with the organization's red, white, and green logo and on the back with its battle cry: "In passionate pursuit of that damnable, dimpled little ball." It's U.S.-made in a cotton/polyester blend and available in small, medium, large, and extra-large unisex sizes.

$27.95 from Enticements; also from Competitive Edge Golf and Las Vegas Discount Golf.

GOLFASAURUS SWEATSHIRT AND T-SHIRT

As a matter of definition, a Golfasaurus is: "1. A links-loving creature who derives great pleasure from the game of golf. 2. Any beast who would forego all responsibility, i.e., work, family, household maintenance, etc., to play golf." If these words fit someone you know, a Golfasaurus sweatshirt or T-shirt undoubtedly will, too. The duffin' dinosaur himself is silk-screened in baby blue on a white background; the definition is, as it should be, in black and white. Both the sweatshirt ($25) and T-shirt ($12.95) are U.S.-made in a 50/50 blend of cotton/polyester and available in medium, large, and extra-large sizes.

From Golf Day Products.

"THE GOLFER" BARBECUE APRON AND HOT MITT

Here it is: sartorial splendor for the barbecue pit. Don this colorful (and colorfast) barbecue apron, which adjusts to fit hackers of all sizes, and in no time you'll be swinging the spit-iron like a pro. What's more, the guests lurking around the Weber grill will know exactly where your allegiance lies; the stain-resistant, cotton/polyester apron

instantly outfits you in an argyle sweater and knickers, with a bag full of clubs. And to make sure that you maintain the proper grillside grip, a "golf glove" hot mitt is included.

$19.95 from The Duck Press.

GORE-TEX GOLF SUIT

For out-of-this world protection, NASA's astronauts wear spacesuits made of Gore-Tex. While your needs may be a little bit more down to earth— braving the nasty weather, say, that threatens to keep you from your appointed rounds— this Gore-Tex Golf Suit from MacGregor is the best protection from wind and rain that money can buy. Sure, you can get a rain suit for under 10 bucks, but you're likely to feel as if you're playing golf in a plastic bag— which, more or less, you are.

The Gore-Tex Golf Suit is waterproof, windproof, breathable, and quiet as a whisper. The secret lies in the Gore-Tex membrane, an ultrathin layer of space-age fabric with 9 billion pores engineered into every square inch. The microscopic pores, which are far too small to let water in and randomly offset to keep wind out, act like a second skin to keep you warm and dry. At the same time, they let your body heat and perspiration vapor escape naturally, keeping you comfortable from the inside out (without a trace of the clammy feeling you get from wearing most rain suits). This excellent water- and wind-proofing system is sandwiched between layers of lightweight, breathable fabric.

MacGregor's Gore-Tex Golf Suit is full-cut for maximum comfort and minimum interference with your swing. The jacket features raglan sleeves, a stand-up collar and adjustable cuffs (both with Velcro), a full-front nylon

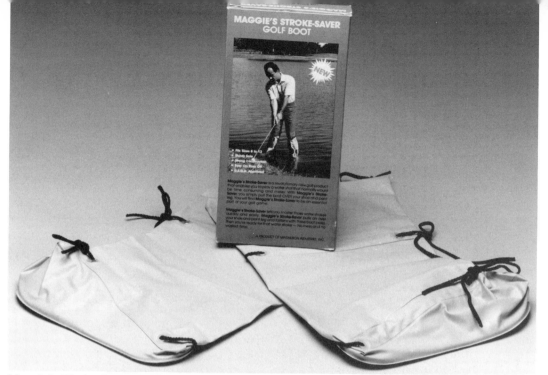

Maggie's Stroke-Saver Golf Boots

zipper and storm flap, and two front flap pockets. The pants feature roomy stovepipe legs with adjustable two-inch hems; 10-inch nylon zippers on each leg let you slip the pants on and off without spiking them on your golf shoes. Both the jacket and pants are available in five different men's sizes.

$219.95 (in navy, navy/white/red, and navy/white/light blue) from Las Vegas Discount Golf.

JOE PRO GOLF CAP

When you're out on the course in the dog days of summer, why not wear the Joe Pro (a.k.a. Snoopy) Golf Cap? Charles Schulz's club-carrying canine is colorfully embroidered on the front of this white cap, which is made of a 50/50 blend of cotton/polyester. And thanks to its adjustable leather back strap, one size fits most adults.

$9.95 from Austad's.

MAGGIE'S STROKE-SAVER GOLF BOOTS

At first you heave a long sigh of relief: Your ball, thank God, didn't wind up in the water. Then, as you approach its resting place near the water's edge, your elation fades with the dawning of the awful truth: Your ball is on terra firma, all right, but your only hope of hitting it with a conventional swing involves getting your feet wet. Oh, but what you would give right then for a pair of Maggie's Stroke-Saver Golf Boots.

These watertight boots allow you to play all of those shots that, for love of dry socks or dignity, you might otherwise have declared unplayable at a penalty of one stroke apiece. Just pull these folding, heavy-bottomed knee-highs out of your golf bag and pull them over your shoes and pant legs. Tie the three drawstrings on each boot tight around your ankles, thighs, and knees, and then wade right in. Hard-gripping rubber spikes give you a dry, secure stance. No more oozing mud or broken

QuicKnicks

glass beneath your bare feet. And, unfortunately, no more stories about the one that got away.

$29.95 from from Las Vegas Discount Golf; also from Magnuson Industries.

QuicKnicks

Maybe you like knickers, but feel just a bit foolish being seen in them on your way to or from the golf course. Maybe you don't want to fill your bedroom closet or country-club locker with clothing that's useless anywhere but on a golf course. Or maybe you just want an easy way to protect the cuffs on your sportiest slacks from golf-course dew, drizzle, and mud.

Now there's an ingenious and inexpensive solution to all three problems: QuicKnicks. They're adjustable elastic garters that turn an ordinary

pair of slacks into knickers in a jiffy. Just fasten the QuicKnicks around your legs slightly below the knees (Velcro makes it a snap) and tuck the bottoms of your trousers up under them; then adjust your trousers so that they "blouse" four to six inches below the garters. Voilà: instant plus fours. When you're ready to return to conventional civilization, simply unfasten the QuicKnicks, roll them up, and stow them in your golf bag, where they'll take up less room than a golf ball.

$6 from Netik Enterprises.

Signature Series Golf Glove

If you can't seem to find a golf glove that really "fits like a glove," maybe it's time you tried one of these on for size. Each Signature Series Golf Glove is individu-

Signature Series Golf Glove

ally table-cut by hand from top-grade, buttery-soft deerskin and contoured to your own hand measurements for a perfect fit. (You trace the outline of your hand on the order form and list its size— measured around the knuckles— in inches.) And instead of a manufacturer's logo, this ivory-colored glove bears your own monogram, which is embroidered on its Velcro closure tab.

Because the Signature Series Golf Glove is made from deerskin, which is more expensive than the goatskin (cabretta) used in most of its cookie-cutter counterparts, it's durable enough to last round after round without ripping, cracking, or losing its velvety feel and custom-tailored fit. Deerskin is also naturally moisture-resistant, which means that a simple hand-washing is all it takes to remove perspiration, salt, dirt, and grime. Best of all, the folks at Signature offer this unconditional guarantee: If the glove they make for you isn't the best-fitting you've ever owned, or if you're dissatisfied in any other way, you can return it for a replacement or a full refund.

$24.95 ($21.95 apiece for three or more) from Signature.

SOLAR-POWERED VENTILATED GOLF CAP

So you tend to get a little hotheaded on the golf course, do you? Well, here's a way to cool down— and keep cool— in style: the Solar-Powered Ventilated Golf Cap. Its visor features a built-in fan that helps you beat the heat by keeping a steady breeze directed at your forehead. The fan's motor normally is powered by six .5-volt solar cells on the top of the cap, but when mother nature lets you down, simply flip a toggle switch and two "AA" batteries will pick up the slack. For extra cooling power, the cap also includes a sponge that can be moistened and attached (via Velcro) inside its headband. The Solar-Powered Ventilated Golf Cap is made of nylon mesh with a nylon front and fits anyone whose hat size is from $6^7/8$ to $7^5/8$.

$29.95 from Hammacher Schlemmer; also from A2Z/The Best of Everything.

TOPTAN SHIRTS

If you're like most golfers, your hands, forearms, neck, and face are tan and the rest of your upper body is stark white. It's enough, as you've no doubt already discovered, to make you the laughingstock of the swimming-pool set. Now, at long last, comes a way to cure this embarrassing condition *while you play golf*: TopTan Shirts. They're made from "Microsol," an ingenious tan-through fabric of 100 percent mercerized cotton lisle. Wear these exceptionally cool shirts on the golf course and you'll get an even, natural tan from the waist up. And because they work like a low to medium sunscreen (about 8-10 SPF), you'll tan gradually, with less risk of burning.

TopTan Shirts are available in small, medium, large, and extra-large sizes for men (light-blue pinstripe, cranberry pinstripe, and blue pencil stripe) and in small, medium, and large sizes for women (light-blue pinstripe and cranberry pinstripe only).

$29.95 each ($80 for three) from Competitive Edge Golf.

BALLS AND RELATED ACCESSORIES

BELT BALL CLIP
This handy little plastic gizmo keeps an extra golf ball at the ready on your belt or bag, and may prove to be a real time-saver for players who pull the old switcheroo every time they set foot on a green. The Belt Ball Clip comes with a ball marker and plastic practice ball.

$1.40 from Everything for Golf.

BIRDIE BALL WASHER
Those ball washers on the local links are vengeful little machines: They're seldom where you really need them, of course, and they're often empty. So why not bring along your own? Just fill the Birdie Ball Washer with a little soap and water and fasten it to your cart or bag; then, whenever you need to clean your golf ball, simply pop it inside and turn the crank. The Birdie Ball Washer is made of durable, high-impact plastic and includes a metal mounting clamp.

$12.95 from Austad's or Las Vegas Discount Golf.

CHECK GO
This portable gizmo is supposed to find a golf ball's optimal spin axis— or "sweet spot." Place a golf ball in Check Go, push a button, and a battery-powered motor spins the ball at 10,000 rpm. After 20 seconds, the ball stops oscillating and rotates steadily on its optimal spin axis. Then, mark the sweet spot with a special pen, place the ball on the tee or green with the mark facing you, and you're ready to hit. Check Go is lightweight (just 4.5 ounces) and small enough (just 4.5 inches high) to stow in a golf bag. Two "AA"z batteries and a marking pen are included.

$25 from The Sharper Image; also from Austad's, Golf Day Products, and Las Vegas Discount Golf.

CONCEPT G PRECISION GOLF BALL GAUGE
There are plenty of gauges on the market that determine whether your golf ball's out of round, but this may be the only one that also checks its size. Most golfers know that an out-of-round ball spins irregularly (much in the way that an unbalanced automobile tire wobbles as it rolls), which can lead to a loss of distance, diminished accuracy, and less-than-true roll on the putting green. Balata and three-piece Surlyn balls, which have windings that can become loose or even break inside the cover, are most likely to go out of round.

Few golfers, however, realize that the size of a golf ball may be just as important as its perfect sphericity. As the diameter of a golf ball increases, so does the air resistance (aerodynamic drag) it encounters in flight, resulting in progressively larger losses of distance. While the United States Golf Association specifies no maximum size for a golf ball, it's prudent to use a ball as close to the USGA's minimum specified size—1.680 inches in diameter—as possible. (According to *The Search for the Perfect Swing*, the authoritative study by Alastair Cochran and John Stobbs, a 4 percent increase in the size of a golf ball leads to a 5 percent higher trajectory, a 4 percent loss in carry, a 10 percent loss in roll, and a 20 to 30 percent increase in sideways deviation.)

The Concept G Precision Golf Ball Gauge renders verdicts on both counts—roundness and size—in just seconds. To check for out-of-roundness, simply rotate your golf ball inside the gauge; a perfectly round ball will rotate freely, but an out-of-round ball will appear to jam or stick on one side. As for size, an acceptable golf ball should freely pass through the "Go" (green) side of the gauge, but not through the "No Go" (red) side. If your ball won't pass through the "Go" ring, it's more than 1.690 inches in diameter, the industry standard for maximum size; if it passes through the "No Go" ring, it's smaller than the USGA's minimum specified size.

The Concept G Precision Golf Ball Gauge is molded from tough, high-impact plastic and comes with a six-inch chain that allows you to attach it to your golf bag or belt.

$7.95 from Advanced Concepts International.

"'84 Gutty" Balls

Back in the late 1800s, golfers played the game with "gutties"—golf balls made from gutta-percha, a rubbery substance derived from the sap of certain tropical trees. The first gutta-percha balls had completely smooth surfaces, but when golfers discovered that their hacked-up balls seemed to fly better, manufactur-

ers began experimenting with various cover markings and patterns. These modern-day gutties, which feature the grooved pattern preferred by most golfers at the turn of the century, are solid, low-compression balls. While you can actually play with these old faithfuls (they're recommended, in fact, for use with wood-shafted clubs), be forewarned that they just don't fly like their dimpled descendants.

$24 a dozen from The Golf Shop Collection; also from The Golf Works.

Executive Golf Ball Holder

You don't really need to be an executive to make use of this handy-dandy dispenser, which keeps a sleeve of golf balls always at the ready, but maybe it will help you get down to business on the golf course. The Executive Golf Ball Holder attaches easily and securely to the side of your golf bag, and its steel-wire frame lets you air-dry those wet balls that come out of the washer.

$12.95 from Competitive Edge Golf.

Floater Golf Balls

Dave Hill, the former PGA touring pro, once said that he'd tried to teach his golf balls to swim by putting them in the bathtub. But the next day, when he hit a couple of them into a water hazard, the balls sank right to the bottom. "They were poor learners," he concluded.

Hill evidently hadn't heard of Floater Golf Balls, which are taught to swim at the factory. These 80-compression, two-piece balls have a Surlyn cover and a special center that renders

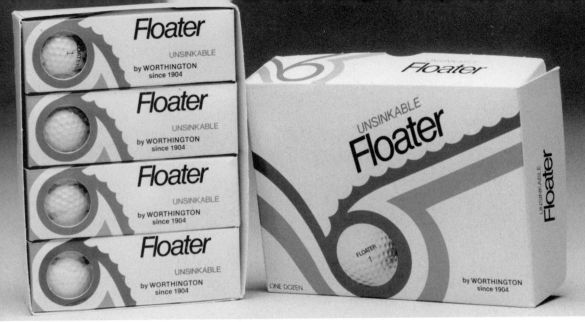

Floater Golf Balls

them unsinkable. They've even been known to cure chronic cases of golfer's hydrophobia— the all-encompassing fear of water hazards. So don't even think of skirting that lake with a safe iron shot; just plop down a Floater and let 'er rip right for the green. If you happen to come up short you'll find your ball bobbing above the breakers, happily waiting to be fished out of the water. What's more, you won't have to dredge up any slime or seaweed in the process. (There is, of course, one minor drawback: If your ball is floating too far from the water's edge, you're going to need either a pair of waders or an awfully long retriever.)

$6 for a sleeve of three from Golf Day Products; also from Austad's, Golfsmith, Hammacher Schlemmer, Herrington, and Northern Golf Ball Company.

GOLF BALL RING GAUGE

This gauge, made of a strong aluminum alloy, will accurately detect a golf ball that's gone out of round— and that's especially important for golfers who use balata balls. Simply pass your golf ball through the gauge while rotating it at the same time; if the ball hangs up in the ring in one direction and not in another, it's out of round (and ready for retirement to the shag bag). The Golf Ball Ring Gauge comes in a cloth drawstring pouch.

$9.75 from The Golf Works.

MIGHTY MIDGET GOLF BALL WASHER

The Mighty Midget looks kind of like a plastic donut, but keep it filled with a soap-and-water solution and you've got a golf ball washer that goes anywhere you go. (How many times could you have used this little gizmo after marking your mud-specked ball on the green?) Simply rotate the ball as you pass it through the middle of the "donut" and it comes out squeaky clean, albeit wet. So clip the Mighty Midget onto your golf bag and it'll always be right where it should be— next to a towel.

NITELITE™

GOLFBALL

- Lights up for evening and night play and NITELITE Tournaments.

- Not a toy. Not a gimmick. Official size & weight.

- Plays like an official golfball.

- Replaceable lightstick lasts up to 6 hours.

- Puts the FUN back into golf!

$5.95 from Las Vegas Discount Golf; also from The Duck Press and Golfsmith.

NITELITE GOLF BALL

Now you can play at dusk— or even in the dark— with the Nitelite Golf Ball. Simply activate a nontoxic Cyalume lightstick (32 reactive chemicals in a durable polyethylene tube) by twisting it. Then insert it in the solid-core Nitelite ball. The result is a bright green glow that illuminates the ball for up to eight hours and from up to 100 yards away. The Nitelite Golf Ball has the same weight, size, click, and feel of a regulation ball, except that it's one club shorter in distance.

$4.95 each or $14 for a sleeve of three from Las Vegas Discount Golf (three extra Nitelite sticks are $3); also from Austad's, Competitive Edge Golf, Florida Golf Warehouse, Golf Day Products, The Golf Works, Golfsmith, Northern Golf Ball Company, Somerton Springs Golf Shoppes, and J. White Industries.

RENEGADE 410 GOLF BALLS

Aptly named because it *purposely* violates the rules of the United States Golf Association, the Renegade 410 may actually be "the longest ball" in golf.

Take one for a test drive, in fact, and if it's not the longest ball you've ever played the manufacturer will give you your money back.

This hot little number is the brainchild of Troy Puckett, a 23-year veteran of the golf-ball manufacturing business and the designer of MacGregor's Muirfield and MT Tourney models, as well as Wilson's ProStaff and Advantage balls. (Ironically, he also developed MacGregor's short-distance Cayman ball.) In designing the Renegade 410, Puckett says that he used "all the ingredients I knew to maximize distance." The three-piece wound ball features 410 dimples of three different sizes on a blended Surlyn cover. The Renegade 410 is slightly smaller (1.65 inches in diameter) and heavier than the USGA's specifications allow, and, according to Puckett, also exceeds the USGA's overall distance standard. The manufacturer's tests, which measured carry and roll with a driver, show that the Renegade's total distance of 292.4 yards surpassed its nearest brand-name competitor by 20.7 yards and the Titleist 384 by 28.0 yards.

Puckett, by the way, never even bothered to submit his ball to the USGA for approval. He knew it wouldn't pass.

$24 a dozen from Competitive Edge Golf; also from Austad's, Golf Day Products, and Herrington.

Left: Nitelite Golf Ball

GRIPS

ENFORCER GRIPS

Jack Nicklaus and other top touring
professionals have been backweighting
their clubs for years, and now you can,
too. Simply by arming your clubs with
Enforcer Grips, according to the manufacturer's tests with a Sportech Golf
Swing Analyzer, you'll get 15, 25, maybe
even 30 extra yards on every shot. Each
Enforcer Grip has a 2.75-ounce metal
insert built into its butt end to put extra
weight above your hands as you swing;
from all outward appearances, however,
it resembles a conventional composition
grip. The backweighting helps you
generate greater clubhead speed, and
that means more distance.

    If it all sounds too good to be true,
fortunately there's an easy and inexpensive way to test the exact feel and effect
of backweighting on every club in your
bag— from driver to sand wedge—
without installing an entire set of new
grips. Simply go to the practice range,
slip the Enforcer Test Cap over the top
of a club's existing grip, and hit away.
(While Enforcer Grips conform to USGA
rules, the test cap doesn't.) The folks
who make Enforcer Grips are betting
that you'll like what you see.

*$4.50 for the the Enforcer Test Cap and
$14.95 for a package of four Enforcer
Grips from Competitive Edge Golf; also
from Austad's, Golf Day Products, and
Pro-Action Golf.*

Tourna Grip

TOURNA GRIP

Losing your grip? This nonslip, all-
weather golf grip is supposed to absorb
moisture 100 times better than conventional composition grips and can be
applied in a matter of minutes. Simply
wrap the adhesive-backed Tourna Grip
over your existing grip one side at a
time, rubbing as you go for a snug fit.
You won't need a golf glove anymore,
say the folks who manufacture Tourna
Grip, and you won't be likely to get
blisters, either.

*$8.50 for a package of four from Com-
petitive Edge Golf or Golf Day Products;
also from Consolidated Service Group,
Golfsmith, and J. White Industries.*

KEEPING SCORES AND STATISTICS

CADDY CARD

Maybe your math is downright atrocious. Maybe you hate those short-as-your-pinkie pencils they give away in the clubhouse— you know, the ones without erasers. Or maybe you'd just like a faster way to figure out, as you tee it up on the 18th hole, whether you have a snowball's chance of breaking 80 for the first time in your life.

Whatever your score-keeping plight or problem, Caddy Card may be the state-of-the-art solution. It's a compact,

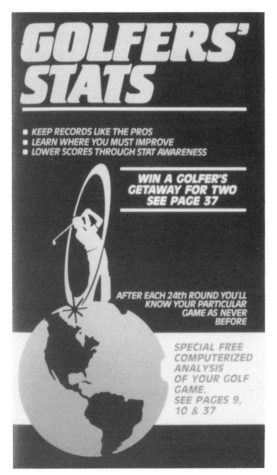

computerized scorecard that keeps track of who's up and who's down as your foursome plays an 18-hole round of golf. Just punch in the scores after each hole, and Caddy Card takes care of the rest: It adds up and displays each player's score, along with par for the course, as you go. Clearing mistakes is a snap, and you can review the entire round— hole by hole, if you'd like— by repeatedly pressing a single key. (The latter feature comes in handy if you want to transfer everything to a conventional scorecard at the end of a round).

Caddy Card measures only five inches high, two-and-a-half inches wide, and a half-inch thick. Batteries are included, as is a simulated suede carrying case that can be conveniently clipped to your golf bag.

$49.95 from A2Z/The Best of Everything, Austad's, Competitive Edge Golf, Golf Day Products, Las Vegas Discount Golf, or The Sharper Image.

GOLFERS' STATS

Keep this handy little booklet in your back pocket or golf bag and you'll be able to record the same 12 statistics— from 24 rounds of golf— that many PGA touring professionals do. After the 5th and 24th rounds, send your statistics in to the manufacturer (Practice House Golf) and, at no additional cost, you'll receive a computerized analysis that compares you to amateurs of comparable ability. Once you know your

Golfers' Stats

game's strengths and weaknesses, you can head to the range and really go to work.

$3.50 from Las Vegas Discount Golf; also from Practice House Golf.

Links 18GX Advanced Golf Scorecard

If you're the designated scorekeeper in your foursome, you already know how tricky toting everything up can be—what with handicaps, hole ratings, and all those incessant questions during the round about who's up, who's down, and by how much. That may be reason enough to carry along the Links 18GX Advanced Golf Scorecard, which keeps scores for up to four players and automatically adjusts them according to individual handicaps.

This hand-held unit displays up to nine holes at a time on its easy-to-read LCD screen, and at the touch of a button it revises handicaps and instantly computes gross, net, and adjusted scores. It also maintains running totals of birdies, pars, bogeys, and double-bogeys; indicates the number of strokes a player is over or under par at any point in the round; and keeps match-play and Stableford scores for any selected pair of players (based on each golfer's handicap and the appropriate hole ratings). The scorecard weighs less than two and a half ounces and measures only four inches wide, three inches high, and a half-inch thick. It's powered by two silver-oxide batteries and comes with a clip that lets you attach it to your golf bag.

$50 from Falk's; also from Hammacher Schlemmer.

Links to the Past

Even if you regularly threaten to burn your scorecards after bad or bruising rounds, chances are they wind up in the trunk of your car, a dresser drawer, or an old cigar box. There must a better way, however, and Links to the Past may be it. This nine-by-seven-inch album neatly organizes and displays up to 50 scorecards at a time; the loose-leaf binder also includes special pages for recording your great (and not-so-great) rounds and for keeping track of other memorable moments in your golfing career. There's even a section devoted to *Golf Digest*'s ranking of the top 100 courses in America—just in case you won't consider your scorecard collection complete until you've played them.

$14.95 from Las Vegas Discount Golf; also from Competitive Edge Golf and Golf Day Products.

Memory Keeper

Maybe you've never heard of Bob Robinson, but he wrote the book on how to store all those old scorecards and other mementos that golfers are wont to collect. Memory Keeper looks like a book on the outside, but inside there's plenty of room for scorecards, photographs, yardage books, and just about anything else you'd want to save—except, of course, for that trusty eight-iron that blessed you with a hole-in-one. This brown, vinyl-covered volume measures roughly nine inches high, six inches wide, and 2.5 inches deep. It's titled *Golf Courses I Have Played*, and for an extra charge you can make yourself (or anyone else) the author.

$15.95 from Memory Keepers; add $10 if you'd like a name imprinted in gold ink on the cover.

Score Caddy

You can use this handy little counter to keep track of your score hole-by-hole or round-by-round, but once you hit 99 you'll be right back where you started. The Score Caddy is made of plastic, with thumbwheels for each digit, and comes with a beaded chain that lets you attach it to your belt, key ring, or golf bag.

$1.95 from Northern Golf Ball Company; also from Golfsmith.

Seiko Golf Scorecard

Your foursome is making its way to the second tee when you discover that no one bothered to pick up a scorecard in the clubhouse— or, worse yet, that no one has a pencil. If it's happened to you more than once, maybe you should pack the Seiko Golf Scorecard in your bag. This marvel of miniaturized electronics, which is about the size of a credit card and only an eighth of an inch thick, keeps score for up to four players over an entire round. Simply enter each hole's number and par, along with each player's total strokes and number of putts, and microchips will take care of everything else. You can instantly retrieve data for any hole or any player with the touch of a button, and the unit will total everything up whenever you'd like. Its easy-to-read Liquid Crystal Display screen will even give you the date and time of day, which means you won't have to play with a watch strapped to your wrist. The Seiko Golf Scorecard runs on a long-life lithium battery and comes with a protective carrying case.

$35 from Roberta Fortune's Almanac; also from Haverhills and Las Vegas Discount Golf.

Memory Keeper

Official PGA Tour Personal Golf Book

Here's the book that many PGA touring pros use to record their scores. Use it to keep track of your driving accuracy, greens in regulation, sand saves, putts, and total scores. Then compare your record with PGA tour statistics and note any areas where you may need lessons or practice.

$3.95 from The Golf Works.

MARKERS, MENDERS, AND MISCELLANEOUS GIZMOS

HL BALLMARK WITH VELCRO

Harold Lerner invented this nifty little number back in 1972, and he's been in the ball-marker business ever since. The HL Ballmark consists of two plastic disks: a penny-sized holder with adhesive on one side and a "woolly" material on the other, and a less-than-dime-sized ball marker backed with Velcro. The first permanently adheres to the end of your putter grip, where it securely holds the ball marker in place until you need it. The marker hugs the surface of the green for a flat, secure "lie," and if you prefer you can carry it on your golf glove or sun visor.

$1.40 for a package of two from HL Ballmark.

MARK'S MARKER

There's something to be said for carrying a ball marker on your putter

Mark's Marker

instead of in your pocket, and that's the idea behind Mark's Marker. It consists of a dime-sized metal ball marker and a magnetic holder that's installed on the grip end of your putter (it easily screws into the pilot holes on most composition grips, and, with a bit more fuss, into the grommet sleeves under most end-capped grips). The coinlike marker, which shows a golfer in follow-through position, sits securely in the holder's recessed top until you need it. And if you happen to drop it, you don't even have to stoop or bend over—just let your putter do the picking up.

$2.85 from Golfsmith; also from Marksman Manufacturing and J. White Industries.

HL Ballmark with Velcro

THE SHRIVOT

Unlike most other ball-mark menders, this one won't take up residence in your dresser drawer, in your clubhouse locker, or in the bottom of your golf bag, and it'll never poke holes in your pockets. The Shrivot slides on the shaft of your putter and stays there until you need it, so it's at your fingertips every time you set foot on a green. (If you prefer to keep it on a key chain, there's also a tiny hole for that purpose.) The Shrivot's twin prongs fix ball marks better than conventional repair tools, and a club-cradle notch at the other end lets you lay down your putter or pitching iron without getting its grip wet or dirty. Because The Shrivot is made of featherweight aluminum and weighs only about a quarter of an ounce, it won't affect your putting stroke in any way. It will, however, make you the greenskeeper's best friend.

$2.95 from Shrivot Corporation; also from Competitive Edge Golf and Herrington.

THE SMITTY

Wear "The Smitty," and you'll never fumble around for a tee or ball marker again. This lightweight, stainless steel gizmo holds two tees and two ball markers and clips onto your belt, pocket, or hat.

$4.49 from Creative Designed Products.

ZIPPO GREENS KEEPER

Zippo lighters have traveled from war zones to singles bars, and probably saved more than a few cool evenings in both. Now the folks at Zippo have come up with another lifesaver: the Greens Keeper. Its brushed stainless steel case is about the size of a silver dollar, with a money clip (or a belt clip, if you prefer) on the back and a thin recess that holds two dime-size ball markers (included) at the ready. The Greens Keeper's forked blade is perfect for repairing ball marks and for cleaning the spikes on your golf shoes. Best of all, the stainless steel blade retracts, jacknife-style, to protect your pocket— and your leg— from close encounters of the unwanted kind.

$8.85 from Golfsmith; also from Austad's.

THE PERSONAL TOUCH

GOLF BALL MONOGRAMMER

This gizmo may look like a big nut-cracker, but it won't open either maca-damias or Maxflis. It will, however, permanently imprint up to three initials on the golf ball of your choice. That should ensure that you'll never get stuck with a one-stroke penalty for playing someone else's ball. The Golf Ball Monogrammer is made in England and includes enough inked marking tape for umpteen dozens of golf balls.

$25 from Abercrombie & Fitch.

GOLF LINKS

Personalizing your golf clubs is the best insurance against accidental loss— How many times have you left a chipping or pitching iron behind at the edge of a green?— and it can add a touch of class, too. Golf Links are featherweight alumi-num end caps, engraved with your monogram and telephone number (including area code), that snap easily and securely into the small holes at the ends of most composition grips. With Golf Links in place, you can rest as-sured that any good Samaritan who finds your missing mashie can find you, too. Golf Links come 14 to a set, along with a matching ball marker, and are available in black with silver-oxide engraving or gold with black-oxide engraving.

$39.95 for a prepaid gift certificate and order form from Herrington; also from Competitive Edge Golf.

THE NAME DROPPER

No doubt you've seen some of the various machines that monogram golf balls, but here's a handy gadget that permanently imprints your entire name on anything— balls, tees, gloves . . . you name it. The Name Dropper works on any surface— flat, round, or curved— and on such materials as plastic, metal, leather, cloth, paper, wood, marble, even glass. In addition to the printing machine itself, The Name Dropper kit includes ball and tee holders, ink, thinner, sealer, and a postage-paid return card for ordering your custom-made metal name plate. (The first one's on the house; additional name plates are available at a nominal charge.)

$22 from Competitive Edge Golf; also from Austad's, Golf Day Products, Las Vegas Discount Golf, and Markline.

RAINY-DAY GEAR

BAG-UMB

Next time it rains while you're on the golf course, you may wish you had one of these: a lightweight, see-through umbrella made especially for your golf clubs. Bag-Umb will keep your clubs dry even in a downpour and won't blow off. Its telescoping handle extends to anchor it among your clubs during use and retracts for convenient storage in your golf bag.

$14.95 from Magnuson Industries.

GOLF BAG RAIN COVER

Whether you're trying to play in a drizzle or a downpour, this full-length, see-through rain cover will protect your clubs, bag, and pull cart— everything, in fact, but you. The Golf Bag Rain Cover fits around any bag and cart— zippers give you easy access to clubs and balls— and folds up for compact storage.

$12.95 from Las Vegas Discount Golf.

THE HURRICANE COVER

Stormy weather? Time to haul out The Hurricane Cover, which will protect all of the clubs in your bag from Mother Nature's wrath. Its zippered top lets you choose your weapon in a matter of seconds, and its elasticized bottom snugly fits golf bags of all sizes. The Hurricane Cover is made of heavy-duty vinyl and can be folded or rolled up for convenient stowage in your golf bag.

$6.95 from Northern Golf Ball Company.

SHADEMASTER UMBRELLA CLAMP

A golf umbrella is something of a mixed blessing: It can protect you from the driving rain, all right, but what do you do with it while you're hitting a shot or holing out a putt? Take the umbrella with you and your clubs get wet; leave the umbrella behind and you run the risk that the wind will carry it into the next fairway.

Now, at least for golfers who use pull carts, comes a real foul-weather friend: the Shademaster Umbrella Clamp. Simply attach it to the handle of your cart, slip the shaft of your golf umbrella into its sleeve, tighten a wing nut, and both you and your clubs are shielded from rain or sun. The clamp securely holds an umbrella at about any angle you'd like, and it easily folds down when not in use. It even comes in handy off the course— at the beach, for example, or on your boat or sun deck.

$17.50 from Golf Day Products.

STAY-N-PLAY

You're on the way to your best round ever when it starts to rain on your parade. What to do? Reach for Stay-n-Play, a clear plastic sleeve that slips right over your clubs and around the rim of your golf bag, keeping the rain out and everything inside dry. An elastic collar holds Stay-n-Play securely on your bag, and a reach-in opening at the other end lets you remove any club without lifting the cover. No frills, maybe, but no fuss, either.

$3 from Competitive Edge Golf; also from Austad's and Golf Day Products.

RETRIEVERS

GOLDEN RETRIEVER

The way some of those scooper-upper retrievers work, you might as well hang a "Gone Fishing" sign on your golf bag every time you hit a ball into the water. But here's one that lets you trap your ball from above (without raking up any mud or muck in the process) and lift it out of the water (without any risk of dropping it back in). The Golden Retriever's patented, two-way locking ring won't let loose of your golf ball until you want it to, and its zinc-plated head rotates 360 degrees for use at any angle— including straight down from a bridge or steep embankment. What's more, its featherweight aluminum shaft extends up to 12 feet, letting you reach well out into water hazards or over fences, and automatically locks in position at the desired length. When not in use, the Golden Retriever telescopes to just three feet for inconspicuous storage in your golf bag. (If you must carry a golf ball retriever, after all, why advertise the awful truth to the whole world?) Next time you hit your ball deep into the water or out of bounds, don't waste time fishing for it; simply let this Golden Retriever out of the bag and say "fetch."

$19.95 from Herrington.

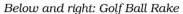

Below and right: Golf Ball Rake

GOLF BALL RAKE

If you've got the muddy-waters blues, this ingenious golf-ball retriever should have you well on the way to a full recovery. It lets you expertly extract your errant balls from water hazards even when you can't see them. Simply attach the Golf Ball Rake to the grip end of any golf club (or to a conventional cup-on-a-pole retriever), position it in the water, and apply a little downward pressure as you slowly pull it in across the bottom of the hazard. Your ball— and, if you're lucky, a couple of others— will nestle in the retriever's 11-inch-wide plastic maw. The Golf Ball Rake weighs only two ounces and can be stored easily in the pocket of your golf bag when it's not in use.

$9.95 from Merv's Retriever.

VEDORO'S BALL PROSPECTOR

Don't get mad at those lakes, ponds, and creeks for stealing your golf balls . . . get even. Just pull Vedoro's Ball Prospector out of your bag and roll its four-track head across the bottom of the water hazard. This ingenious picker-upper will retrieve a ball you can't even see, and you're likely to hook a few more while you're fishing for yours.

$39.95 from Vedoro, Ltd.

TAKING CARE OF YOUR EQUIPMENT

CARBIDE TIP GROOVE CLEANER

"Bite, baby, bite!" Oh, but there's no hope if the grooves on your irons are filled with rust, grime, or hard-packed dirt. It's the grooves, after all, that put backspin on a golf ball, and what good is there in landing your shot on the dance floor if it won't stay there? Carry the Carbide Tip Groove Cleaner in your golf bag and you can keep your irons in tiptop playing condition; its super-hard point should last a lifetime and features four 90-degree cleaning angles to match the 90-degree grooves in conventional (nonbox-grooved) irons. Yes, it costs a lot more than a tee, but it works a lot better, too.

$14.95 from Golf Day Products.

DELUXE VINYL IRON COVERS

Once you've invested hundreds of dollars in a brand new set of irons, why not spend a few dollars more to protect them from nicks and scratches? These covers fit any size or style of irons—wraparound zippers do the trick—and have large identification numbers that let you quickly find the club you need. Deluxe Vinyl Iron Covers come 10 to a set (2-9, pitching wedge, and sand wedge) in black, brown, navy blue, or red.

$16 from Austad's.

DENTAL PICKS

A dental pick is the perfect tool for dislodging the dirt that's embedded deep in the face grooves of your driver and other woods, for cleaning screwheads and scoring lines, or for any other club-cleaning job that requires a strong, sharp point. These dental picks, which are made from tempered carbon steel and can be resharpened many times, are offered in a random assortment of tip shapes. You can ask your dentist for one, of course, but why risk the horrified stare you're likely to get in return?

$2 each from The Golf Works.

GOLF CLUB CLEANING KIT

If your clubs take a licking, this handy little kit will help keep them ticking in top playing condition. It includes a 2.5-ounce tin of "Golf Club Cleaner Wax," which removes ball marks, dirt, and grass stains from woods and irons (not to mention those maddening marks from driving-range mats), and a 2-ounce can of "The Gripper," an aerosol conditioner that restores tackiness to leather grips and gloves. There's also a nylon brush for woods, a wire brush for irons, four sponge polish applicators, and a polishing cloth.

$11.95 from Golf Day Products; also from The Golf Works, Las Vegas Discount Golf, and Nevada Bob's Discount Golf.

GOLF CLUB DESIGN, FITTING, ALTERATION & REPAIR

If you're interested in golf clubs, this

Golf Club Cleaning Kit

step-by-step photographs, illustrations, tables, and charts, and nine appendixes (including all of the USGA's rules on club design, a glossary of terms, tables of manufacturers' club specifications, and explanations of exactly what happens to a golf club and ball at the moment of impact). As you make your way through this encyclopedic volume you'll learn, among many other things, how to repair and refinish all makes and models of woods, irons, and putters; how to install leather and composition grips; how to change lofts, lies, shafts, and swingweights; how to assemble golf clubs from components; how clubs are designed and manufactured; and how clubs should be fitted to individual players. And should you be interested in all of this as something more than a hobby, you'll even learn how to start your own clubmaking and repair business.

$38.50 from The Golf Works; also from GolfSmart and National Golf Foundation.

book is the Bible. In it Ralph Maltby of The Golf Works will tell you everything you need to know about the tools of the golfer's trade— and then some. Since 1973 Maltby has conducted more than 200 seminars on the subject for PGA professionals, and his 725-page book is widely regarded as the industry's standard reference work. First published in 1974, this updated and expanded edition of *Golf Club Design, Fitting, Alteration & Repair* contains 60 chapters organized into nine comprehensive sections; more than 1,500

Golf Glove Dryer

No matter what kind of golf glove you wear, it's likely to last a lot longer if you use this handy plastic drying frame after every round. Keep the Golf Glove Dryer clipped to your bag, in fact, and you'll never again have to force your hand into a stiff, shapeless, dried-out wad of leather. The hand-shaped frame not only keeps your glove stretched in its original size, but also allows air to circulate inside and prevents sweat-soaked leather from sticking together. Your golf glove will dry wrinkle-free and in shape for your next round.

$3.75 from The Golf Works; also from Austad's, Golf Day Products, and J. White Industries.

Golfer's Repair and Maintenance Handbook

If the only thing you learn from this do-it-yourself guide is how to put new grips on your clubs (the process for replacing composition grips is shown here in six simple steps), the *Golfer's Repair and Maintenance Handbook* undoubtedly will pay for itself many times over. But with 11 chapters, 95 pages, and 125 photographs and other illustrations, it can teach you much, much more. Written by John Harvey, the president of Golf Day Products, this step-by-step instruction manual shows you virtually everything you'll need to know to maintain, repair, and refinish your golf clubs— from removing soleplates to adjusting swingweights.

$6.95 from Golf Day Products.

Grip Life

If the composition grips on your clubs are hard and slick, chances are that body oils, perspiration, and golf-course grime have taken their toll. You can undo the damage with Grip Life, a pump-spray product that's specially formulated to penetrate, clean, and condition rubber (not leather) golf grips. Just spray it on the grip and wait 15 minutes; then rinse away the resultant film with clean water. A four-ounce bottle of Grip Life is enough to keep your grips soft and tacky for a full season.

$5.95 from Austad's, Golf Day Products, or Las Vegas Discount Golf.

Lacquer-Stiks

Your golf clubs were given nice paint jobs at the factory, but over the years the manufacturer's original markings have worn off. What to do? Many professional refinishers rely on Lacquer-Stiks— a no-muss, no-fuss form of fill-in paint— to put the color back in clubhead stampings (the recessed numbers, lettering, logos, and lines on irons and wood soleplates). Simply fill the various indentations with this fast-drying paint, one color at a time, wiping away the excess as you go. Lacquer-Stiks can be used on all kinds of metals, woods, plastics, and ceramics— even glass— and come in six colors: red, white, blue, green, black, and gold.

$1.30 apiece or $5.50 for a set of six from The Golf Works; also from Florida Golf Warehouse and Golfsmith.

McDivot's Clubscrub

Next time you take a foot-long divot with your five-iron, you may wish that you had a Clubscrub clipped to your

McDivot's Clubscrub

bag. Its refillable cylinder dispenses a soap-and-water solution (or just plain water) through a tough nylon brush to clean dirt, mud, and grass from the grooves of your irons and woods. To saturate the brush, simply pull up on the cap and gently squeeze on the cylinder; push the cap back down and Clubscrub is leakproof.

$9.95 from Golf Day Products.

McSpike

There you are, precariously balanced on one leg as you try to clean the mud-encrusted spikes on your golf shoes with the pointed end of a wooden golf tee. It's the wrong tool for the job— and besides, you deserve a break today. So why not use McSpike, a little round

gizmo that cleans your spikes right down to the shine with a twist or two of the wrist?

$3.50 from Everything for Golf.

MAGNETIC PROTRACTOR

Most top professionals constantly tinker with the tools of their trade. By fine-tuning such key specifications as lofts and lies, they aim to extract every possible ounce of performance from their clubs. Most amateur golfers would do well, as it turns out, to follow the leaders; it's been estimated that more than two-thirds of them carry clubs with the wrong lofts and lies. Are you among them? You can easily find out with the Magnetic Protractor, which lets you accurately measure (to within one-half of a degree) the loft and lie of every club in your bag— from driver to putter. Simply sole a club in proper playing position and have someone hold the gauge's magnetic base flat against the clubface; the loft is shown on a com-pass-like dial. Then, to measure the club's lie, move the gauge to the lower portion of its shaft. The Magnetic Pro-tractor's easy-to-read plastic dial is four inches in diameter and has loft and lie specifications listed on its reverse side.

$12.85 from The Golf Works; also from Golfsmith.

MAGNUM FORCE I RATCHET SPIKE WRENCH

"Go ahead," you say to that evil spike as you take aim with the Magnum Force I Ratchet Spike Wrench. "Make my day." The spike gives up without a fight, however, and for good reason: Your chrome-plated steel weapon packs so much torque that anything short of surrender would be foolish. This wrench, in fact, makes removing even the oldest and most obstinate spikes just about as easy as installing new ones, and its rubber-coated handle makes sure that you won't lose your grip in the process. Best of all, the wrench's ratcheting action lets you get the job done with no wasted motion.

$7.95 from Las Vegas Discount Golf.

New Zealand Lambskin Headcovers

Once you've invested hundreds of dollars in a beautiful set of woods, why cut corners in the headcover department? These classy golf-club covers are made from genuine New Zealand lambskin and may well represent the ultimate in both luxury and protection. The fleece, which is shorn to an approximate depth of three-quarters of an inch, is as soft as a baby's bottom, pleasant to touch, and exceptionally durable. An elastic waist five inches from the bottom of each headcover keeps it snugly secured to the club.

New Zealand Lambskin Headcovers

Phillips Spike Wrench

come four to a set, measure 16 inches from top to bottom, and are available in four colors (camel, champagne, light grey, or yellow). Each set includes five leather tags, embossed with numbers 1 through 5, which are attached to the headcovers on dog-leash clasps. While the driver cover is slightly larger than the others in the set, the numbered tags are otherwise interchangeable, and the folks at Shepherd's Pack will even substitute blank tags on request. And when these headcovers get dirty, a simple hand-washing in Woolite— what else?— will leave them looking like new.

$55 from Shepherd's Pack.

Phillips Spike Wrench

Spike wrenches are something like tire irons: Having one ill-designed for the

New Zealand Lambskin Headcovers

job may be worse than not having one at all. In the Phillips Spike Wrench, however, you can behold utter perfection in form and function. Manufactured by F.C. Phillips, Inc., of Stoughton, Massachusetts, this wrench will last a lifetime. Its T-shaped handle lets you undo even the most stubborn rust-bound spikes with a minimum of elbow grease. The Phillips Spike Wrench, unlike most others on the market, has replaceable tungsten prongs; an extra set is included.

$4.95 from Las Vegas Discount Golf; also from Golfsmith and Northern Golf Ball Company.

PING WEIGHT BALANCE SCALE

If you like to tinker with the tools of your trade— regripping, refinishing, reshafting, or otherwise repairing them— you can't afford to ignore swingweight, which is a statistical proxy for clubhead feel. Swingweight relates the weight of the clubhead to the club's total weight, and is expressed in a letter (A, B, C, D, E, F) followed by a number (0 to 9). The higher up the letter-number scale, the higher the swingweight.

This lightweight, precision-calibrated, easy-to-read scale provides the same accuracy as its bigger brethren at less than half the size and cost. The Ping Weight Balance Scale gives you direct readings of both swingweight and dead weight (to tenths of an ounce), which means you don't need to use those cumbersome conversion charts, and measures only 22 inches long, 2 inches deep, and 3.5 inches high.

$40 from Florida Golf Warehouse or Golfsmith; also from Golf Day Products.

SPIKE CADDY

There's one problem with most golf shoes: the spikes. You're asking for trouble if you try to pack them in your golf bag or suitcase (unless, in the latter instance, you don't happen to mind if your golf shirts are perforated). Spike Caddy's ingenious double-pouch design solves the packing problem— and protects your golf shoes from each other at the same time. For starters, Spike Caddy is made from reinforced 1,000-denier Dupont Cordura, a rugged material that won't rip, snag, or puncture, and dual vents on both pouches allow moisture to escape and guard against mildew. The pouches cling together (via Velcro) for easy carrying to and from the course, or hinge out like saddle bags for packing in your suitcase or golf bag. And when you finish a round, Spike Caddy will keep your dirty golf shoes from dirtying up anything else.

$19.95 from Herrington; also from Austad's, Competitive Edge Golf, and The Golf Works.

SUPER GRIP DRYER/SUBERAANAI

Slippery golf grips can send your score soaring, so why not keep 'em dry with Suberaanai? Simply slip a wet grip into the Super Grip Dryer (which absorbs moisture and leaves behind a nontoxic, resin-based powder), wring gently, and the tack will be back before you can say the magic word.

$2.95 for a package of six from Miya Epoch.

TEES

The Dream Tee

It's illegal for real play, but the Dream Tee just might force you to build a better swing. When you use this odd-looking plastic tee, the clubface contacts only the tee— not the ball. Your shot goes straighter because the club-imparted spin can't take hold. So you don't think you have an outside-in swing? You can check it out on the practice range by hitting balls with a Dream Tee and then switching to a regular tee.

$2.25 for a package of five from The Golf Works; also from The Duck Press.

ExacTee

"The average player tees the ball too low for the drive," Tommy Armour, the legendary shotmaker and teacher, wrote more than 35 years ago in *How To Play Your Best Golf All the Time.* "The fine player tees the ball high, usually with about half of the ball being above the top of the driver when it is soled behind the ball. . . . When I'm teaching the drive, I have my assistant tee the first 20 balls. Then I have the pupils tee the next 20, and every time the pupils will tee the ball about a half-inch lower until I say to them that they'll have to learn how to use a tee before they can expect much about using a club."

If Armour's admonition applies to you, ExacTee might be ExactLee what you need. It's engineered to provide, in foolproof fashion, what Armour and many others have generally recommended as the optimum tee height. The plastic ExacTee resembles a conventional $2^1/_{16}$-inch tee, except for a circular collar a little more than an inch from the bottom that prevents it from penetrating too deep into the turf. (Imagine a tee that's been poked through a washer and you've got the picture.) Because ExacTee ensures that your golf ball is always in the same position for every drive, it should help you hit the big stick with greater consistency.

$1 for a package of six from Sutherland Products.

Flex-Tee

At last . . . a golf tee that won't break. This flexible, three-piece tee is the brainchild of Frank Liccardello, a model maker for Chrysler Corporation, who got so tired of carrying around a pocketful of tees that he decided to invent one that would last virtually forever. Flex-Tee's top half is made of Dupont Hytrel, a polyester elastomer that bends with the impact of the clubhead and then returns to its original position; the bottom half is made of Dupont Delrin, an acetal resin that's rigid enough to penetrate the toughest turf— even hardpan— without breaking. (The third piece is a handy ball marker that snaps on top.) By minimizing impact resistance (the ball is hit *off* of the tee, not *out* of the tee), it's supposed to maximize driving distance. Thanks to its yielding nature, Flex-Tee lasts a lot longer than conventional wood tees— indefinitely, the manufacturer says—

Flex-Tee

and won't nick, chip, or mar clubheads. And thanks to its bigger-than-average top surface, Flex-Tee is unlikely to embarrass you by letting your golf ball fall off before you have a chance to hit it. Finally, Flex-Tees come in various eye-catching fluorescent colors to help make sure you don't leave them behind after you've hit— which, aside from giving them away, is just about the only reason you'll ever need extras. And if it all sounds too good to be true, rest assured that Flex-Tees conform with USGA rules.

$9.95 a dozen from Herrington.

POW'R TEE
This two-piece plastic tee is a real pushover. Its top section, which is

joined to the bottom in ball-and-socket fashion, simply swivels out of the way as your clubhead speeds through the impact zone. The less the resistance, the theory goes, the greater your distance. What's more, Pow'r Tees take much of the guesswork out of teeing up. You can choose from three different heights and each tee tells you when to stop pushing it into the turf (a collar on its lower section fixes the depth of penetration). Pow'r Tees are made of indestructible plastic, conform to USGA rules, and come three to a package (one of each height), with two ball markers tossed in for good measure.

$9.95 from Las Vegas Discount Golf.

REV-TEE
Imagine this: a tee that you'll never

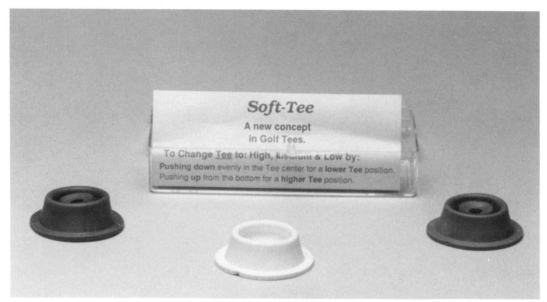

Soft-Tee

break, that you can't lose, and that just may help you drive longer and straighter. Rev-Tee consists of a metal spike that you insert into the ground (it easily slides into even the hardest hardpan) and, attached perpendicularly to it, a revolving arm on which you tee up your golf ball. A raised line that runs down the middle of the arm helps you square your clubface to the target, and a crosshair helps you correctly sight your intended line. Rev-Tee's revolving arm is made of DuPont Surlyn, the same stuff used in golf-ball covers, so it won't damage or discolor your club-heads. And if this all sounds way too good to be true, don't worry: The United States Golf Association has ruled that Rev-Tee conforms to the official Rules of Golf.

$5.95 from The Duck Press.

SOFT-TEE

This thimble-shaped rubber tee has a lot going for it, but the best part is that you don't even have to force it into the ground. Simply adjust Soft-Tee to the desired height (high, medium, or low) by pushing up or down from the center, plop your ball on top, and hit away. It won't break like a wooden tee or poke holes in your pockets, either. And because your golf ball is always posi-tioned at one of three fixed heights, it may even improve your consistency off the tee. What's more, you'll never again struggle to penetrate hardpan or frozen ground, and you can say goodbye once and for all to those infernal rubber tees at the local driving range.

$9 for a package of three (in red, white, and blue) from Soft-Tee Enterprises.

THROWING A GOLF PARTY

BOGEY ICE

Here's an ice-cube tray that makes the only kind of golf balls you'd intentionally drop in the drink. Just fill this two-piece, snap-together tray with water, stick it in the freezer, and in a little while you'll have 10 ice cubes the same size and shape as real golf balls— right down to the dimples.

$6.50 from Golf Day Products; also from Somerton Springs Golf Shoppes.

BOGEY ICE BUCKET

This insulated, three-quart ice bucket is ideal for chilling down the drinks at any 19th-hole setting. The Bogey Ice Bucket resembles your basic golf ball, except that it's fully 10 inches high and has a tee on top— as the handle that lifts the lid— rather than at the bottom. It's made to order for stowing your Bogey Ice (see above), of course, but it'll also keep more conventional cubes at the ready.

$21.95 from Enticements.

Bogey Ice

GOLF BALL "ICE CUBES"

When the guests at your next 19th-hole gathering see you walk into the kitchen and take a bunch of golf balls out of the freezer, they may shake their heads and wonder to themselves whether the game's finally gotten to you. And when they see you plop a couple of them into someone's glass or drop a dozen into the punch bowl, they may even conclude that you've gone off the deep end. But not to worry: These dimpled, smaller-than-regulation-size spheres are *supposed* to be submerged. Thanks to the quick-freezing solution that's permanently sealed inside their white plastic covers, they keep drinks ice-cold without watering them down. What's more, these Golf Ball "Ice Cubes" are fully washable and endlessly reusable. Each package of one dozen "cubes" includes a handy plastic freezer tray that keeps them from rolling around aimlessly inside your refrigerator.

$4 from The Duck Press; also from Somerton Springs Golf Shoppes.

GOLF QUOTE GLASSES

Next time you host the 19th-hole happy hour, you can keep your guests smiling by serving their drinks in these 14-ounce, old-fashioned-size tumblers. Each glass in the set of six is delicately etched with a humorous saying about the game's truths or consequences. To wit: "Golf is 90 percent inspiration and 10 percent inspiration."—Johnny Miller. "Give me golf clubs, fresh air, and a beautiful partner, and you can keep my golf clubs and the fresh air."—Jack Benny. "I'm hitting the woods just great, but I'm having a terrible time getting out of them."—Harry Toscano. "You can talk to a fade, but a hook won't listen."—Lee Trevino. "I play in the low '80s. If it's any hotter than that, I won't play."—Joe E. Lewis. "Nothing increases your score like witnesses."—Anonymous. Golf Quote Glasses are dishwasher-safe.

$24.95 from Austad's.

GOLF PARTY ACCESSORIES

Whether you're throwing an informal golf get-together or hosting a happy hour at the 19th hole, here's just about everything you might need in the way of paper party accessories: invitations with matching envelopes (eight for $1.85); cocktail napkins (20 for $1.50); luncheon napkins (20 for $1.65); seven-inch plates (10 for $1.85); nine-inch plates (10 for $2.20); eight-ounce hot and cold cups (10 for $1.90); salt and pepper shakers (one of each, unfilled, for $.99); and a 54-by-102-inch table cover ($3). All feature the same lighthearted cartoon of a colorfully attired duffer poised in midswing.

From Maryco Products; also from Golf Day Products.

GOLF PARTY-PAK

"Behold the golfer, he riseth up early in the morning and disturbeth the whole household. Mighty are his preparations. He goeth forth full of hope and when the day is spent, he returneth smelling of strong drink, and the truth is not in him."

That's just one of the bits of wisdom you can bestow upon your guests when you entertain with the Golf Party-Pak. This cocktail-party-in-a-kit features a foursome of frosted, 14-ounce acrylic tumblers decorated with clever cartoons and quotations about the lighter side of golf, 80 matching cocktail napkins, and a 10.5-inch-square clear acrylic serving tray that keeps everything in order. (The glasses and tray are top-rack dishwasher safe.)

$19.50 from Golf Day Products ($11.50 for a set of four extra tumblers); also from Competitive Edge Golf and Enticements.

TOWELS

IMPORTED BRITISH GOLF TOWELS

Why carry an ordinary golf towel when you can class up your on-the-course act with one of these? Each member of this terrycloth threesome is imprinted with the name and crest of a world-famous Scottish golf course: Carnoustie, The Old Course at St. Andrews, and Turnberry (all historic sites of the British Open). They're made of thick, 100 percent cotton toweling, measure 15 by 19 inches, and have grommets and hooks for easy attachment to your golf bag.

$11.50 each ($33 for the set of three) from Golf Day Products.

RAGTAIL GOLF TOWEL

You step onto the green, mark and pick up your ball, and—yecch!—it's covered with mud or, even worse yet, goose doo-doo. Where's your golf towel when you really need it? Hanging on your golf bag, that's where . . . over at the edge of the green, or near the next tee (and you thought you were thinking ahead by leaving it there).

Tucking an ordinary golf towel under your belt or waistband is one solution, of course, but the RagTail goes its conventional cousins one step better. Thanks to a flexible plastic insert that's permanently sewn into one end, the RagTail Golf Towel fits perfectly—and stays neatly folded—in your hip pocket or waistband. It's made from 100 percent cotton terrycloth, with a metal grommet for good measure—just in case

you don't want your golf towel to go everywhere you do.

$7.50 from Competitive Edge Golf; also from Pursuit of Par Enterprises.

"STAYCLEAN" GOLF TOWEL

If you don't carry two golf towels— one for your equipment and another for

"Stayclean" Golf Towel

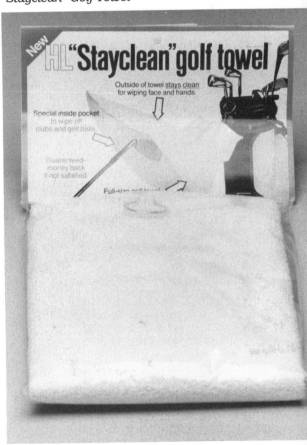

your face and hands—you may walk off the 18th green looking like a ditch-digger. This full-sized, two-in-one golf towel has a special inside pocket for wiping the dirt, grass, and mud off your clubs and balls, which leaves the outside clean for your face and hands. The "Stayclean" Golf Towel is made of white terrycloth, with a buttonhole-stitched grommet and clip for easy attachment to your golf bag.

$6.98 from HL Ballmark Company.

THE ULTIMATE GOLF TOWEL

You don't need to save The Ultimate Golf Towel for a rainy day, but that's when it's bound to come in the handiest. Unlike conventional cotton towels, this one won't ever get waterlogged; it stays dry and absorbent even in a downpour. Because it's made of chamois, The Ultimate Golf Towel absorbs moisture like a sponge and wrings out like one, too.

$11.50 from Golf Day Products.

ETCETERA

CADDI-SAK

Here's one for the golfer with everything but no place to put it. Caddi-Sak is an attractive drawstring pouch that's designed to let you safely and conveniently store your golf paraphernalia and personal items— on the course, at the practice range, or, for that matter, just about anywhere. Just dump everything— car keys, coins, jewelry, glasses, watch, wallet, whatever— into the pouch, tighten the drawstring, and drop it in the pocket of your golf bag or on the dashboard rack of your golf cart. Caddi-Sak's ingenious double-pocket design even lets you separate and protect any scratchable valuables. The pouch is made of tough, long-wearing nylon suede cloth, embroidered with the Caddi-Sak logo, and can be machine-washed and -dried. And now the best news: When you head to the parking lot, you won't have to fish around in your golf bag anymore for your wallet and car keys.

$9.95 (in burgundy, hunter green, or navy blue) from The Golf Works; also from The Duck Press and Golf Day Products.

Caddi-Sak

CAD-EZE

If you're forever fumbling around in your pockets or golf bag for balls and tees, Cad-Eze can ease— and maybe even eliminate— the chaos. This see-through plastic dispenser features two built-in tubes that feed you one ball or tee at a time. The Cad-Eze unit easily clips onto any golf bag and comes filled with four tees and practice balls.

$19.95 from Enticements.

DELUXE FACE SAVER IRON COVERS

Your irons may be their own worst enemies. Let them bang around in your bag and pretty soon they'll be covered with nicks, scratches, dents, and other battle scars. These snap-on plastic covers, which are contoured to securely fit any type of irons (including low-

Golf-Buoy

profile models), will protect your club-heads from wear and tear both on and off the course. Deluxe Face Saver Iron Covers are packaged eight to a set (three-iron through pitching wedge), numbered or lettered on top for easy club selection, and strung together on an elastic lanyard to guard against loss. They're available for either right- or left-handed irons and come in four different colors (black, brown, red, and white). Matching covers for two-irons and sand wedges are sold individually.

$9.95 a set ($1.50 each for individual covers) from Northern Golf Ball Company; also from Golf Day Products, Golfsmith, and Edwin Watts Golf Shops.

FLEX-TIPS

You're burning up the course, but your

approach shot on the 16th hole has just fallen short of the green and trickled into a water hazard. Should you try to play it as it lies— in the water— or swallow hard and take the penalty stroke? Well, if you happened to be carrying Flex-Tips in your hip pocket or golf bag, you could turn to its section on "Trouble Shots" and read this bit of quick advice: "If the ball is no more than a half-inch under water take a pitching wedge and play the shot like a sand explosion."

That's just one of more than 100 tips on everything from uphill lies to downhill putts— even golf-course etiquette and safety— you'll find inside Flex-Tips, an 18-page memory-refresher that's barely bigger than a credit card. This illustrated quick-reference guide opens like an accordion and snaps shut between two flexible, magnetic covers. It's far from encylopedic, of course, but

Flex-Tips does have one big advantage over your home library of golf instruction books: You *can* take it with you.

$2.95 from Bricker Enterprises.

GOLF-BUOY

The typical golf course is anything but a level playing field, which means that any drink you try to bring along could be headed for a spill. This free-swiveling beverage caddy, which can be attached in minutes to a pull cart or golf car, keeps virtually any kind of liquid— hot or cold— on the level. If you're not quite awake as you head to the first tee, the Golf-Buoy, thanks to a vertical slot on one side, will hold your mug of coffee safely at the ready; later, when you're ready for something cooler, simply insert the insulated Coaster-Buoy and slip a can, bottle, or glass inside. The Golf-Buoy comes with a chrome-plated steel clamp (for mounting on tubular handles and frames) and a plastic clip (for mounting on dashboards and other flat surfaces).

$8.95 from Las Vegas Discount Golf; also from Austad's and Golfsmith.

GOTCHA

Who's away? No need to guess, pace it off, or flip a coin if you've got Gotcha, a simple little gadget that settles the question scientifically. Just place a plastic hook around the base of the flagstick and pull Gotcha out to the first ball, unwinding up to 40 feet of nylon string as you go. Then press Gotcha in the middle to lock the string at that distance and swing it around to the

next ball . . . and so on, until it's time to stop arguing and start putting. If your next tournament includes a closest-to-the-pin contest, this baby may be worth its weight in gold.

$4.95 from Golf Day Products.

THE GRAND LUXE GOLF CART

Bag Boy has been making pull carts for golfers since 1945 (its first model rolled on two lawn-mower wheels), but this one looks like something out of the 21st century. The Grand Luxe, which is made mostly of superstrong graphite composites, weighs in at only six pounds and rolls along at the slightest suggestion of the fingertips. What's more, once you remove its snap-off wheels and "J"-hook handle, this scissor-folding showpiece of computer-aided design collapses to a size of only 26 inches high, 16 inches wide, and five inches thick— a virtual disappearing act. The cart won't corrode, can cradle a bag of any size (quick-release straps secure it to the cart), and, owing to its wide stance, is nearly impossible to tip over. The Grand Luxe is available in red, black, or blue and comes with Bag-Boy's standard five-year warranty.

$79.95 from Edwin Watts Golf Shops; also from Las Vegas Discount Golf.

HIDDEN-CART GOLF BAG

Just say "presto chango" and you're ready to roll: This standard-sized vinyl golf bag has a built-in pull cart that comes out of hiding whenever you need it. As you unfold the cart's galvanized steel frame from its zippered compartment, its rubber-rimmed steel wheels snap into place and a spring-loaded latch securely locks the legs and handle in playing position. The bag has an extra-large pocket that holds both accessories and apparel (including your golf shoes) and comes with a snap-on travel cover. The Hidden-Cart Golf Bag is handmade in England, stands 36 inches high, and at 17 pounds weighs less, than some of its cartless cousins.

$134.50 from Hammacher Schlemmer.

"LINKS TO THE PAST" BALL MARKER DISPLAY

If you're among the many golfers who like to save ball markers as souvenirs of the courses they've played, why keep your collection stashed away where no one can see it? This framed showcase from Links to the Past hangs handsomely on the wall and attractively displays up to four dozen ball markers below a colorful and nostalgic clubhouse scene.

$14.95 from Las Vegas Discount Golf.

19TH HOLE FLAG

What good is any 19th hole without its own flag? This one is made of heavy-duty cotton in fire-engine red with white numbers, and, at 18 inches wide by 13 inches deep, is regulation-size. Three metal grommets sewn into the reinforced edge let you easily attach the 19th Hole Flag to any flagstick, or fly it from your golf cart, clubhouse locker, boat, or tailgate— or, for that matter, anywhere else you and your friends gather after a round of golf.

$6.50 from Golf Day Products.

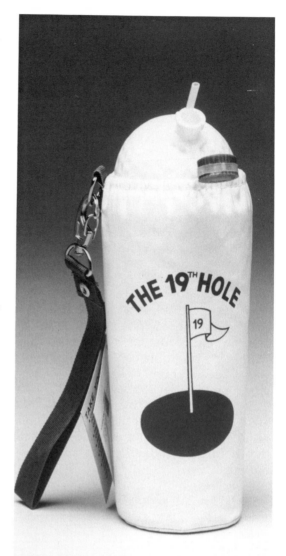

The 19th Hole Sipper

THE 19TH HOLE SIPPER

If the beverage of your choice happens to be carrot juice instead of Coca-Cola, The 19th Hole Sipper may be just what the dietitian ordered. It's an insulated drink caddy that keeps up to 23 ounces of liquid— coffee, orange juice, lemonade, Gatorade, you name it— hot or cold. Thanks to its screw-on "golf-ball" top, you can fill it up without any fuss (and, if you'd like, add ice); twist a dial and out comes a pop-up drinking straw. The 19th Hole Sipper is 11 inches high, and a clip-on carrying strap lets you sling it from your golf bag or cart.

$9.95 from Maryco Products; also from Golf Day Products.

pull carts and golf cars, and is manufactured in three different colors (burgundy, charcoal grey, and French blue). There are no zippers to snag or break, and you can keep it looking like new with a little bit of water and Armour All. Whether you carry it 7,000 yards or ship it 7,000 miles, here, at long last, is a lightweight bag that's durable enough to go the distance.

$159.95 from Austad's; also from Hammacher Schlemmer.

PROTECH GOLF BAG

If you take your clubs along with you when you travel, you know how the airlines can manhandle— even mangle— your golf bag. The ultimate solution to the problem may well be this ingenious and virtually indestructible "clubhouse," which is molded from a high-impact plastic alloy that's designed to withstand plenty of punishment and weighs only about 10 pounds. Snap on and latch its double-walled travel cover and your clubheads will be protected from car trunk to baggage carousel; remove the cover at the course and you're all ready to play.

The PROTECH Golf Bag's built-in club dividers and four separate storage compartments give your equipment and accessories maximum protection on and off the course, and a swinging door gives you easy access to everything that's packed away inside. There's a nifty golf-ball dispenser on top (which keeps up to a sleeve of balls at the ready); a handy compartment that will fit tees, gloves, ball markers, and the like; and two larger compartments for your golf shoes and outerwear. The PROTECH Golf Bag comes with a double-padded shoulder strap and carrying handle, is designed to fit all

PUT'R THERE/THE PUTTER CADDY

There oughta be a Murphy's Law: The one golf club you need on every hole— your putter— invariably is the hardest to find. Why? As the shortest club in the bag, the putter tends to get lost in the thicket of woods and irons. Now comes Put-r There, a clever little gizmo that ends the fumbling at every green by keeping your putter on the outside of your golf bag. (The only catch is that your bag must be on a golf cart or otherwise maintained in vertical position.)

Simply fasten Put'r There to the edge of your golf bag, slip the slimmer end of your putter's tapered shaft into it, and then slide the club down, head first, until it's held firmly in place. When you next need your putter, simply reverse the process. And because Put'r There is made of Delrin plastic, it won't scratch or mar your putter's shaft.

$6.95 from The Duck Press; also from Herrington.

PUTTER GRIPPER

Oh, your aching back? Attach this little rubber gizmo to the grip end of your putter and relief is on the way. You'll never again have to reach down into the cup to pick up your golf ball. Just turn your putter upside down, press the Putter Gripper against the ball, and bingo— you're on the way to the next tee. It's nothing new, of course, but the folks who manufacturer this black-rubber model claim at least two improvements over the original: "We've made the lip a little thinner for better suction. It comes in black. And that goes with more things than green."

$1.95 from Las Vegas Discount Golf.

Redi Club

If you play golf with something less than a full set, Redi Club may be better than

Sav-A-Scratch

a bag. This lightweight carrier, made of engineering-grade plastic and looks a little bit like a sawhorse with a handle, holds eight clubs in horizontal position (keeping them within reach but off wet grass), eight balls, six tees, and a pencil. Whether you carry it by hand or use the adjustable shoulder strap, Redi Club folds flat whenever you pick it up. Store it in your trunk, in fact, and you'll always have a handy way to tote your clubs to and from the practice range.

$26.95 from Austad's; also from Golf Day Products and Las Vegas Discount Golf.

St. Andrews Headcovers

These classic— and classy— tartan

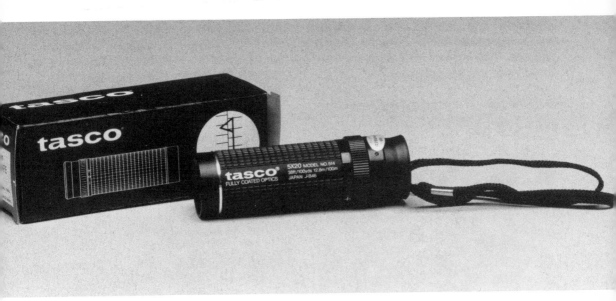

Tasco Golf Scope

headcovers are imported from Scotland, and for good reason: They wear the embroidered crest of the Old Course at St. Andrews, the home of golf. The tartan is Hunting MacLean, a colorful plaid of red, blue, and green, and the fabric is a rich blend of wool and polyester. Each St. Andrews Headcover has a sewn-in waterproof barrier to keep moisture out and a soft inner liner to keep your clubs in fine finish, along with a decorative pompom and a leather tag that identifies the wood inside (1, 3, 5, or X). A matching, drawstringed shoe bag is $18.95.

$12.95 each from Golf Day Products.

Sav-A-Scratch

Here's a padded mat, complete with shoe horn and brush, that hooks onto the trunk lip of your car and protects your bumper from nicks and scratches while you change into— and out of— your golf shoes. If you're real lucky,

Sav-A-Scratch may even Sav-A-Back, too.

$7.95 from Sav-A-Scratch.

Tasco Golf Scope

This one's a no-no, if you play by the Rules of Golf, but it nonetheless may put everything on the golf course in its proper perspective. The Tasco Golf Scope is a precision-made, roof-prism monocular with a yards-to-the-pin scale etched on its lens. Simply sight the flagstick through the scope, making sure that the lowermost crossbar on the yardage scale is aligned with the cup. (If you can't see the cup with the naked eye, don't worry; the scope's five-power magnification will bring it into focus.) Then, where the top of the flag intersects the yardage scale, read off the remaining distance to the pin. The Tasco Golf Scope is accurate anywhere from 40 to 200 yards out, measures only 4.3 inches long by 1.3 inches in diameter, and, thanks to its aluminum and magnesium barrel, weighs only 3.5 ounces. Two rubber lens caps and a vinyl case are included.

$79.95 from Haverhills; also from The Golf Shop Collection.

TEA-TIME AT THE MASTERS

If you'd just as soon be Craig Claiborne as Craig Stadler, this collection of recipes from the Junior League of Augusta, Georgia, may help you keep the honors in the kitchen. Now in its ninth printing, *Tea-Time at the Masters* is one part culinary tour de force, one part tribute to Augusta's most famous annual event. The cookbook's 17 chapters cover everything from appetizers to desserts, and sprinkled throughout are recipes from some of the world's finest golf clubs (including the Royal and Ancient Golf Club of St. Andrews, Pebble Beach Golf Links, Pinehurst Country Club, and, of course, Augusta National Golf Club), as well as from many former Masters champions and their spouses. Byron Nelson, for example, offers a Mustard Ring, Spanish Pork Chops ("All is done for a favorite meal of ours. I usually serve with a green salad."), and Lemon Whipped Cream Sauce. Barbara Nicklaus, wife of the winningest Master of them all,

shares her recipes for a Crab Casserole, Skillet Pineapple Upside Down Cake, and Glazed Wine Bars. Added bonuses include Rosalynn Carter's recipe for peanut soup and Mamie Eisenhower's formula for the perfect piecrust. Even if you're a duffer in the kitchen, no need to worry: "Each recipe in Tea-Time has been prepared over and over on the practice range," the editors note, "and is therefore suitable for the big course under any playing conditions." And who knows? Maybe you'll even learn to slice as well indoors as you do out.

$9.95 from Tea-Time at the Masters; also from Maryco Products.

TRAVELS WITH A GOLF TOUR GOURMET

Betty Hicks won the U.S. Women's Amateur championship in 1941 and went on to become one of the pioneers of the LPGA Tour. In *Travels with a Golf Tour Gourmet*, a 208-page memoir that's generously laced with anecdotes and photographs, she offers a behind-the-scenes look at life on the ladies' tour. But this fascinating book has as much to do much with chicken legs as doglegs; sprinkled throughout the text are Hicks's favorite recipes and cooking tips.

$12.95 from The Duck Press; also from The Golf Shop Collection.

GOLF EQUIPMENT MANUFACTURERS

CLUBS AND COMPONENTS

Accuform Golf Limited
76 Fordhouse Boulevard
Toronto, Ontario
Canada M8Z 5X7
(416) 259-3259
(800) 387-3227

Adams Golf
17 East Windmill Circle
Abilene, Texas 79605
(915) 695-2010
(800) 622-0609

Allied Golf Corporation
4538 West Fullerton Avenue
Chicago, Illinois 60639
(312) 772-7710
(800) 346-5346

American Precision Golf of Pinehurst
1510 U.S. Highways 15 & 501
Southern Pines, North Carolina 28387
(919) 692-5080

American Tour, Inc.
9514-4 Reseda Boulevard
Northridge, California 91324
(818) 701-0296
(800) 443-8222

Tommy Armour Golf Company
8350 North Lehigh Avenue
Morton Grove, Illinois 60053
(312) 966-6300
(800) 742-4653; in Illinois, (800) 742-
    4244

Auld Golf, Inc.
P.O. Box 1607
Concord, North Carolina 28025
(704) 786-4653
(800) 732-4677

B & M Golf Company
P.O. Box 634
16 Church Street
Kings Park, New York 11754
(516) 269-1188
(800) 752-9727

Barber-Goldentouch Golf, Inc.
P.O. Box 1687
San Marcos, California 92069-1687
(619) 471-8950
(800) 423-2220

Beauwood California, Inc.
2915 Daimler Street
Santa Ana, California 92705
(714) 756-1220

Bel Air Golf
23769 Madison Street
Torrance, California 90505
(213) 373-1633

Bridgestone Sports (U.S.A.)
3000 Northwoods Parkway, Suite 105
Norcross, Georgia 30071
(404) 449-6123
(800) 358-6319

Browning Golf Company
Route 1
Morgan, Utah 84050
(801) 876-2711

Cactus Golf
FTM Sports
P.O. Box 165203
Miami, Florida 33116
(305) 255-2272
(800) 292-5589

Callaway Golf
2345 Camino Vida Roble
Carlsbad, California 92009
(619) 931-1771
(800) 228-2767

Chicago Golf & Sports
15251 Roosevelt Boulevard, Suite 201
Clearwater, Florida 34620
(813) 530-0666
(800) 438-6082

Roger Cleveland Golf Company, Inc.
14508 South Garfield Avenue
Paramount, California 90723
(213) 630-6363
(800) 632-6363

Cobra Golf Inc.
4645 North Avenue
Oceanside, California 92056
(619) 941-9550
(800) 223-3537

Compass Golf Products Inc.
1685 Scenic
Costa Mesa, California 92626
(714) 557-6090
(800) 322-4653

Contax Sports, Inc.
1437 North Carolan Avenue
Burlingame, California 94010
(415) 697-9500
(800) 692-9500

Ray Cook Company
2233 Faraday Avenue
Carlsbad, California 92008
(619) 931-0141
(800) 531-7252

Cougar Golf
Roger Dunn Golf Shops
2803 South Yale Street
Santa Ana, California 92704
(714) 966-0310
(800) 682-5351

Crackshot Golf U.S.A. Inc.
8714 Darby Avenue
Northridge, California 91325
(818) 886-9773
(800) 821-1854

Otey Crisman Golf Company
P.O. Box 386
201 Faulk Avenue
Selma, Alabama 36702-0386
(205) 872-8486
(800) 633-2575

Custom Craft Golf Corporation
2725 West Prindiville Street
Chicago, Illinois 60647
(312) 772-1142

Custom Golf Clubs, Inc.
10206 North Interregional Highway
Austin, Texas 78753
(512) 837-8810
(800) 531-5025; in Texas, (800) 252-
8108

Daiwa Golf Company
7421 Chapman Avenue
Garden Grove, California 92641
(714) 895-6689
(800) 824-8981; in California, (800)
826-8081

Delta Golf Company
4410 North Ravenswood Avenue
Chicago, Illinois 60640
(312) 275-7220

Diamondhead Golf Company
11351 Trade Center Drive
Rancho Cordova, California 95670
(916) 638-7220

Dunlop Slazenger Corporation
P.O. Box 3070
Greenville, South Carolina 29602
(803) 271-9767
(800) 845-8875

Dynacraft Golf Products, Inc.
71 Maholm Street
Newark, Ohio 43055
(614) 344-1191
(800) 321-4833; in Ohio, (800) 423-
2968

Dynapro
400 Skokie Road, Suite 5901
Northbrook, Illinois 60062
(312) 480-0063

Falcon Golf, Inc.
24000 Woodward Avenue
Pleasant Ridge, Michigan 48069
(313) 547-4800
(800) 546-3252

Foxbat Precision Golf Equipment
15105 Surveyor Boulevard
Dallas, Texas 75244
(214) 239-5200

Gator Sports
3565 South West Temple, Number 5
Salt Lake City, Utah 84115
(801) 261-3729

Golf Clubs Ltd. (Logistics)
P.O. Box 2606
Canoga Park, California 91306
(818) 700-0493

Golf Design and Manufacturing, Inc.
10865 Portal Drive
Los Alamitos, California 90720
(213) 430-3586 or (714) 995-3612
(800) 854-6148

The Golf Works
Ralph Maltby Enterprises, Inc.
4820 Jacksontown Road
P.O. Box 3008
Newark, Ohio 43055
(614) 323-4193
(800) 848-8358; in Ohio, (800) 762-
   1831

The John Rouzee Green Company, Inc.
P.O. Box 379
York, South Carolina 29745
(803) 684-6853

Hubby Habjan
P.O. Box 442
Lake Forest, Illinois 60045
(312) 234-8225

Harris International Inc. (Nomad International)
9999 North East Glisan Street
P.O. Box 20729
Portland, Oregon 97220
(503) 256-2302
(800) 547-2880
Catalog: $1 postage/handling

Heritage Golf Company
145 Burt Road
Lexington, Kentucky 40503
(606) 277-0005

Hillerich & Bradsby Company, Inc.
   (PowerBilt)
P.O. Box 35700
Louisville, Kentucky 40232-5700
(502) 585-5226
(800) 282-2287

Hireko, Inc.
220 Mason Way
City of Industry, California 91746
(818) 330-5525
(800) 367-8912

Ben Hogan Company
2912 West Pafford Street
P.O. Box 11276
Fort Worth, Texas 76109
(817) 921-2661
(800) 631-9000; in Texas, (800) 772-
   2307

Inpro Companies, Inc. (Optima)
3407 78th Avenue West
P.O. Box 940
Rock Island, Illinois 61204-0940
(309) 787-4971
(800) 447-0524

International Golf Manufacturing
P.O. Box 9463
Fountain Valley, California 92728
(714) 731-1646

Marty Irving Custom Club Company
3885 Miller Trunk Highway
Duluth, Minnesota 55811
(218) 729-6925
(800) 223-2774, ext. 173

Karsten Manufacturing Corporation
   (Ping)
2201 West Desert Cove
P.O. Box 9990
Phoenix, Arizona 85068
(602) 277-1300

Kentucky Golf Classics, Inc. (Middleground)
P.O. Box 1646
Garden City, Kansas 67846-1646
(316) 275-0557

King Bilt Golf Company
5430 Greenwood Road
Shreveport, Louisiana 71109
(318) 636-2447
(800) 524-5464

Las Vegas Discount Golf & Tennis (St. Andrews)
5325 South Valley View Boulevard, Suite 10
Las Vegas, Nevada 89118
(702) 798-5500
(800) 634-6743

Lion of California
68929 Perez Road
Cathedral City, California 92234
(619) 324-3217

Louisville Golf Club Company
2601 Grassland Drive
Louisville, Kentucky 40299
(502) 491-1631
(800) 626-6379

Lynx Golf Inc.
16017 East Valley Boulevard
P.O. Box 1611
City of Industry, California 91749-1611
(818) 961-0222
(800) 233-5969, ext. 251

MacGregor Golf Company
1601 South Slappey Boulevard
Albany, Georgia 31708
(912) 888-0001
(800) 841-4358
Catalog: $10

Mario's Golf Shop
511 North Eureka Street
P.O. Box 253
Redlands, California 92373
(714) 798-3548

Matzie Golf Company, Inc.
112 Penn Street
El Segundo, California 90245
(213) 322-1301
(800) 722-7125

Merit Golf Company
P.O. Box 622
Kennesaw, Georgia 30144
(404) 499-1415
(800) 828-1445

Mitsushiba International, Inc.
4055 East La Palma Avenue, Unit C
Anaheim, California 92807
(714) 630-4138
(800) 722-4061

Mizuno Golf Company
5125 Peachtree Industrial Boulevard
Norcross, Georgia 30092
(404) 441-5553
(800) 554-5694

Nassau Investment Casting Company
99 Russell Place
Freeport, New York 11520
(516) 867-8018

Nine Eagles Golf Company, Inc.
1030 North Batavia Street #A
Orange, California 92667
(714) 538-5810

Northwestern Golf Company
4701 North Ravenswood Avenue
Chicago, Illinois 60640
(312) 275-0500
(800) 621-5156

Novadyne Golf Equipment
749 Green Valley Road
Watsonville, California 95076
(408) 724-9324

Ofer Custom Golf Clubs
2559 Blake Avenue, N.W.
Canton, Ohio 44718
(216) 456-5357

Oregon Golf Works
7410 S.W. Macadam Avenue
Portland, Oregon 97219
(503) 244-8143
(800) 262-8143

Orizaba Golf Products, Inc.
5839 Mission Gorge Road, Suite A
San Diego, California 92120
(619) 584-4458
(800) 325-1634; in California, (800)
    533-9969

Orlimar Golf Company
25673 Nickel Place
Hayward, California 94545-3221
(415) 783-1883

Pal Joey Golf Company, Inc.
99 South Pine Street
Newark, Ohio 43055
(614) 344-2390
(800) 358-9881

Palm Springs Golf Company
74-824 Lennon Street
Palm Desert, California 92260
(619) 341-3220
(800) 821-9735

Par Ace Company, Inc.
12033 East Independence Boulevard,
    Suite 11-B
Matthews, North Carolina 28105
(800) 438-6082

Paragon Sports
4055 East La Palma Avenue, Unit C
Anaheim, California 92807
(714) 630-4138
(800) 443-9120; in California, (800)
    521-0890

Pedersen Custom Golf Clubs, Inc.
312 Howard Avenue
Bridgeport, Connecticut 06602
(203) 367-1155 or 367-1264

The Penna Golf Company, Inc.
400 Toney Penna Drive
Jupiter, Florida 33458
(305) 746-5146

Perflex International, Inc.
50 South 800 West
Salt Lake City, Utah 84104
(801) 595-6900, ext. 125

Joe Phillips Golf
479 Willis Avenue
Williston Park, New York 11596
(516) 741-7867

Pinseeker Golf Corporation
3502 South Susan Street
Santa Ana, California 92704
(714) 979-4500 or (213) 582-7650
(800) 824-4656

Players Golf
P.O. Box 1516
Rancho Santa Fe, California 92067
(619) 756-0360
(800) 922-7529

Positive Putter Company, Inc.
5532 North High School Road
Indianapolis, Indiana 46254
(317) 632-3759

Joe Powell Golf, Inc.
3909 Clark Road
Sarasota, Florida 33583
(813) 921-6257
(800) 237-4660

PRGR U.S.A.
2539 West 237th Street, Suite D
Torrance, California 90505
(213) 534-3700
(800) 333-7747

Prima
5380 South Valley View Boulevard
Las Vegas, Nevada 89118
(702) 736-8801
(800) 932-1622

Pro-Action Golf Company
3123 North Pulaski Road
Chicago, Illinois 60641
(312) 736-5000
(800) 642-5868

ProGroup, Inc.
6201 Mountain View Road
Ooltewah, Tennessee 37363
(615) 238-5890
(800) 251-6300

Pro-Swing
P.O. Box 6225
Akron, Ohio 44312
(216) 644-2599

Pure Golf
1452 East Katella Avenue
Anaheim, California 92805
(714) 634-1348

Rainbow Sports
22500 South Vermont Avenue
Torrance, California 90502-2553
(213) 328-8418

Ram Golf Corporation
2020 Indian Boundary Drive
Melrose Park, Illinois 60160
(312) 681-5800
(800) 833-4653

Reflex, Inc.
10304 N. Hayden Road, Suite 4
Scottsdale, Arizona 85258
(602) 951-1721
(800) 232-2711; in California, (800)
    654-8368

John Riley Golf Company
585 Cannery Row
Monterey, California 93940
(408) 373-8855
(800) 538-9505

Royal Scottish Clubmakers, Ltd.
3435 St. Mary's Road
Lafayette, California 94549
(800) 235-6646, ext. 274; in California,
    (800) 235-6647, ext. 274

Ryobi-Toski Corporation
160 Essex Street
P.O. Box 576
Newark, Ohio 43055
(614) 345-9683
(800) 848-2075; in Ohio, (800) 824-
    6691

Sasse Golf, Inc.
2101 Sandhills Boulevard
Southern Pines, North Carolina
    28387
(919) 692-2205
(800) 334-3451

Scottsdale Golf Corporation
6938 Fifth Avenue
Scottsdale, Arizona 85251
(602) 994-5093

Sea Island Custom Clubs
P.O. Box 423
Retreat Avenue
St. Simons Island, Georgia 31522
(912) 638-3611

Shamrock Golf
17622 Armstrong Avenue
Irvine, California 92714
(714) 250-0873

Shapton International Corporation
39 Winding Hill Drive
Hockessin, Delaware 19707
(302) 239-0599

Shear-Line Putters
Division of Kiser Corporation
P.O. Box 908
Muncie, Indiana 47305-0908
(317) 284-8525
(800) 222-8545

Sidekick Golf
1940 East Camelback Road, Suite
    101
Phoenix, Arizona 85016
(602) 277-6630
(800) 528-1174

Slazenger
David Geoffrey & Associates
P.O. Box 7259
Brandon Mill Complex #202
25 Draper Street
Greenville, South Carolina 29610
(803) 295-4444
(800) 843-1027

Slotline Golf
5252 McFadden Avenue
Huntington Beach, California 92649
(714) 898-2888
(800) 854-8169

J.C. Smith, Inc.
P.O. Box 4588
Palm Desert, California 92261
(619) 568-2422
(800) 828-4653

Kenneth Smith Golf Clubs
1801 Baltimore
Kansas City, Missouri 64108
(816) 221-6644

Sounder International, Inc.
Milford Industrial Park
107 Research Drive
Milford, Connecticut 06460
(203) 877-8737
(800) 243-9234

Spalding Sports Worldwide
425 Meadow Street
P.O. Box 901
Chicopee, Massachusetts 01021-0901
(413) 536-1200

Square Two Golf
18 Gloria Lane
Fairfield, New Jersey 07006
(201) 227-7783
(800) 526-2250

Arthur Swanson Golf Clubs
9501 West Devon Avenue
Rosemont, Illinois 60018
(312) 696-2088

Taurus Golf Ltd.
998 South Robertson Boulevard
Los Angeles, California 90035
(213) 659-8383
(800) 222-6703

Taylor Made Golf Company, Inc.
2440 Impala Drive
Carlsbad, California 92008
(619) 931-1991
(800) 325-7579; in California, (800)
   772-6464

Tech 21 Golf Company
5757 Westheimer, Suite 3-200
Houston, Texas 77057
(713) 789-1800
(800) 827-7888

Tech-Line
3975 South Highway 89
Star Route, Box 9
Jackson, Wyoming 83001
(307) 733-4952
(800) 451-8858

Stan Thompson Golf Club Company
2707 South Fairfax Avenue
Culver City, California 90230
(213) 870-7228
(800) 421-3126

Tiger Shark Golf
Building 60— Sabovich Street
Mojave, California 93501
(805) 824-4551
(800) 654-9892; in California, (800)
   533-6294

Titleist Golf Division
Acushnet Company
P.O. Box B965
New Bedford, Massachusetts 02741
(508) 997-2811
(800) 225-8500

Tour Fit Golf Products
5008 West Linebaugh Avenue, Suite 46
Tampa, Florida 33624
(813) 962-8863
(800) 999-7888

Triumph Golf Company
7617 Narcoossee Road
Orlando, Florida 32822
(407) 277-4300

USTech, Inc. (Heritage Classics)
17720 North East 65th Street
Redmond, Washington 98052-4903
(206) 881-8989

Weatherford
P.O. Box 5231
Reno, Nevada 89513
(702) 747-1914
(800) 752-9464

John Wheatley Clubmaker
1073 Farmington Avenue
Farmington, Connecticut 06032
(203) 674-9384

Wilson Sporting Goods Company
2233 West Street
River Grove, Illinois 60171
(312) 456-6100

World Class Products Limited
Confidence Sports Division
220 Queen S.W.
Albany, Oregon 97321
(503) 928-5700
(800) 421-1833

Wright Weight Corporation
67 Laurel Lane
Ludlow, Massachusetts 01056
(413) 583-4640

Yamaha Golf
6600 Orangethorpe Avenue
P.O. Box 6600
Buena Park, California 90620
(714) 522-9011
(800) 854-3849; in California, (800)
   824-4866

Yonex Corporation
350 Maple Avenue
Torrance, California 90503-2603
(213) 553-6014
(800) 992-6639; in California, (800)
   772-5522

CARS AND CARTS

Bag Boy, Inc.
5675 International Way
Milwaukie, Oregon 97222
(800) 426-2697

Bridgeport Industries, Inc.
1623 Broadway Street, P.O. Box 159
Superior, Wisconsin 54880
(715) 392-9700
(800) 223-2774, ext. 700

Cadd'x of North America Corporation
50 Chestnut Ridge Road
Montvale, New Jersey 07645
(201) 930-8808
(800) 223-0919

Columbia PARCAR Corporation
One Golf Car Road
Deerfield, Wisconsin 53531
(608) 764-5474
(800) 222-4653

E-Z-GO Division of Textron Inc.
P.O. Box 388
Augusta, Georgia 30913-2699
(404) 798-4311

Geo-Sport
536 Main Street, P.O. Box 499
Allenton, Wisconsin 53002
(414) 629-5506
(800) 558-1005

Gettig Technologies, Inc.
One Streamside Place
Spring Mills, Pennsylvania 16875
(814) 422-8892

Go-Fer Products, Inc.
337 Airport-Pulling Road North
Naples, Florida 33942
(813) 643-1844

Harris International Inc. (Nomad International)
9999 North East Glisan Street
P.O. Box 20729
Portland, Oregon 97220
(503) 256-2302
(800) 547-2880
Catalog: $1 postage/handling

Kangaroo Products Company
108 Mill Spring Road
P.O. Box 607
Columbus, North Carolina 28722
(704) 894-8241

Lo Pro Industries
P.O. Box 244
Novi, Michigan 48050
(313) 626-7362

Melex USA, Inc.
1221 Front Street
Raleigh, North Carolina 27609
(919) 828-7645

PowaKaddy International Ltd.
965 Central Avenue
St. Petersburg, Florida 33705
(813) 894-5036

U.S. Indoor Golf (Caddymatic Electric Golf Trolley)
220 Bush Street, Suite 660
San Francisco, California 94104
(415) 781-7430

GRIPS

Avon Illinois Inc.
395 Kent Avenue
Elk Grove Village, Illinois 60007
(312) 439-2190

Consolidated Service Group, Inc.
5032 North Royal Atlanta Drive
Tucker, Georgia 30084
(404) 938-1900
(800) 438-1900

Golf Pride
P.O. Box 1848
Laurinburg, North Carolina 28352
(919) 276-6901

Harmony Golf
1036 Irvine Boulevard
Tustin, California 92680
(714) 838-9371

R. Neumann & Company
300 Observer Highway
P.O. Box MD
Hoboken, New Jersey 07030
(201) 659-3400
(800) 372-4141

Tacki-Mac Grips, Inc.
21500 Osborne Street
Canoga Park, California 91304
(714) 944-9681
(800) 423-2549

SHOES

Bostonian Golf Shoes
520 South Broad Street
Kennett Square, Pennsylvania 19348
(215) 444-6550
(800) 426-3708

Dexter Shoe Company
1230 Washington Street
West Newton, Massachusetts 02165
(617) 332-4300

Etonic Inc.
147 Centre Street
Brockton, Massachusetts 02403
(617) 583-9100

Foot-Joy, Inc.
144 Field Street
Brockton, Massachusetts 02403
(508) 586-2233

Harris International Inc. (Nomad International)
9999 North East Glisan Street
P.O. Box 20729
Portland, Oregon 97220
(503) 256-2302
(800) 547-2880
Catalog: $1 postage/handling

Johnston & Murphy
Genesco Park
Nashville, Tennessee 37202
(615) 367-8101
(800) 826-2690; in Tennessee, (800) 342-5705, ext. 9102

Lazy-Bones
Carnation Drive, P.O. Box 331
Aurora, Missouri 65605
(417) 678-2181

Nike, Inc.
9000 S.W. Nimbus
Beaverton, Oregon 97005
(503) 644-9000

Reebok International, Ltd.
150 Royall Street
Canton, Massachusetts 02021
(617) 821-2800
(800) 843-4444

Signature Tour Quality Footwear
1100 East Main Street
Endicott, New York 13760
(607) 757-4004
(800) 321-2111

SHAFTS

Aldila
15822 Bernardo Center Drive
San Diego, California 92127
(619) 592-0404
(800) 854-2786

Apollo Golf Inc.
85 Kelly Street
Elk Grove Village, Illinois 60007
(312) 956-0330

Kerband, Inc.
1940 East Camelback Road, Suite 101
Phoenix, Arizona 85016
(602) 277-6630
(800) 528-1174

Kunnan Sports Technology
9590 Candida Street
San Diego, California 92126
(619) 566-9200
(800) 874-7206

Paragon Sports
4055 East La Palma Avenue, Unit C
Anaheim, California 92807
(714) 630-4138
(800) 443-9120; in California, (800) 521-0890

Sandvik Special Metals Corporation
P.O. Box 6027
Kennewick, Washington 99336
(509) 586-4131
(800) 874-2387

True Temper Sports Division
Emhart Consumer Group
871 Ridgeway Loop Road, Suite 201
Memphis, Tennessee 38119
(901) 767-9411

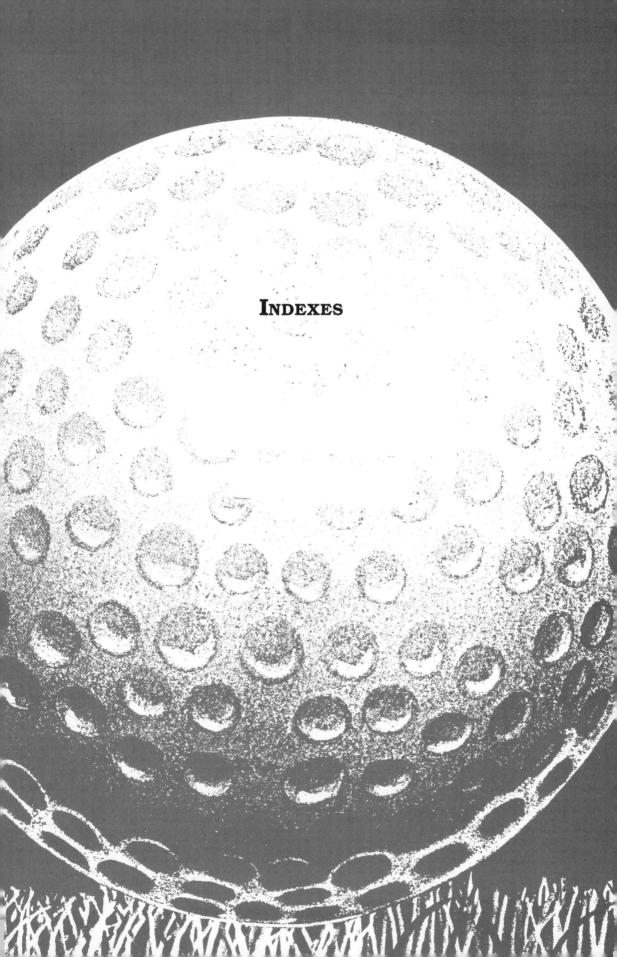

INDEXES

INDEX TO SOURCES

A2Z/The Best of Everything
Miami Somers Building
505 New Road
Somers Point, New Jersey 08244
(609) 645-5577
(800) 445-9618
    The Reel Putter, 57
    Bob Hope Golfer, 114
    Pro Golf, 121
    Executive Golf Tool, 141
    Solar-Powered Ventilated Golf Cap,
      196
    Caddy Card, 203

Abercrombie & Fitch At Home, Inc.
P.O. Box 70858
Houston, Texas 77270-9990
(800) 777-3330
    The Duke and The Duchess Putters,
      63
    The Golf Game Par Excellence, 108
    Mini Golf, 117
    Carpet Coasters, 141
    Golf Glasses, 142
    Difficult Shots Made Easy with Hale
      Irwin, 165
    Golf with Al Geiberger, 168
    Golf with Patty Sheehan, 168
    How I Play Golf with Bobby Jones,
      176
    Power Driving with Mike Dunaway,
      186
    Precision Putting with Dave Stockton,
      186
    Golf Ball Monogrammer, 208

Access Software, Inc.
545 West 550 South, Suite 130
Bountiful, Utah 84010
(801) 298-9077
    World Class Leader Board, 126

Acorn Sports, Inc.
5816 Shakespeare Road
P.O. Box 5977
Columbia, South Carolina 29250
(803) 735-0733
(800) 633-2252, ext. 4250
    The Art of Putting with Ben Crenshaw,
      162
    Automatic Golf with Bob Mann, 162
    The Jimmy Ballard Golf Connection,
      163
    Better Golf Now! with Ken Venturi,
      164
    Difficult Shots Made Easy with Hale
      Irwin, 165
    Feel Your Way to Better Golf with
      Wally Armstrong, 166
    Golden Greats of Golf, 167
    The Golden Tee, 167
    Golf with Al Geiberger, 168
    Golf with Patty Sheehan, 168
    *The Golf Digest Schools Learning
      Library*, 169
    Golf for Winners with Hank Haney
      and Mark O'Meara, 171
    Golf the Miller Way with Johnny
      Miller, 173
    Golf My Way with Jack Nicklaus, 174
    The Golf Swing with Tom Weiskopf,
      174
    Golf—The Winner's Edge with Kermit
      Zarley, 174
    The Greater Golfer in You with Dr.
      Gary Wiren, 174
    How To Golf with Jan Stephenson,
      178
    *An Inside Look at the Game for a
      Lifetime* with Bob Toski, Jim Flick,
      Peter Kostis, and John Elliott, 181
    *The John Jacobs Series—The Full
      Swing, The Short Game, and Faults
      and Cures*, 181
    1986 Masters Tournament, 184
    One Move to Better Golf, 185
    Play Your Best Golf—Volumes 1 and
      2, 185
    Power Driving with Mike Dunaway,
      186

Precision Putting with Dave Stockton, 186

Bob Toski Teaches You Golf, 189

Activision, Inc.
3885 Bohannon Drive
Menlo Park, California 94025
(415) 329-0500
   Championship Golf— The Great
   Courses of the World (Volume One:
   Pebble Beach), 105

Adams Golf
17 East Windmill Circle
Abilene, Texas 79605
(915) 695-2010
(800) 622-0609
   Dave Pelz Putting Track, 50
   Dave Pelz Teacher Putter, 50

Advanced Concepts International
3 Golf Center, Suite 285
Hoffman Estates, Illinois 60195
(312) 882-3695
   Concept G Precision Golf Ball Gauge,
   197

Alexander Associates
251 West 97 Street
New York, New York 10025
(212) 662-4362
   "Ginger Beer Hole" Print, 151

APBA Game Company, Inc.
1001 Millersville Road
P.O. Box 4547
Lancaster, Pennsylvania 17604-4547
(717) 394-6161
   APBA Professional Golf Game, 104

Ardent Video Publishing, Inc.
P.O. Box 41854
Memphis, Tennessee 38174-1854
(800) 453-7600; in Canada, (800) 543-
   1006
   Jack Grout Tee Square, 34

Keys to Consistency with Jack Grout,
182

Tommy Armour Golf Company
8350 North Lehigh Avenue
Morton Grove, Illinois 60053
(312) 966-6300
(800) 742-4653; in Illinois, (800) 742-
   4244
   Silver Scot Collector Putter, 77

Austad's
4500 East 10th Street
P.O. Box 1428
Sioux Falls, South Dakota 57196-1428
(605) 336-3135
(800) 759-4653
   ASSIST, 9
   Head Up Preventer, 15
   Impact Bag, 16
   Mitsubishi Golf Trainers, 17
   Power Trainer, 21
   Pro-Tater, 21
   The Spiro Swinger, 22
   Swing Groover, 24
   Swing Memory, 24
   TruSwing, 30
   Shotmaker Golf Glove, 32
   Training Grip, 32
   Force II Putter Grip, 45
   The 19th Hole Putting Green, 49
   The 19th Hole Ultimate Electric
      Putting Cup, 49
   The Reel Putter, 57
   Tiger Shark P-Squared Putter Grip,
      58
   The Duke and The Duchess Putters,
      63
   Power Pod, 68
   Dishner Concept Putter, 71
   TourHawk Putter, 74
   Ray Cook Original M-1 Putter, 77
   Chip-N-Pitch Net, 82
   The Clikka Bag, 84
   Gull-Wing Practice Net, 84
   "Perfect Stroke" Golf Practice Net, 87
   Tee Wizz, 90
   GolfGym, 96
   The Marcy Wedge, 97
   Warm-Up Practice Weight, 101

Bob Hope Golfer, 114
"In Pursuit of Par"— Par 72 Edition,
    114
Mini-Putt, 117
Pro Golf, 121
Cloud-Flite Trick Golf Ball, 130
Laid Back Golfer's Association, 133
Putter Power, 134
Slice Repellent, 136
Off-the-Wall Golf-Ball Alarm Clock,
    146
The Jimmy Ballard Golf Connection,
    163
Golf with Patty Sheehan, 168
Golf My Way with Jack Nicklaus, 174
How To Golf with Jan Stephenson,
    178
Play Your Best Golf— Six Lessons, 186
Golf Rubbers, 192
Joe Pro Golf Cap, 192
Birdie Ball Washer, 197
Check Go, 197
Floater Golf Balls, 198
Nitelite Golf Ball, 201
Renegade 410 Golf Balls, 201
Enforcer Grips, 202
Caddy Card, 203
Zippo Greens Keeper, 207
The Name Dropper, 208
Stay-n-Play, 209
Deluxe Vinyl Iron Covers, 212
Golf Glove Dryer, 214
Grip Life, 214
Spike Caddy, 217
Golf Quote Glasses, 222
Golf Buoy, 227
PROTECH Golf Bag, 229
Redi Club, 230

Ban Products, Inc.
1156 Berwick Lane
South Euclid, Ohio 44121
(216) 381-6189
    Putt-Caster, 55, 89

Banff Golf Company
Nemacolin Woodlands
Farmington, Pennsylvania 15437
(412) 329-6200
    The Jimmy Ballard Swing Connector,
    9

Flying Elbows, 11
Graph-Check Sequence Camera, 14
The Stable Flexor, 24
Swing Memory, 24
Ball Flight Visualizer, 33
Pro-Align, 35
The Bunkerboard, 39
The Kostis Krutch, 40
The Separator, 41
Puttband-Swingband, 54
The Window-Wedge, 76
The Distance Builder, 95

Barber-Goldentouch Golf, Inc.
P.O. Box 1687
San Marcos, California 92069-1687
(619) 471-8950
(800) 423-2220
    Jerry Barber Practice Swing Driver,
    94

Paul Bertholy
P.O. Box 408
Foxfire Village, North Carolina 27281
(919) 281-3093
    The Bertholy Swing Pipe, 9

B L & S Enterprises
P.O. Box 27538
San Diego, California 92128
(619) 487-9981
    PAR 5 Golf Handicap and Statistics
    System, 118

B.N. Genius
22121 Crystal Creek Boulevard S.E.
Bothell, Washington 98021
(206) 483-6000
(800) 468-4410
    Pro Golf, 121

Bricker Enterprises
P.O. Box 344
Novelty, Ohio 44072
(216) 338-1448
    Flex-Tips, 226

Brooks Brothers
350 Campus Plaza
P.O. Box 4016
Edison, New Jersey 08818-4016
(201) 225-4870
(800) 274-1815
    Ballpoint Pen With Golf-Club Clip,
      140

Mike Calbot Golf Studio
9701 Foxglove Circle
Fort Myers, Florida 33907
(813) 481-8734
    Learning Golf with Mike Calbot, 183

The Cat's Pyjamas
20 Church Street
Montclair, New Jersey 07042
(201) 667-5938
(800) 228-7757
    Wacky Golf Cap, 137

Competitive Edge Golf
51 West 14th Street, Suite 3F
New York, New York 10011
(212) 206-0760
(800) 255-9141
    Shotmaker Golf Glove, 32
    Putt Master Putting Carpet, 55
    Tru-Stroke Putting Guide, 59
    The Bomber, 62
    The Giant Niblick, 64
    Hero Driver, 64
    Mercury-Loaded Driver, 66
    Perflex Driver, 68
    Shurfire Alma Mater Putters, 70
    Slim Jim Putter, 72
    Super Stick Adjustable Golf Club, 72
    Triple Crown Wedge, 74
    The Clikka Bag, 84
    Practice Golf Range, 88
    GolfGym, 96
    Power Tone Exerciser, 99
    "In Pursuit of Par"— TPC at Sawgrass
      Edition, 115
    Pro Golf, 121
    The Golfaholics Anonymous Official
      Driving Kit, 131
    Pure Silk Golf Ties, 148

Putter Tie Clip, 148
The Art of Putting with Ben Crenshaw,
   162
Automatic Golf with Bob Mann, 162
The Jimmy Ballard Golf Connection,
   163
Better Golf Now with Ken Venturi,
   164
Feel Your Way to Better Golf with
   Wally Armstrong, 166
Golden Greats of Golf, 167
The Golden Tee, 167
Golf with Al Geiberger, 168
Golf with Patty Sheehan, 168
*The Golf Digest Schools Learning
   Library*, 169
Golf Lessons with Sam Snead, 172
Golf Like a Pro with Billy Casper, 172
Golf the Miller Way with Johnny
   Miller, 173
Golf My Way with Jack Nicklaus, 174
How To Golf with Jan Stephenson,
   178
*The John Jacobs Series— The Full
   Swing, The Short Game*, and *Faults
   and Cures*, 181
Play Great Golf with Arnold Palmer—
   Mastering the Fundamentals and
   Course Strategy, 185
The Short Way to Lower Scoring with
   Paul Runyan— *Volume I: Putting
   and Chipping; Volume II: Pitching
   and Sand Play*, 187
*So You Stand on the Wrong Side of the
   Ball, Too!* with Jay Edgar, 188
Bob Toski Teaches You Golf, 189
Golfaholics Anonymous Official
   Sweatshirt, 192
TopTan Shirts, 196
Executive Golf Ball Holder, 198
Nitelite Golf Ball, 201
Renegade 410 Golf Balls, 201
Enforcer Grips, 202
Tourna Grip, 202
Caddy Card, 203
Links to the Past, 204
The Shrivot, 207
Golf Links, 208
The Name Dropper, 208
Stay-n-Play, 209
Spike Caddy, 217
Golf Party Pak, 222
RagTail Golf Towel, 223

Consolidated Service Group, Inc.
5032 North Royal Atlanta Drive
Tucker, Georgia 30084
(404) 938-1900
(800) 438-1900
Blue Finger, 31
Tourna Grip, 202

J.M. Cooper
1110 Oklahoma Street
Kannapolis, North Carolina 28081
(704) 782-2493
A.G. Spalding & Bros.— Pre-1930 Clubs, Trademarks,and Collectibles, 158

Correct Swing
P.O. Box 16028
Phoenix, Arizona 85011
(602) 279-3631
(800) 447-9464
Correct Swing, 10

Creative Designed Products
69 Carla Way
P.O. Box 10
Broomfield, Colorado 80020-0010
(303) 469-9383
The Smitty, 207

Creative Specialties of South Dakota
P.O. Box Par 72
Wall, South Dakota 57790
(605) 279-2961
Shake-a-Round, 123

Critics' Choice Video, Inc.
800 Morse Avenue
Elk Grove Village, Illinois 60007
(800) 367-7765
The Art of Putting with Ben Crenshaw, 162
Automatic Golf with Bob Mann, 162
Better Golf Now! with Ken Venturi, 164
Feel Your Way to Better Golf with Wally Armstrong, 166
Golf for Kids of All Ages with Wally Armstrong, 171
Golf Like a Pro with Billy Casper, 172
Golf My Way with Jack Nicklaus, 174
How To Golf with Jan Stephenson, 178
One Move to Better Golf with Carl Lohren, 185

Crossroads International
11625 South Mayfield Avenue
Worth, Illinois 60482
(312) 388-3072
Business-Card Golfer in a Bottle, 140

Richard E. Donovan Enterprises
P.O. Box 7070
1904 East Main Street
Endicott, New York 13760
(607) 785-5874
Jack Grout Tee Square, 34
The Golf Club Identification and Price Guide, 155
The Art of Putting with Ben Crenshaw, 162
The Jimmy Ballard Golf Connection, 163
Better Golf Now! with Ken Venturi, 164
Challenge Golf with Peter Longo, 164
Difficult Shots Made Easy with Hale Irwin, 165
Exercises for Better Golf, 166
Feel Your Way to Better Golf with Wally Armstrong, 166
Golden Greats of Golf, 167
The Golden Tee, 167
Golf with Al Geiberger, 168
Golf with Patty Sheehan, 168
Golf Club Repair— The Knowledge & Bench Skills with Tom Wishon and Mark Wilson, 169
The Golf Digest Schools Learning Library, 169
Golf for Kids of All Ages with Wally Armstrong, 171
Golf for Winners with Hank Haney and Mark O'Meara, 171

Golf Lessons with Sam Snead, 172
Golf Like a Pro with Billy Casper, 172
Golf the Miller Way with Johnny
   Miller, 173
Golf My Way with Jack Nicklaus, 174
The Golf Swing with Tom Weiskopf,
   174
Golf—The Winner's Edge with Kermit
   Zarley, 175
Golf's Greats Quick Tips— Volumes I
   and II, 175
The Greater Golfer in You with Dr.
   Gary Wiren, 175
How I Play Golf with Bobby Jones,
   176
How To Golf with Jan Stephenson,
   178
*How To Play Your Best Golf All the
   Time* with Tommy Armour, 179
*An Inside Look at the Game for a
   Lifetime* with Bob Toski, Jim Flick,
   Peter Kostis, and John Elliott, 181
*The John Jacobs Series—The Full
   Swing, The Short Game*, and *Faults
   and Cures*, 181
Junior Golf "The Easy Way" with
   Mark Steinbauer, 182
Keys to Consistency with Jack Grout,
   182
Keys to Great Golf! with JoAnne
   Carner, 183
*The Master System to Better Golf:
   Volume 1* with Craig Stadler, Davis
   Love III, Tom Purtzer, and Gary
   Koch, 183
1986 Masters Tournament, 184
One Move to Better Golf with Carl
   Lohren, 185
Play Great Golf with Arnold Palmer—
   Mastering the Fundamentals and
   Course Strategy, 185
Play Your Best Golf— Volumes 1 and
   2, 185
Power Driving with Mike Dunaway,
   186
Precision Putting with Dave Stockton,
   186
The Short Way to Lower Scoring with
   Paul Runyan— *Volume I: Putting
   and Chipping; Volume II: Pitching
   and Sand Play*, 187
*So You Stand on the Wrong Side of the
   Ball, Too!* with Jay Edgar, 188
Bob Toski Teaches You Golf, 189
Total Golf with Bruce Crampton, 189

The Duck Press
144 Avenida Serra
San Clemente, California 92672
(714) 498-3859
(800) 233-2730
   Cloud-Flite Trick Golf Ball, 130
   Putter Power, 134
   Slice Repellent, 136
   Streamin' Mimi Joke Golf Ball, 136
   Wacky Tees, 137
   Flagpin "Great American Golf Holes"
      Playing Cards, 142
   "The Golfer" Barbecue Apron and Hot
      Mitt, 193
   Mighty Midget Golf Ball Washer, 197
   The Dream Tee, 218
   Rev-Tee, 219
   Golf Ball "Ice Cubes," 221
   Caddi-Sak, 225
   Put'r There/The Putter Caddy, 229
   Travels with a Golf Tour Gourmet, 232

Dynacomp, Inc.
178 Phillips Road
Webster, New York 14580
(716) 265-4040
(800) 828-6772
   Golf Handicapper, 109
   Professional-Class Golf, 122

"18 Tips"
P.O. Box 2459
Secaucus, New Jersey 07094
(800) 321-5700
   18 Tips from 18 Legends of Golf, 165

Electronic Arts
1820 Gateway Drive
San Mateo, California 94404
(415) 571-7171
   World Tour Golf, 127

Enticements
P.O. Box 7070
Mount Vernon, New York 10551-7070
(914) 668-4842
(800) 243-4300
    Putt Wizz, 56
    Tee Wizz, 90
    PLA-GOLF Miniature Golf Game, 119
    Pro Golf, 121
    Wastepaper Golfer, 125
    Wacky Golf Cap, 137
    Golf Tee Tie Rack, 143
    Golfaholics Anonymous Official
      Sweatshirt, 192
    Bogey Ice Bucket, 221
    Golf Party-Pak, 222
    Cad-Eze, 225

Everything for Golf
3543 West Braddock Road
Alexandria, Virginia 22302
(703) 671-0202
    Groove-E-Swing Trainer, 14
    Wrist-Magic, 30
    The Slicebuster, 36
    Swing-R Sway Control, 37
    Golf Putt Stroke Guide, 45
    NoRamp, 49
    The 19th Hole Chip & Putt, 86
    The Golferciser, 96
    The Bent One, 130
    Fisherman's Par-Tee Pak, 131
    Jumbo Golf Tees, 133
    McSpike, 215

Exec-U-Putt, Inc.
P.O. Box 124
Northfield, New Jersey 08225
(609) 786-1588
    The Reel Putter, 57

Falk's
539 Glenrose Lane
Cincinnati, Ohio 45244
(513) 528-5858
(800) 543-3255
    Nerf Indoor Golf, 118
    Golf Quotes, 143
    Links 18GX Advanced Golf Score-
      card, 204

Florida Golf Warehouse, Inc.
4085 L.B. McLeod, Suite D
Orlando, Florida 32811
(305) 423-5343
(800) 346-6574
    Training Grip, 32
    Golfsmith XL Design Putter Grip, 46
    The Track, 59
    Classic Golf Clubs: A Pictorial Guide,
      155
    The Art of Putting with Ben Crenshaw,
      162
    Automatic Golf with Bob Mann, 162
    The Jimmy Ballard Golf Connection,
      163
    Nitelite Golf Ball, 201
    Lacquer-Stiks, 214
    Ping Weight Balance Scale, 217

Roberta Fortune's Almanac
150 Chestnut Street
San Francisco, California 94111-1004
(800) 321-2232 [customer service]
(800) 331-2300 [orders]
    Seiko Golf Scorecard, 205

Garrett Hypnosis Clinic
7151 West Berwyn
Chicago, Illinois 60656
(312) 775-6100
    Improve Your Golf Game with Larry
      Garrett, 180

Gator Golf Enterprises, Inc.
P.O. Box 1911
Maitland, Florida 32751
(407) 699-0688
    Feel Your Way to Better Golf with
      Wally Armstrong, 166
    Golf for Kids of All Ages with Wally
      Armstrong, 171

GOAL! Incorporated
P.O. Box 678
Niantic, Connecticut 06357
(203) 739-4467
Practice Golf Cage, 87

Godiva Chocolatier, Inc.
260 Madison Avenue
New York, New York 10016
(212) 951-2888
Godiva Golf Balls, 142

Golf Arts & Imports
Dolores near 6th
P.O. Box 5217
Carmel, California 93921
(408) 625-4488
"Famous British Golf Clubs" Place-
mats and Coasters, 141
Terence Legg Golf Sign, 153

Golf Day Products, Inc.
3015 Commercial Avenue
Northbrook, Illinois 60062
(312) 398-1400
(800) 433-4653
Hit & Tell Decals, 15
Swingthing, 27
Shotmaker Golf Glove, 32
Training Grip, 32
Chalk It, 33
Pro-Align, 35
Swing-Guide, 38
Top-Tips, 38
Electric Putting Partner, 45
Oversize Putting Green, 50
Putt-a-Bout Auto Return Putting
Green, 53
Putting Trainer, 56
Iron Driver, 64
Power Pod, 68
Side Saddle Putters, 72
Super Stick Adjustable Golf Club, 72
Triple Crown Wedge, 74
Ball Boy, 82
Indoor/Outdoor Practice Net, 85
The Original Bag Shag, 86
Tee Wizz, 90
BioCurve Hand Developer, 94
The Distance Builder, 95
Warm-Up Practice Weight, 101
Compu-Golf, 107
Golfer's Cribbage, 110
Mini-Putt, 117
PLA-GOLF Miniature Golf Game, 119
Pro Golf, 121
Ultimate Golf, 124
World Class Leader Board, 126
19th Hole Toilet Seat, 134
Vassisdat Putter, 136
Wacky Tees, 137
Golfer's Welcome Mat, 143
The Art of Putting with Ben Crenshaw,
162
Automatic Golf with Bob Mann, 162
The Jimmy Ballard Golf Connection,
163
Better Golf Now! with Ken Venturi,
164
Difficult Shots Made Easy with Hale
Irwin, 165
Feel Your Way to Better Golf with
Wally Armstrong, 166
Golden Greats of Golf, 167
Golf for Kids of All Ages with Wally
Armstrong, 171
Golf My Way with Jack Nicklaus, 174
The Golf Swing with Tom Weiskopf,
174
Golf's Greats Quick Tips— Volumes I
and II, 175
How To Golf with Jan Stephenson,
178
*The John Jacobs Series— The Full
Swing, The Short Game*, and *Faults
and Cures*, 181
One Move to Better Golf with Carl
Lohren, 185
Play Great Golf with Arnold Palmer—
Mastering the Fundamentals and
Course Strategy, 185
Play Your Best Golf— Six Lessons, 186
Power Driving with Mike Dunaway,
186
Precision Putting with Dave Stockton,
186
The Short Way to Lower Scoring with
Paul Runyan— *Volume I: Putting
and Chipping; Volume II: Pitching
and Sand Play*, 187
So You Stand on the Wrong Side of

the Ball, Too! with Jay Edgar, 188
Bob Toski Teaches You Golf, 189
"British Open" Caps, 192
"Certainly I Love Him ..." Sweatshirt
  and T-Shirt, 192
Golfasaurus Sweatshirt and T-Shirt,
  193
Check Go, 197
Floater Golf Balls, 198
Nitelite Golf Ball, 201
Renegade 410 Golf Balls, 201
Enforcer Grips, 202
Tourna Grip, 202
Caddy Card, 203
Links to the Past, 204
The Name Dropper, 208
Shademaster Umbrella Clamp, 209
Stay-n-Play, 209
Carbide Tip Groove Cleaner, 212
Golf Club Cleaning Kit, 212
Golf Glove Dryer, 214
*The Golfer's Repair and Maintenance
  Handbook,* 214
Grip Life, 214
McDivot's Clubscrub, 214
Ping Weight Balance Scale, 217
Bogey Ice, 221
Golf Party Accessories, 222
Golf Party-Pak, 222
Imported British Golf Towels, 223
The Ultimate Golf Towel, 224
Caddi-Sak, 225
Deluxe Face Saver Iron Covers, 225
Gotcha, 227
19th Hole Flag, 228
The 19th Hole Sipper, 228
Redi Club, 230
St. Andrews Headcovers, 230

Golf Digest
P.O. Box 68618
Indianapolis, Indiana 46268
(800) 451-7020, operator #39
  The Art of Putting with Ben Crenshaw,
    162
  The Jimmy Ballard Golf Connection,
    163
  Golden Greats of Golf, 167
  *The Golf Digest Schools Learning
    Library,* 169
  Golf My Way with Jack Nicklaus, 174

How To Golf with Jan Stephenson,
  178
*An Inside Look at the Game for a
  Lifetime* with Bob Toski, Jim Flick,
  Peter Kostis, and John Elliott, 181
*The John Jacobs Series—The Full
  Swing, The Short Game,* and *Faults
  and Cures,* 181
1986 Masters Tournament, 184
Play Great Golf with Arnold Palmer—
  Mastering the Fundamentals and
  Course Strategy, 185
The Short Way to Lower Scoring with
  Paul Runyan— *Volume I: Putting
  and Chipping; Volume II: Pitching
  and Sand Play,* 187
Bob Toski Teaches You Golf, 189

Golf House
United States Golf Association
P.O. Box 708
Far Hills, New Jersey 07931-0708
(201) 234-2300
(800) 336-4446
  Rules Master, 122
  "American Golf Courses" Placemats
    and Coasters, 140
  Crystal Golf Ball, 141
  "Famous British Golf Clubs" Place-
    mats and Coasters, 141
  Golf House Ball Marker, 142
  Golf Ornaments, 143
  Golf Sundial, 143
  "The Golfer" Character Jug, 143
  "Golfing Hazards" Towel, 144
  "It's Tee Time! Mug, 145
  "Major Green" Character Mug, 145
  Douglas Adams Prints, 150
  Bobby Jones Concentration, 153
  Tom Morris Print, 153
  W. Dendy Sadler Prints, 154
  The Triumverate, 154
  The Club Makers, 155
  The Golf House Rare Book Collection,
    156
  *The Golf Club Identification and Price
    Guide,* 155
  How I Play Golf with Bobby Jones,
    176

Golf Rite Products
61 Fulton Street
Brentwood, New York 11717
(516) 231-9530
  Stance Guide, 37

The Golf Shop Collection
325 West 5th Street
Cincinnati, Ohio 45202
(513) 241-7789
(800) 227-9700
  "Famous British Golf Clubs" Place-
    mats and Coasters, 141
  Golf Ornaments, 143
  Golf Sundial, 143
  Hole-In-One Trophy Case, 144
  Douglas Adams Prints, 150
  "The Bogey Man" and "St. Andrews
    Caddie," 150
  British Cigarette Cards:"Famous
    Golfers 1930" and "Golf 1939," 150
  "Ginger Beer Hole" Print, 151
  "The Golfers" Print, 152
  Lealand Gustavson Prints, 152
  Bobby Jones Concentration, 153
  Tom Morris Print, 153
  W. Dendy Sadler Prints, 154
  The Triumverate, 154
  "'84 Gutty" Balls, 198
  Tasco Golf Scope, 231
  Travels with a Golf Tour Gourmet, 232

Golf Sports Engineering
1813 Mark Street N.E.
Olympia, Washington 98506
(206) 491-8067
  Right Touch, 58

The Golf Works
Ralph Maltby Enterprises, Inc.
4820 Jacksontown Road
P.O. Box 3008
Newark, Ohio 43055-7199
(614) 323-4193
(800) 848-8358
  ASSIST, 9
  Flying Elbows, 11
  Foot Wedge, 12
  Head Up Preventer, 15

Impact Decals, 15
Impact Bag, 16
Labelon Tape, 16
The Lone Eagle Swing Plane Trainer,
  16
Pro-Swing, 21
Swing Memory, 24
Swing Mirror, 25
Swing-O-Meter, 25
Swingrite, 26
Tempo Training Club, 28
TruSwing, 30
Training Grip, 32
Ball Flight Visualizer, 33
Chalk It, 33
Jack Grout Tee Square, 34
Magnetic Lie Angle Tool, 34
Pro-Align, 35
Sam Snead's Power Stance Mat, 35
Set-Up Master, 35
Stretch-Aligner, 37
Top-Tips, 38
Blast Master, 39
The Bunkerboard, 39
Chip Trainer, 40
The Separator, 41
Wrist Lock, 41
Clyde Guide and Arm Guide, 44
Indoor Putting Mat, 47
The 19th Hole Par Putting Cup, 49
Oak Putter Stand, 50
Puttband-Swingband, 54
Putt-R-Buddy, 56
Putt Square, 56
Tru-Stroke Putting Guide, 59
Adjustable Swingweight Five-Iron, 62
Hero Driver, 64
Tunstall Putter, 76
Hitting Mat, 84
The "Par"-Fect Golf Net, 87
Pitching Net, 87
Short Flyte Golf Balls, 89
Target Green Kit, 90
The Aircast Pneumatic Armband, 94
The Distance Builder, 95
GolfGym, 96
The Marcy Wedge, 97
Power Builder, 98
Tour Belt, 101
Warm-Up Practice Weight, 101
Douglas Adams Prints, 150
The Triumverate, 154

Classic Golf Clubs: A Pictorial Guide, 155

The Golf Club Identification and Price Guide, 155

Hillerich & Bradsby: History-Catalogs (1922-1980), 157

MacGregor Golf: History-Catalogs (1935-1970), 157

Wilson Golf: History-Catalogs (1931-1979), 159

The Art of Putting with Ben Crenshaw, 162

Automatic Golf with Bob Mann, 162

The Jimmy Ballard Golf Connection, 163

Better Golf Now! with Ken Venturi, 164

Challenge Golf with Peter Longo, 164

Difficult Shots Made Easy with Hale Irwin, 165

Exercises for Better Golf, 166

Feel Your Way to Better Golf with Wally Armstrong, 166

Get Rid of Your Back Problems and Play Better Golf with Sam Snead and Dr. J.K. Keggi, 167

Golden Greats of Golf, 167

The Golden Tee, 167

Golf with Al Geiberger, 168

Golf with Patty Sheehan, 168

Golf Club Design, Specifications & Fitting with Ralph Maltby, 169

Golf Club Repair—The Knowledge & Bench Skills with Tom Wishon and Mark Wilson, 169

The Golf Digest Schools Learning Library, 169

Golf for Kids of All Ages with Wally Armstrong, 171

Golf for Winners with Hank Haney and Mark O'Meara, 171

Golf Lessons with Sam Snead, 172

Golf My Way with Jack Nicklaus, 174

Golf Secrets with Walter Hagen, 174

The Golf Swing with Tom Weiskopf, 174

Golf Your Way with Phil Ritson, 175

Golf's Greats Quick Tips—Volumes I and II, 175

The Greater Golfer in You with Dr. Gary Wiren, 175

How To Golf with Jan Stephenson, 178

How To Play Your Best Golf All the Time with Tommy Armour, 179

An Inside Look at the Game for a Lifetime with Bob Toski, Jim Flick, Peter Kostis, and John Elliott, 181

The John Jacobs Series—The Full Swing, The Short Game, and *Faults and Cures*, 181

Junior Golf "The Easy Way" with Mark Steinbauer, 182

Keys to Consistency with Jack Grout, 182

The Master System to Better Golf: Volume 1 with Craig Stadler, Davis Love III, Tom Purtzer, and Gary Koch, 183

1986 Masters Tournament, 184

One Move to Better Golf with Carl Lohren, 185

Play Great Golf with Arnold Palmer—*Mastering the Fundamentals* and *Course Strategy*, 185

Play Your Best Golf—Volumes 1 and 2, 185

Play Your Best Golf—Six Lessons, 186

The Short Way to Lower Scoring with Paul Runyan—*Volume I: Putting and Chipping; Volume II: Pitching and Sand Play*, 187

So You Stand on the Wrong Side of the Ball, Too! with Jay Edgar, 188

Bob Toski Teaches You Golf, 189

Total Golf with Bruce Crampton, 189

"'84 Gutty" Balls, 198

Golf Ball Ring Gauge, 199

Nitelite Golf Ball, 201

Official PGA Tour Personal Golf Book, 205

Dental Picks, 212

Golf Club Cleaning Kit, 212

Golf Club Design, Fitting, Alteration & Repair, 212

Golf Glove Dryer, 214

Lacquer-Stiks, 214

Magnetic Protractor, 215

Spike Caddy, 217

The Dream Tee, 218

Caddi-Sak, 225

GolfSmart

Post Office Box 639
Chicago Park, California 95712-0639
(916) 272-1422
(800) 637-3557

Compu-Golf, 107
The Golf Club Identification and Price Guide, 155
Hillerich & Bradsby: History-Catalogs (1922-1980), 157
MacGregor Golf: History-Catalogs (1935-1970), 157
Wilson Golf: History-Catalogs (1931-1979), 159
The Art of Putting with Ben Crenshaw, 162
Automatic Golf with Bob Mann, 162
The Jimmy Ballard Golf Connection, 163
Better Golf Now! with Ken Venturi, 164
Challenge Golf with Peter Longo, 164
Difficult Shots Made Easy with Hale Irwin, 165
Exercises for Better Golf, 166
Feel Your Way to Better Golf with Wally Armstrong, 166
Golden Greats of Golf, 167
The Golden Tee, 167
Golf with Al Geiberger, 168
Golf with Patty Sheehan, 168
The Golf Digest Schools Learning Library, 169
Golf for Kids of All Ages with Wally Armstrong, 171
Golf for Winners with Hank Haney and Mark O'Meara, 171
Golf Lessons with Sam Snead, 172
Golf the Miller Way with Johnny Miller, 173
Golf My Way with Jack Nicklaus, 174
The Golf Swing with Tom Weiskopf, 174
Golf—The Winner's Edge with Kermit Zarley, 175
Golf's Greats Quick Tips—Volumes I and II, 175
The Greater Golfer in You with Dr. Gary Wiren, 175
How I Play Golf with Bobby Jones, 176
How To Golf with Jan Stephenson, 178
How To Play Your Best Golf All the Time with Tommy Armour, 179
An Inside Look at the Game for a Lifetime with Bob Toski, Jim Flick, Peter Kostis, and John Elliott, 181
The John Jacobs Series—The Full Swing, The Short Game, and *Faults and Cures*, 181
The Keys to Great Golf! with JoAnne Carner, 183
The Master System to Better Golf: Volume 1 with Craig Stadler, Davis Love III, Tom Purtzer, and Gary Koch, 183
1986 Masters Tournament, 184
One Move to Better Golf with Carl Lohren, 185
Play Your Best Golf—Volumes 1 and 2, 185
Power Driving with Mike Dunaway, 186
Precision Putting with Dave Stockton, 186
The Short Way to Lower Scoring with Paul Runyan—*Volume I: Putting and Chipping; Volume II: Pitching and Sand Play*, 187
So You Stand on the Wrong Side of the Ball, Too! with Jay Edgar, 188
Bob Toski Teaches You Golf, 189
Total Golf with Bruce Crampton, 189
Golf Club Design, Fitting, Alteration & Repair, 212

Golfsmith

Custom Golf Clubs, Inc.
10206 North Interregional Highway
Austin, Texas 78753
(512) 837-4810
(800) 531-5025; in Texas, (800) 252-8108

Labelon Tape, 16
Mitsubishi Golf Trainers, 17
Swing Right, 22
Swingrite, 26
Tee-Off, 27
Training Grip, 32
Golf Green Speed-Meter, 45
Golfsmith XL Design Putter Grip, 46
The 19th Hole Par Putting Cup, 49
The 19th Hole Putting Green, 49
Pro Practice Putting Green, 53

The Track, 59
Super Stick Adjustable Golf Club, 72
No-Fore Practice Ball, 86
The Original Bag Shag, 86
Practice Golf Range, 88
The Aircast Pneumatic Armband, 94
Heavy Weighted Practice Club, 96
"Limber-Up" Golf Mitt, 96
Swing Developer, 100
Warm-Up Practice Weight, 101
Baby Golf Shoes, 130
Classic Golf Clubs: A Pictorial Guide,
    155
The Art of Putting with Ben Crenshaw,
    162
Automatic Golf with Bob Mann, 162
Golden Greats of Golf, 167
Golf with Al Geiberger, 168
Golf with Patty Sheehan, 168
The Golf Digest Schools Learning
    Library, 169
Golf My Way with Jack Nicklaus, 174
Bob Toski Teaches You Golf, 189
Golf Rubbers, 192
Floater Golf Balls, 198
Mighty Midget Golf Ball Washer, 197
Nitelite Golf Ball, 199
Tourna Grip, 202
Score Caddy, 205
Mark's Marker, 206
Zippo Greens Keeper, 207
Lacquer-Stiks, 214
Magnetic Protractor, 215
Phillips Spike Wrench, 216
Ping Weight Balance Scale, 217
Deluxe Face Saver Iron Covers, 225
Golf-Buoy, 227

GolfTek
0203 Third Street
Lewiston, Idaho 83501
(208) 743-9037
    GolfTek Swing Analyzer/Pro III
        Model, 13
    GolfTek Personal Model Golf Com-
        puter, 13

Golfware Originals
4510 Regent Street
P.O. Box 5148
Madison, Wisconsin 53705

(608) 233-6059
    The Secret Weapon Driver, 69

Hammacher Schlemmer
9180 Le Saint Drive
Fairfield, Ohio 45014
(800) 543-3366
    Oncourse Instructor, 18
    Sony CaddyCam, 22
    Indoor Practice Green, 46
    Two-Way Indoor Putting Green, 60
    Super Stick Adjustable Golf Club, 72
    Pro Golf, 121
    Vassisdat Putter, 136
    Solar-Powered Ventilated Golf Cap,
        196
    Floater Golf Balls, 198
    Links 18GX Advanced Golf Score-
        card, 204
    Hidden-Cart Golf Bag, 227
    PROTECH Golf Bag, 229

Hancock Techtronics, Inc.
101 East Main Street
Hancock, Maryland 21750
(301) 678-6000
    TRS-80 Golf Handicapping System,
        123

Haverhills
131 Townsend Street, Suite 360
San Francisco, California 94107
(800) 888-9920 [customer service]
(800) 621-1203 [orders]
    Condo Golf, 107
    Seiko Golf Scorecard, 205
    Tasco Golf Scope, 231

Head Freezer
P.O. Box 209
Jackson, Michigan 49204
(800) 426-7973
    Head Freezer, 14

Head Trainer
P.O. Box 17215
Mesa, Arizona 85212
    Head Trainer, 15

Herrington/The Enthusiasts' Catalog
3 Symmes Drive
Londonberry, New Hampshire 03053
(603) 437-4939
  Pro-Green, 53
  Puttband-Swingband, 54
  Driver and a Half, 63
  The Duke and The Duchess Putters, 63
  Positive Putter, 68
  Golf with Al Geiberger, 168
  Golf with Patty Sheehan, 168
  Floater Golf Balls, 198
  Renegade 410 Golf Balls, 201
  The Shrivot, 207
  Golf Links, 208
  Golden Retriever, 210
  Spike Caddy, 217
  Flex-Tee, 218
  Put'r There/The Putter Caddy, 229

HL Ballmark Company
P.O. Box 402
Conshohocken, Pennsylvania 19428
(215) 825-0210
  HL Ballmark With Velcro, 206
  "Stayclean" Golf Towel, 224

Hollrock Engineering Inc.
P.O. Box 780
150 Salmon Brook Street
Granby, Connecticut 06035
(203) 653-7973
  Shag King, 89

How To Play Better Golf
P.O. Box 7005
State College, Pennsylvania 16803
(814) 237-1774 or (814) 234-1177
  How To Play Better Golf with Bob
    Intrieri, 179

Hurley Style
P.O. Box 4127
Portsmouth, New Hamsphire 03801
(603) 436-7983
  Wooden Golf Jigsaw, 126
  Brass Club-and-Ball Doorknocker, 140

  Ceramic Golf-Ball Teapot, 141
  Golf Caddy Fire Iron Set, 142
  Golfers' Pewter Hip Flasks, 144
  Golfing Coasters, 144
  "Golfing Hazards" Towel, 144
  Hexagonal Golf Tidy Box, 144
  Terence Legg Golf Sign, 153
  "Old Tom Morris" Toby Jug, 153

Image Links
522 Stevenson Street
Salinas, California 93907
(408) 422-6266
  Own Your Own Golf Course, 147

Indoor Golf
P.O. Box 665
Meridian, Idaho 83642
(208) 888-7183
  Putting Tutor, 56

Inpro Companies, Inc.
3407 78th Avenue West
P.O. Box 940
Rock Island, Illinois 61204-0940
(309) 787-4971
  Optima Driver, 66

Joe Jahraus
7509 East 60th Street
Tulsa, Oklahoma 74145
(918) 663-1167
  Look-Alike Caricatures by Joe Jah-
    raus, 145

R.L. Kays and Associates
P.O. Box 4116
Lake San Marcos, California 92069-
    1015
(619) 744-2932
  The Inner Solution with Dr. Robert
    Metzger, 181

Kerdad, Inc.
688 Williams Street
San Leandro, California 94577

(415) 352-8662
  Golf Swinger, 12

Las Vegas Discount Golf & Tennis
5325 South Valley View Boulevard,
  Suite 10
Las Vegas, Nevada 89118
(702) 798-5500
(800) 634-6743
  ASSIST, 9
  Golf Swinger, 12
  Mitsubishi Golf Trainers, 17
  Oncourse Instructor, 18
  Swingthing, 27
  The Hooker Golf Glove, 31
  Training Grip, 32
  Electric Putting Partner, 45
  The Klanger, 47
  Pro Practice Putting Green, 53
  The Reel Putter, 57
  Tiger Shark P-Squared Putter Grip,
    58
  Vision Putt, 60
  The Giant Niblick, 64
  Perflex Driver, 68
  Power Pod, 68
  Shurfire Alma Mater Putters, 70
  Jack Nicklaus Twenty-Fifth Anniver-
    sary Commemorative Clubs, 77
  Jerry Barber Practice Swing Driver,
    94
  GolfGym, 96
  "Limber-Up" Golf Mitt, 96
  Warm-Up Practice Weight, 101
  Compu-Golf, 107
  Condo Golf, 107
  Pro Golf, 121
  Cloud-Flite Trick Golf Ball, 130
  Laid Back Golfer's Association, 133
  Plumber's Putter, 134
  Vassisdat Putter, 136
  Executive Golf Tool, 141
  Off-the-Wall Golf-Ball Alarm Clock,
    146
  The Otey Cane, 146
  The Art of Putting with Ben Crenshaw,
    162
  The Jimmy Ballard Golf Connection,
    163
  Golf with Al Geiberger, 168
  Golf with Patty Sheehan, 168

*The Golf Digest Schools Learning
    Library,* 169
Golf for Kids of All Ages with Wally
    Armstrong, 171
Golf My Way with Jack Nicklaus, 174
How I Play Golf with Bobby Jones,
    176
How To Golf with Jan Stephenson,
    178
*The Master System to Better Golf:
    Volume 1* with Craig Stadler, Davis
    Love III, Tom Purtzer, and Gary
    Koch, 183
Play Great Golf with Arnold Palmer—
    Mastering the Fundamentals and
    Course Strategy, 185
*So You Stand on the Wrong Side of the
    Ball, Too!* with Jay Edgar, 188
  Famous-Logo Visors, 192
  Golf Rubbers, 192
  Golfaholics Anonymous Official
    Sweatshirt, 192
  Gore-Tex Golf Suit, 193
  Maggie's Stroke-Saver Golf Boots,
    194
  Birdie Ball Washer, 197
  Check Go, 197
  Mighty Midget Golf Ball Washer, 199
  Nitelite Golf Ball, 201
  Caddy Card, 203
  Golfers' Stats, 203
  Links to the Past, 204
  Seiko Golf Scorecard, 205
  The Name Dropper, 208
  Golf Bag Rain Cover, 209
  Golf Club Cleaning Kit, 212
  Grip Life, 214
  Magnum Force I Ratchet Spike
    Wrench, 215
  Phillips Spike Wrench, 216
  Pow'r Tee, 219
  Golf-Buoy, 227
  The Grand Luxe Golf Cart, 227
  "Links to the Past" Ball Marker
    Display, 228
  Putter Gripper, 229
  Redi Club, 230

Leister Game Company, Inc.
511 Sumner Street
Toledo, Ohio 43609

(419) 248-4449
(800) 282-3186
  Foot Wedge, 131
  Golfer's Crotch Hook, 131
  Kneel 'n' Pray Putter, 133
  Vassisdat Putter, 136

Lion Tool & Die Company
P.O. Box 66
Algonquin, Illinois 60102
(312) 658-8898
(800) 255-6389
  Dynasight, 11

Louisville Golf Club Company
2601 Grassland Drive
Louisville, Kentucky 40299
(502) 491-1631
(800) 626-6379
  The Bomber, 62
  Pro Golf, 121
  Persimmon Seeds ("Grow Your Own
    Golf Clubs"), 134

Magnuson Industries, Inc.
P.O. Box 5444
Rockford, Illinois 61125
(815) 229-2970
(800) 435-2816
  Maggie's Stroke-Saver Golf Boots,
    194
  Bag-Umb, 209

Markline
P.O. Box 13807
Philadelphia, Pennsylvania 19101-
    3807
(215) 244-9610
(800) 225-8390
  Chipper Net, 83
  Tee Wizz, 90
  The Marcy Wedge, 97
  The Name Dropper, 208

Marksman Manufacturing
1118 Tobias Drive
Chula Vista, California 92011-1108

(619) 426-2366
  Mark's Marker, 206

Maryco Products
The Golf People
7215 Pebblecreek Road
West Bloomfield, Michigan 48322
(313) 851-4597
(800) 334-7757
  International Duffers Association,
    133
  Off-the-Wall Golf-Ball Alarm Clock,
    146
  The Art of Putting with Ben Crenshaw,
    162
  Exercises for Better Golf, 166
  Golf for Kids of All Ages with Wally
    Armstrong, 171
  Golf My Way with Jack Nicklaus, 174
  How To Golf with Jan Stephenson,
    178
  Keys to Great Golf! with JoAnne
    Carner, 183
  Play Great Golf with Arnold Palmer—
    Mastering the Fundamentals and
    Course Strategy, 185
  Bob Toski Teaches You Golf, 189
  Golf Party Accessories, 222
  The 19th Hole Sipper, 228
  Tea-Time at the Masters, 231

Matzie Golf Company, Inc.
112 Penn Street
El Segundo, California 90245
(213) 322-1301
(800) 722-7125
  ASSIST, 9
  Putt-R-Buddy, 56
  Slim Jim Putter, 72
  Hot Dog Putter, 132
  Plumber's Putter, 134
  Hillerich & Bradsby: History-Catalogs
    (1922-1980), 157
  MacGregor Golf: History-Catalogs
    (1935-1970), 157
  Wilson Golf: History-Catalogs (1931-
    1979), 159
  The Art of Putting with Ben Crenshaw,
    162
  Automatic Golf with Bob Mann, 162
  The Jimmy Ballard Golf Connection,

163

Better Golf Now! with Ken Venturi, 164

Difficult Shots Made Easy with Hale Irwin, 165

Exercises for Better Golf, 166

Feel Your Way to Better Golf with Wally Armstrong, 166

Golden Greats of Golf, 167

The Golden Tee, 167

Golf with Al Geiberger, 168

Golf with Patty Sheehan, 168

The Golf Digest Schools Learning Library, 169

Golf for Kids of All Ages with Wally Armstrong, 171

Golf for Winners with Hank Haney and Mark O'Meara, 171

Golf Lessons with Sam Snead, 172

Golf the Miller Way with Johnny Miller, 173

Golf My Way with Jack Nicklaus, 174

The Golf Swing with Tom Weiskopf, 174

Golf— The Winner's Edge with Kermit Zarley, 175

Golf's Greats Quick Tips— Volumes I and II, 175

The Greater Golfer in You with Dr. Gary Wiren, 175

How I Play Golf with Bobby Jones, 176

How To Golf with Jan Stephenson, 178

How To Play Your Best Golf All the Time with Tommy Armour, 179

An Inside Look at the Game for a Lifetime with Bob Toski, Jim Flick, Peter Kostis, and John Elliott, 181

The John Jacobs Series— The Full Swing, The Short Game, and *Faults and Cures,* 181

Keys to Great Golf! with JoAnne Carner, 183

1986 Masters Tournament, 184

One Move to Better Golf with Carl Lohren, 185

Play Great Golf with Arnold Palmer— *Mastering the Fundamentals* and *Course Strategy,* 185

Play Your Best Golf— Volumes 1 and 2, 185

Power Driving with Mike Dunaway, 186

Precision Putting with Dave Stockton, 186

The Short Way to Lower Scoring with Paul Runyan— *Volume I: Putting and Chipping; Volume II: Pitching and Sand Play,* 187

So You Stand on the Wrong Side of the Ball, Too! with Jay Edgar, 188

Bob Toski Teaches You Golf, 189

Total Golf with Bruce Crampton, 189

Memory Keepers
P.O. Box 558264
Cincinnati, Ohio 45255
(513) 232-2664
Memory Keeper, 204

Merv's Retriever, Inc.
P.O. Box 39
Ransomville, New York 14131
(716) 689-9690
Golf Ball Rake, 211

Milliken Publishing Company
1100 Research Boulevard
St. Louis, Missouri 63132
(314) 991-4220
(800) 643-0008
Golf Classic, 107

MindPower Golf, Inc.
1607 Colonial Parkway
Inverness, Illinois 60067
(312) 934-4163
Subliminal Golf Improvement Program, 188

Mitsubishi Electric Sales America, Inc.
5757 Plaza Drive, P.O. Box 6007
Cypress, California 90630-0007
(714) 220-2500
(800) 626-5485; in California, (800) 626-5482
Mitsubishi Golf Trainers, 17

Miya Epoch Inc.
1635 Crenshaw Boulevard
Torrance, California 90501
(213) 320-1172
Head Up Preventer, 15
Miya Computer Shot Analyzer, 18
Miya Computer Putting Checker, 48
Miya Putting Trainer, 48
Super Grip Dryer/Suberaanai, 217

Morris Video
2730 Monterey, Suite 105
Torrance, California 90503
(213) 533-4800
Chipping & Putting with Charlie
Schnaubel, 164
Golf Like a Pro with Billy Casper, 172
Golf the Miller Way with Johnny
Miller, 173
The Ultimate Drive with Art Sellinger,
190

Motivation Media, Inc.
1245 Milwaukee Avenue
Glenview, Illinois 60025
(312) 297-4740
Challenge Golf with Peter Longo, 164

National Golf Foundation
1150 South U.S. Highway One
Jupiter, Florida 33477
(407) 744-6006
(800) 872-1150
The Toski Trainer, 28
*The Golf Club Identification and Price
Guide*, 155
*Hillerich & Bradsby: History-Catalogs
(1922-1980)*, 157
*MacGregor Golf: History-Catalogs
(1935-1970)*, 157
*Wilson Golf: History-Catalogs (1931-
1979)*, 159
The Art of Putting with Ben Crenshaw,
162
The Jimmy Ballard Golf Connection,
161
Better Golf Now! with Ken Venturi,
164
Challenge Golf with Peter Longo, 164

Difficult Shots Made Easy with Hale
Irwin, 165
Exercises for Better Golf, 166
Feel Your Way to Better Golf with
Wally Armstrong, 166
*Get Rid of Your Back Problems and
Play Better Gol* with Sam Snead
and Dr. K.J. Keggi, 167
Golden Greats of Golf, 167
The Golden Tee, 167
Golf with Al Geiberger, 168
Golf with Patty Sheehan, 168
*The Golf Digest Schools Learning
Library*, 169
Golf for Kids of All Ages with Wally
Armstrong, 171
Golf for Winners with Hank Haney
and Mark O'Meara, 171
Golf Lessons with Sam Snead, 172
Golf the Miller Way with Johnny
Miller, 173
Golf My Way with Jack Nicklaus, 174
The Golf Swing with Tom Weiskopf,
174
Golf's Greats Quick Tips— Volumes I
and II, 175
The Greater Golfer in You with Dr.
Gary Wiren, 175
How I Play Golf with Bobby Jones,
176
How To Golf with Jan Stephenson,
178
*How To Play Your Best Golf All the
Time* with Tommy Armour, 179
*An Inside Look at the Game for a
Lifetime* with Bob Toski, Jim Flick,
Peter Kostis, and John Elliott, 181
*The John Jacobs Series— The Full
Swing, The Short Game,* and *Faults
and Cures*, 181
Keys to Great Golf! with JoAnne
Carner, 183
*The Master System to Better Golf:
Volume 1* with Craig Stadler, Davis
Love III, Tom Purtzer, and Gary
Koch, 183
1986 Masters Tournament, 184
One Move to Better Golf with Carl
Lohren, 185
Play Great Golf with Arnold Palmer—
Mastering the Fundamentals and
Course Strategy, 185

Play Your Best Golf– Volumes 1 and 2, 185

Power Driving with Mike Dunaway, 186

Precision Putting with Dave Stockton, 186

The Short Way to Lower Scoring with Paul Runyan— *Volume I: Putting and Chipping; Volume II: Pitching and Sand Play,* 187

So You Stand on the Wrong Side of the Ball, Too! with Jay Edgar, 188

Bob Toski Teaches You Golf, 189

Total Golf with Bruce Crampton, 189

Golf Club Design, Fitting, Alteration & Repair, 212

Netik Enterprises
500 Glenwood Circle, Suite 522
Monterey, California 93940
(408) 375-4543
   QuicKnicks, 195

Nevada Bob's Discount Golf
3333 East Flamingo Road
Las Vegas, Nevada 89121
(702) 451-9913
   Mitsubishi Golf Trainers, 17
   Electric Putting Partner, 45
   MacGregor Putting Green, 48
   The Wilson 8802, 78
   The Wilson 8813, 78
   MacGregor Chip and Drive Mat, 85
   Pro Golf, 121
   The Art of Putting with Ben Crenshaw, 162
   The Jimmy Ballard Golf Connection, 163
   Better Golf Now! with Ken Venturi, 164
   Golf with Al Geiberger, 168
   Golf with Patty Sheehan, 168
   Golf for Winners with Hank Haney and Mark O'Meara, 171
   Golf My Way with Jack Nicklaus, 174
   The Golf Swing with Tom Weiskopf, 174
   How To Golf with Jan Stephenson, 178
   The Master System to Better Golf:

Volume 1 with Craig Stadler, Davis Love III, Tom Purtzer, and Gary Koch, 183

Play Great Golf with Arnold Palmer— *Mastering the Fundamentals* and *Course Strategy,* 185

Bob Toski Teaches You Golf, 189

   Golf Club Cleaning Kit, 212

Northern Golf Ball Company
2350 West Roscoe Street
Chicago, Illinois 60618
(312) 472-1760 or (312) 935-1420
   Training Grip, 32
   Electric Putting Partner, 45
   Professional Golf Putting Cup, 52
   Putting Trainer, 56
   Super Stick Adjustable Golf Club, 72
   Chip Shot Target, 82
   Indoor Golf Net and Frame, 84
   "Perfect Stroke" Golf Practice Net, 87
   Shag King, 89
   "Limber-Up" Golf Mitt, 96
   Warm-Up Practice Weight, 101
   Foot Wedge, 131
   Goofy Golf Balls, 131
   Jumbo Golf Tees, 133
   Kneel 'n' Pray Putter, 133
   Vassisdat Putter, 136
   Golf Rubbers, 192
   Floater Golf Balls, 198
   Nitelite Golf Ball, 201
   Score Caddy, 205
   The Hurricane Cover, 209
   Phillips Spike Wrench, 216
   Deluxe Face Saver Iron Covers, 225

Objective Golf, Inc.
9100 South Dadeland Boulevard, Suite 1406
Miami, Florida 33156
(305) 665-9222
   The Toski Trainer, 28

Ofer Custom Golf Clubs
2559 Blake Avenue, N.W.
Canton, Ohio 44718
(216) 456-5357
   "3 in 1" Club, 74

1 Step Software, Inc.
510 Griffith Road
Charlotte, North Carolina 28210
(704) 525-6688
(800) 525-4653
   Golf Doctor, 108
   Golf's Best—Pinehurst No. 2, 110
   Golf's Best—St. Andrews, 112
   Play Golf—Pineview, 120
   Play Golf—Ye Old Course, 120

Oregon Golf Works, Inc.
7410 S.W. Macadam Avenue
Portland, Oregon 97219
(503) 244-8143
(800) 262-8143
   Fore 7-4-7 Jumbo Driver, 63

Par-Buster
1 East 26th Place
Tulsa, Oklahoma 74114
(918) 585-8542
   Indoor/Outdoor Practice Net, 85
   Par-Buster Target and Chart, 86
   T-Mats, 91

Par-Phernalia Golf Products
P.O. Box 28475
San Diego, California 92128
(619) 485-8850
   Plumb Bob Training Tool, 51

Perflex International
50 South 800 West
Salt Lake City, Utah 84104
(801) 595-6900, ext. 125
   Perflex Driver, 68

The Pilcher Company
14827 Bluegrass/Silver Lakes
P.O. Box 1456
Helendale, California 92342
(619) 245-8996
   Pug-Ugly Putter, 69

Polar Golf
301 West G Street
San Diego, California 92101
(619) 233-3186
(800) 334-7741
   ASSIST, 9
   Golf Swinger, 12
   Mitsubishi Golf Trainers, 17
   Electric Putting Partner, 45
   Super Stick Adjustable Golf Club, 72
   The Wilson 8802, 78
   The Wilson 8813, 78
   Power Swing, 99

Potpourri
Department 146
120 North Meadows Road
Medfield, Massachusetts 02052
(508) 359-5440
(800) 225-9848
   "American Golf Courses" Placemats
     and Coasters, 140
   Executive Golf Tool, 141

Powerstroke, Inc.
202 Auburn Avenue
Auburn, Washington 98002
(202) 939-1493
   Powerstroke, 99

Practical Golfers Aid, Inc.
P.O. Box 457
66 Prospect Street
Manchester, New Hampshire 03105
(603) 625-8931
   Iron Driver, 64

Practice House Golf, Inc.
P.O. Box 1496
South Bend, Indiana 46624
(219) 288-4991
(800) 348-5162
   Chalk It, 33
   Blast Master, 39
   Wrist Lock, 41
   The Klanger, 47
   Reed & Barton Ball Mark Repair Tool,
     148
   Golfers' Stats, 203

Precision Putting Systems, Inc.
P.O. Drawer 147
Somerdale, New Jersey 08083
(609) 232-1345
(800) 627-7888
    Precision Putting System, 51

The Price of His Toys
1800 Washington Boulevard, Suites A,
    B & C
Venice, California 90291
(213) 578-6800
(800) 447-8697; in California, (800)
    448-8697
    Golf Attaché, 107
    Bob Hope Golfer, 114
    PLA-GOLF Miniature Golf Game, 119
    Off-the-Wall Golf-Ball Alarm Clock,
    146

Prism Marketing, Inc.
P.O. Box 501
LaVerne, California 91750
(714) 986-2425
(800) 443-5444
    The Marcy Wedge, 97

Pro-Action Golf Company
3123 North Pulaski Road
Chicago, Illinois 60641
(312) 736-5000
(800) 642-5868
    Mercury-Loaded Driver, 66
    Enforcer Grips, 202

Pursuit of Par Enterprises
7151 West Highway 98
Panama City, Florida 32407
(904) 235-1818
    "In Pursuit of Par"— Par 72 Edition,
    114
    "In Pursuit of Par"— TPC at Sawgrass
    Edition, 115
    RagTail Golf Towel, 223

Rebound Systems, Inc.
145 Dogwood Avenue
Roslyn Harbor, New York 11576
(516) 484-0992
    Power Flexor, 98

Reflex Inc.
10304 North Hayden Road, Suite 4
Scottsdale, Arizona 85258
(602) 274-7976
    TourHawk Putter, 74
    Putting with Confidence with Duff
    Lawrence and Barb Thomas, 187

Ryobi-Toski Corporation
160 Essex Street
P.O. Box 576
Newark, Ohio 43055
(614) 345-9683
(800) 848-2075
    Driver and a Half, 63
    Mighty-Mite SS, 71

Sav-A-Scratch
3835 Southeast 11th Place
Cape Coral, Florida 33904
(813) 945-0651
    Sav-A-Scratch, 231

The Sharper Image
650 Davis Street
San Francisco, California 94111
(415) 445-6000
(800) 344-4444
    Power Trainer, 21
    The Marcy Wedge, 97
    Pro Golf, 121
    Check Go, 197
    Caddy Card, 203

Shepherd's Pack Ltd.
P.O. Box 318
Allenhurst, New Jersey 07711
(201) 531-9233
    New Zealand Lambskin Headcovers,
    216

Shrivot Corporation
50 East 50th Street
New York, New York 10022
(212) 308-2198
   The Shrivot, 207

Signature, Inc.
P.O. Box 2086
Ann Arbor, Michigan 48106
(313) 761-7300
   Signature Series Golf Glove, 195

Snyder Golf Creations
5415 Countryside Road
Minneapolis, Minnesota 55436
(612) 929-1111
   The Edge Putter, 44
   Professional Golf Putting Cup, 52

Soft-Tee Enterprises
P.O. Box 3785
Kent, Washington 98032
   Soft-Tee, 220

Somerton Springs Golf Shoppes
53 Bustleton Pike
Feasterville, Pennsylvania 19047
(215) 355-1776
(800) 523-5204
   Pro Golf, 121
   Ultimate Golf Game, 124
   Cloud-Flite Trick Golf Ball, 130
   Laid Back Golfer's Association, 133
   19th Hole Toilet Seat, 134
   Putter Power, 134
   Slice Repellent, 136
   Wacky Tees, 137
   Ceramic Golf-Ball Teapot, 141
   Difficult Shots Made Easy with Hale
      Irwin, 165
   Golf with Al Geiberger, 168
   Golf with Patty Sheehan, 168
   *The Golf Digest Schools Learning
      Library,* 169
   essons with Sam Snead, 172
   Way with Jack Nicklaus, 174
   with Jan Stephenson,

*The John Jacobs Series— The Full
   Swing, The Short Game,* and *Faults
   and Cures,* 181
Play Great Golf with Arnold Palmer—
   Mastering the Fundamentals and
   Course Strategy, 185
Precision Putting with Dave Stockton,
   186
The Short Way to Lower Scoring with
   Paul Runyan— *Volume I: Putting
   and Chipping; Volume II: Pitching
   and Sand Play,* 187
*So You Stand on the Wrong Side of the
   Ball, Too!* with Jay Edgar, 188
Nitelite Golf Ball, 201
Bogey Ice, 221
Golf Ball "Ice Cubes," 221

Specialty Video Marketing, Inc.
274 Westport Road
Wilton, Connecticut 06897
(203) 454-5910
   *Get Rid of Your Back Problems and
      Play Better Golf* with Sam Snead
      and Dr. K.J. Keggi, 167

Sportime
Select Service & Supply Company, Inc.
2905-E Amwiler Road
Atlanta, Georgia 30360
(404) 449-5700
(800) 444-5700
   Wiffle Golf Balls, 91
   Nerf Indoor Golf, 118
   PLA-GOLF Miniature Golf Game, 119
   The Art of Putting with Ben Crenshaw,
      162
   Golf— The Winner's Edge with Kermit
      Zarley, 175

Sports Technology, Inc.
P.O. Box 800
Old Saybrook, Connecticut 06475
(203) 767-2677
   Sportech Golf Swing Analyzer, 23

SportsWare Ltd.
P.O. Box 120
Hyde Park, New York 12538
(914) 229-0102
   Golf Tournament Scoring Program,
      112

Sunland Marketing, Inc.
P.O. Box 4096
Lake San Marcos, California 92069
(619) 727-4212 or (619) 471-7232
(800) 443-0466
   Power Swing, 99

Sutherland Products
P.O. Box 52491
Livonia, Michigan 48152
(313) 538-5458
   ExacTee, 218

Swing-O-Meter
400 South Dean Street
Englewood, New Jersey 07631
   Swing-O-Meter, 25

Swing Ring, Inc.
2137 Dixie Avenue
Smyrna, Georgia 30080
(404) 432-0340 or (404) 434-5215
   Swing Ring, 26

Swing's the Thing Golf Schools
P.O. Box 200
Shawnee-on-Delaware, Pennsylvania
      18356
(717) 421-6666
(800) 221-6661
   Swing Plane Trainer, 25

SyberVision Systems, Inc.
7133 Koll Center Parkway
Pleasanton, California 94566
(415) 846-3388
(800) 888-9980
   Difficult Shots Made Easy with Hale
      Irwin, 165
   Golf with Al Geiberger, 168

Golf with Patty Sheehan, 168
How I Play Golf with Bobby Jones,
   176
Power Driving with Mike Dunaway,
   186
Precision Putting with Dave Stockton,
   186

Tea-Time at the Masters
P.O. Box 3232
Augusta, Georgia 30904
   Tea-Time at the Masters, 231

Tee-Off Company
5610 Flagstone Street
Long Beach, California 90808
(213) 425-4128
   Tee-Off, 27

Think Big!
390 West Broadway
New York, New York 10012
(212) 925-7300
(800) 221-7019
   Think Big! Golf Ball, 136

Top Sight Putting Aid, Inc.
P.O. Box 588
Deerfield, Illinois 60015
   Top Sight Putting Aid, 59

Traders Marketing Company
137 Tartan Drive
Nepean, Ontario
Canada K2J 3T2
(613) 825-6655
   Golf Partner, 110
   Handicap Manager, 113

Triple Tee Ltd.
1203 Dove Street
Oshkosh, Wisconsin 54901
(414) 426-3255
   Chip 2 Par Practice Net, 83

U.S. Indoor Golf
220 Bush Street, Suite 660
San Francisco, California 94104
(415) 781-7430
   Par T Golf— The Incredible Golf
      Machine, 118

Ultimate Golf, Inc.
P.O. Box 920
Worcester, Massachusetts 01602
   Ultimate Golf, 124

Vedoro, Ltd.
1906 South Kessler
Wichita, Kansas 67213
(316) 943-0440
(800) 323-4676
   Vedoro's Ball Prospector

Video Reel, Inc.
28231 North Avenue Crocker, Suite 120
Valencia, California 91355
(805) 257-1035
(800) 458-2183
   Automatic Golf with Bob Mann, 162

Vintage Golf
7825 Hollywood Boulevard
Pembroke Pines, Florida 33024
(305) 981-0155
(800) 432-0158
   Tiger Shark P-Squared Putter Grip,
      58
   Hillerich & Bradsby: History-Catalogs
      (1922-1980), 157
   MacGregor Golf: History-Catalogs
      (1935-1970), 157
   Wilson Golf: History-Catalogs (1931-
      1979), 159
   How To Play Your Best Golf All the
      Time with Tommy Armour, 179

Twin Watts Golf Shops
   Drawer 1806
      ... Beach, Florida 32549
         ...: in Florida, (800) 342-

Mitsubishi Golf Trainers, 17
Swingthing, 27
The Bomber, 62
Lynx Parallax Putter with Transmitter
   Shaft, 66
The Wilson 8802, 78
The Wilson 8813, 78
Pro Golf, 121
The Art of Putting with Ben Crenshaw,
   162
Automatic Golf with Bob Mann, 162
The Jimmy Ballard Golf Connection,
   163
Golf with Al Geiberger, 168
Golf with Patty Sheehan, 168
Golf My Way with Jack Nicklaus, 174
The Golf Swing with Tom Weiskopf,
   174
Golf Your Way with Phil Ritson, 175
Golf's Greats Quick Tips— Volumes I
   and II, 175
How I Play Golf with Bobby Jones,
   176
How To Golf with Jan Stephenson,
   178
An Inside Look at the Game for a
   Lifetime with Bob Toski, Jim Flick,
   Peter Kostis, and John Elliott, 181
The John Jacobs Series— The Full
   Swing, The Short Game, and *Faults*
   and Cures, 181
Keys to Great Golf! with JoAnne
   Carner, 183
Play Great Golf with Arnold Palmer—
   Mastering the Fundamentals and
   Course Strategy, 185
Play Your Best Golf— Volumes 1 and
   2, 185
So You Stand on the Wrong Side of the
   Ball, Too! with Jay Edgar, 188
Bob Toski Teaches You Golf, 189
Deluxe Face Saver Iron Covers, 225
The Grand Luxe Golf Cart, 227

Westminster Graphics
3830 Ray Street
San Diego, California 92104
(619) 295-8672
(800) 426-1776
   British Cigarette Cards: "Famous
      Golfers 1930" and "Golf 1939," 150

J. White Industries
405 Bradford Drive
P.O. Box 132
Canfield, Ohio 44406-0132
(216) 533-5986
  ASSIST, 9
  Head Up Preventer, 15
  Mitsubishi Golf Trainers, 17
  The Spiro Swinger, 22
  Swingthing, 27
  Tee-Off, 27
  Training Grip, 32
  Wrist Lock, 41
  Miya Computer Putting Checker, 48
  Miya Putting Trainer, 48
  Putt-in-Cup, 55
  Putt-R-Buddy, 56
  Iron Driver, 64
  Power Pod, 68
  Super Stick Adjustable Golf Club, 72
  The Original Bag Shag, 86
  Sand Trap Practice Net, 89
  "Limber-Up" Golf Mitt, 96
  Swing Developer, 100
  Warm-Up Practice Weight, 101
  Pro Golf, 121
  Cloud-Flite Trick Golf Ball, 130
  Golf with Patty Sheehan, 168
  Golf Lessons with Sam Snead, 172
  Golf My Way with Jack Nicklaus, 174
  One Move to Better Golf with Carl
    Lohren, 185
  Bob Toski Teaches You Golf, 189
  Golf Rubbers, 192
  Nitelite Golf Ball, 201
  Tourna Grip, 202
  Mark's Marker, 206
  Golf Glove Dryer, 214

Gary Wiren's "Golf Around the World"
564 Greenway Drive
North Palm Beach, Florida 33408
(305) 626-4176
  Impact Bag, 16
  Sam Snead's Power Stance Mat, 35
  The Distance Builder, 95
  The Greater Golfer in You with Dr.
    Gary Wiren, 175
  Play Your Best Golf— Volumes 1 and
    2, 185

Wood Wand Corporation
2101 Sandhills Boulevard
Southern Pines, North Carolina 28387
(919) 692-2205
  Wood Wand, 76

Wright Weight Corporation
67 Laurel Lane
Ludlow, Massachusetts 01056
(413) 583-4640
  Just-Rite Putter, 65

Wrong Side Enterprises, Inc.
9794 Forest Lane, Suite 448
Dallas, Texas 75243
(800) 527-2814
  *So You Stand on the Wrong Side of the
    Ball, Too!* with Jay Edgar, 188

XOR Corporation
7607 Bush Lake Road
Minneapolis, Minnesota 55435
(612) 831-0444
(800) 635-2425
  MacGolf Classic, 116

INDEX TO PRODUCTS

Douglas Adams Prints, 150
Adjustable Swingweight Five-Iron, 62
The Aircast Pneumatic Armband, 94
"American Golf Courses" Placemats and
    Coasters, 140
APBA Professional Golf Game, 104
Approach Shot and Sand Play, 186
The Art of Putting with Ben Crenshaw, 162
ASSIST, 9
Automatic Golf with Bob Mann, 162
"Awarding the First USGA Trophy, 1895,"
    152

Baby Golf Shoes, 130
Bag-Umb, 209
Ball Boy, 82
Ball Flight Visualizer, 33
The Jimmy Ballard Golf Connection, 163
The Jimmy Ballard Swing Connector, 9
Ballpoint Pen with Golf-Club Grip, 140
Jerry Barber Practice Swing Driver, 94
Belt Ball Clip, 197
The Bent One, 130
The Bertholy Swing Pipe, 9
Better Golf Now! with Ken Venturi, 164
BioCurve Hand Developer, 94
Birdie Ball Washer, 197
Blast Master, 39
Blue Finger, 31
Bogey Ice, 221
Bogey Ice Bucket, 221
"The Bogey Man," 150
The Bomber, 62
Brass Club-and-Ball Doorknocker, 140
British Cigarette Cards: "Famous Golfers
    1930" and "Golf 1939," 150
"British Open" Caps, 192
The Bunkerboard, 39
Business-Card Golfer in a Bottle, 140

Cad-Eze, 225
Caddi-Sak, 225
Caddy Card, 203
Carbide Tip Groove Cleaner, 212
Carpet Coasters, 141
Ceramic Golf-Ball Teapot, 141
"Certainly I Love Him . . ." Sweatshirt and T-
    Shirt, 192
Chalk It, 33

Challenge Golf with Peter Longo, 164
Championship Golf— The Great Courses of
    the World (Volume One: Pebble
    Beach), 105
Check Go, 197
Chip-N-Pitch Net, 82
Chip Shot Target, 82
Chip Trainer, 40
Chip 2 Par Practice Net, 83
Chipper Net, 83
Chipping & Putting with Charlie Schnaubel,
    164
Classic Golf Clubs: A Pictorial Guide, 155
The Clikka Bag, 84
Cloud-Flite Trick Golf Ball, 130
The Club Makers, 155
The Clubs, 186
Clyde Guide and Arm Guide, 44
Compu-Golf, 107
Concept G Precision Golf Ball Gauge, 197
Concerning Golf, 156
Condo Golf, 107
Ray Cook Original M-1 Putter, 77
Correct Swing, 10
Course Strategy with Arnold Palmer, 185
Crystal Golf Ball, 141

Deluxe Face Saver Iron Covers, 225
Deluxe Vinyl Iron Covers, 212
Dental Picks, 212
"A Difficult Bunker," 150
Difficult Shots Made Easy with Hale Irwin,
    165
Dishner Concept Putter, 71
The Distance Builder, 95
The Dream Tee, 218
"The Drive," 150
Driver and a Half, 63
Driving with Davis Love III, 184
Driving for Distance with John Elliott, 170
The Duke and The Duchess Putters, 63
Dynasight, 11

The Edge Putter, 44
18 Tips from 18 Legends of Golf, 165
"'84 Gutty" Balls, 198
Electric Putting Partner, 45
Enforcer Grips, 202
ExacTee, 218

Executive Golf Ball Holder, 198
Executive Golf Tool, 141
Exercises for Better Golf, 166

**"Famous British Golf Clubs" Placemats
    and Coasters, 141**
Famous-Logo Visors, 192
Faults and Cures with John Jacobs, 181
Feel Your Way to Better Golf with Wally
    Armstrong, 166
A Few Rambling Remarks on Golf, 156
Fifty Years of Golf, 156
Find Your Own Fundamentals with Bob
    Toski and Jim Flick, 170
"The First Clubhouse in America, 1892," 152
"The First Tee," 154
Fisherman's Par-Tee Pak, 131
Flagpin "Great American Golf Holes" Playing
    Cards, 142
Flex-Tee, 218
Flex-Tips, 226
Floater Golf Balls, 198
Flying Elbows, 11
Foot Wedge, 12
Foot Wedge, 131
Force II Putter Grip, 45
Fore 7-4-7 Jumbo Driver, 63
"Francis D. Ouimet Wins United States
    Open Title, 1913," 152
The Full Swing with John Jacobs, 181

**Get Rid of Your Back Problems and Play
    Better Golf with Sam Snead and
    Dr. K.J. Keggi, 167**
The Giant Niblick, 64
"Ginger Beer Hole" Print, 151
Godiva Golf Balls, 142
Golden Greats of Golf, 167
Golden Retriever, 210
The Golden Tee, 167
Golf with Al Geiberger, 168
Golf with Patty Sheehan, 168
Golf Attaché, 107
Golf Bag Rain Cover, 209
Golf Ball "Ice Cubes," 221
Golf Ball Monogrammer, 208
Golf Ball Rake, 211
Golf Ball Ring Gauge, 199
⌐lf-Buoy, 227
        ⌐ddy Fire Iron Set, 142
          ⌐ 107
            ⌐ng Kit, 212
              ⌐ting, Alteration & Repair,

Golf Club Design, Specifications & Fitting,
    169
The Golf Club Identification and Price Guide,
    155
*Golf Club Repair—The Knowledge & Bench
    Skills* with Tom Wishon and Mark
    Wilson, 169
The Golf Digest Schools Learning Library,
    169
Golf Doctor, 108
Golf for Kids of All Ages with Wally Arm-
    strong, 171
Golf for Winners with Hank Haney and Mark
    O'Meara, 171
The Golf Game Par Excellence, 108
Golf Glasses, 142
Golf Glove Dryer, 214
Golf Green Speed-Meter, 45
Golf Handicapper, 109
Golf House Ball Marker, 142
The Golf House Rare Book Collection, 156
Golf in America, 156
Golf Lessons with Sam Snead, 172
Golf Like a Pro with Billy Casper, 172
Golf Links, 208
Golf the Miller Way with Johnny Miller, 173
Golf My Way with Jack Nicklaus, 174
Golf Ornaments, 143
Golf Partner, 110
Golf Party Accessories, 222
Golf Party-Pak, 222
Golf Putt Stroke Guide, 45
Golf Quote Glasses, 222
Golf Quotes, 143
Golf Rubbers, 192
Golf Secrets with Walter Hagen, 174
Golf Sundial, 143
The Golf Swing, 186
The Golf Swing with Tom Weiskopf, 174
Golf Swinger, 12
Golf Tee Tie Rack, 143
Golf Tournament Scoring Program, 112
Golf Your Way with Phil Ritson, 175
Golf—The Winner's Edge with Kermit Zarley,
    175
The Golfaholics Anonymous Official Driving
    Kit, 131
Golfaholics Anonymous Official Sweatshirt,
    192
Golfasaurus Sweatshirt and T-Shirt, 193
"The Golfer" Barbecue Apron and Hot Mitt,
    193
"The Golfer" Character Jug, 143
The Golferciser, 96

Golfer's Cribbage, 110
Golfer's Crotch Hook, 131
Golfer's Repair and Maintenance Handbook, 214
Golfer's Welcome Mat, 143
"The Golfers" Print, 152
Golfers' Pewter Hip Flasks, 144
Golfers' Stats, 203
GolfGym, 96
Golfing Coasters, 144
"Golfing Hazards" Towel, 144
Golf's Best— Pinehurst No. 2, 110
Golf's Best— St. Andrews, 112
Golf's Greats Quick Tips— Volumes I and II, 175
Golfsmith XL Design Putter Grip, 46
GolfTek Personal Model Golf Computer, 13
GolfTek Swing Analyzer/Pro III Model, 13
Goofy Golf Balls, 131
Gore-Tex Golf Suit, 193
Gotcha, 227
The Grand Luxe Golf Cart, 227
Graph-Check Sequence Camera, 14
Great Golfers in the Making, 156
The Greater Golfer in You with Dr. Gary Wiren, 175
Grip Life, 214
Groove-E-Swing Trainer, 14
Jack Grout Tee-Square, 34
Gull-Wing Practice Net, 84
Lealand Gustavson Prints, 152

Handicap Manager, 113
Head Freezer, 14
Head Trainer, 15
Head Up Preventer, 15
Heavy Weighted Practice Club, 96
Hero Driver, 64
Hexagonal Golf Tidy Box, 144
Hidden-Cart Golf Bag, 227
Hillerich & Bradsby: History-Catalogs (1922-1980), 157
Hit & Tell Decals, 15
Hitting the Long Shots with Davis Love, Jr., 171
Hitting Mat, 84
HL Ballmark With Velcro, 206
Hole-In-One Trophy Case, 144
The Hooker Golf Glove, 31
Bob Hope Golfer, 114
Hot Dog Putter, 132
How I Play Golf with Bobby Jones, 176
How To Golf with Jan Stephenson, 178

How To Play Better Golf with Bob Intrieri, 179
How To Play Your Best Golf All the Time with Tommy Armour, 179
The Hurricane Cover, 209

Impact Bag, 16
Impact Decals, 15
Imported British Golf Towels, 223
Improve Your Golf Game with Larry Garrett, 180
"In Pursuit of Par"— Par 72 Edition, 114
"In Pursuit of Par"— TPC at Sawgrass Edition, 115
Indoor Golf Net and Frame, 84
Indoor/Outdoor Practice Net, 85
Indoor Practice Green, 46
Indoor Putting Mat, 47
The Inner Solution with Dr. Robert Metzger, 181
An Inside Look at the Game for a Lifetime with Bob Toski, Jim Flick, Peter Kostis, and John Elliott, 181
International Duffers Association, 133
Iron Accuracy with Tom Purtzer, 184
Iron Driver, 64
"It's Tee Time!" Mug, 145

The John Jacobs Series—The Full Swing, The Short Game, and Faults and Cures, 181
Joe Pro Golf Cap, 194
Bobby Jones Concentration, 153
Jumbo Golf Tees, 133
Junior Golf "The Easy Way" with Mark Steinbauer, 182
Just-Rite Putter, 65

***Keys to Consistency* with Jack Grout, 182**
Keys to Great Golf! with JoAnne Carner, 183
The Klanger, 47
Kneel 'n' Pray Putter, 133
The Kostis Krutch, 41

Labelon Tape, 16
Lacquer-Stiks, 214
Laid Back Golfer's Association, 133
Learning Golf with Mike Calbot, 183
Terence Legg Golf Sign, 153
"Limber-Up" Golf Mitt, 96
Links 18GX Advanced Golf Scorecard, 204
Links to the Past, 204
"Links to the Past" Ball Marker Display, 228

"A Little Practise," 154
The Lone Eagle Swing Plane Trainer, 16
Look-Alike Caricatures by Joe Jahraus, 145
Lynx Parallax Putter with Transmitter Shaft,
      66

MacGolf Classic, 116
MacGregor Chip and Drive Mat, 85
MacGregor Golf: History-Catalogs (1935-
      1970), 157
MacGregor Putting Green, 48
McDivot's Clubscrub, 214
McSpike, 215
Maggie's Stroke-Saver Golf Boots, 194
Magnetic Lie Angle Tool, 34
Magnetic Protractor, 215
Magnum Force I Ratchet Spike Wrench, 215
"Major Green" Character Mug, 145
The Marcy Wedge, 97
Mark's Marker, 206
The Master System to Better Golf: Volume 1
      with Craig Stadler, Davis Love III,
      Tom Purtzer, and Gary Koch, 183
Mastering the Fundamentals with Arnold
      Palmer, 185
Memory Keeper, 204
Mercury-Loaded Driver, 66
Mid and Short Irons, 186
Mighty Midget Golf Ball Washer, 199
Mighty-Mite SS, 71
Mini Golf, 117
Mini-Putt, 117
Mitsubishi Golf Trainers, 17
Miya Computer Putting Checker, 48
Miya Computer Shot Analyzer, 18
Miya Putting Trainer, 48
Tom Morris Print, 153

The Name Dropper, 208
Nerf Indoor Golf, 118
New Zealand Lambskin Headcovers, 216
Jack Nicklaus Twenty-Fifth Anniversary
      Commemorative Clubs, 77
1986 Masters Tournament, 184
The 19th Hole Chip & Putt, 86
19th Hole Flag, 228
The 19th Hole Par Electric Putting Cup, 49
The 19th Hole Putting Green, 49
19th Hole Sipper, 228
le Toilet Seat, 134
le Ultimate Electric Putting Cup,

Oak Putter Stand, 50
Off-the-Wall Golf-Ball Alarm Clock, 146
Official PGA Tour Personal Golf Book, 205
"The Old Apple Tree Gang, 1888," 152
"Old Tom Morris" Toby Jug, 153
Oncourse Instructor, 18
One Move to Better Golf with Carl Lohren,
      185
Optima Driver, 66
The Original Bag Shag, 86
The Otey Cane, 146
Oversize Putting Green, 50
Own Your Own Golf Course, 147

Par-Buster Target and Chart, 86
PAR 5 Golf Handicap and Statistics System,
      118
Par T Golf—The Incredible Golf Machine,
      118
The "Par"-Fect Golf Net, 87
Dave Pelz Putting Track, 50
Dave Pelz Teacher Putter, 50
"Perfect Stroke" Golf Practice Net, 87
Perflex Driver, 68
Persimmon Seeds ("Grow Your Own Golf
      Clubs"), 134
Phillips Spike Wrench, 216
Ping Weight Balance Scale, 217
Pitching and Sand Play with Paul Runyan,
      187
Pitching Net, 87
PLA-GOLF Miniature Golf Game, 119
Play Golf—Pineview, 120
Play Golf—Ye Old Course, 120
Play Great Golf with Arnold Palmer—
      Mastering the Fundamentals and
      Course Strategy, 185
Play Your Best Golf—Six Lessons, 186
Play Your Best Golf—Volumes 1 and 2, 185
"Playoff for Masters Championship, 1954,"
      152
Plumb Bob Training Tool, 51
Plumber's Putter, 134
Positive Putter, 68
Power Builder, 98
Power Driving with Mike Dunaway, 186
Power Flexor, 98
Power Pod, 68
Power Swing, 99
Power Tone Exerciser, 99
Power Trainer, 21
Powerstroke, 99
Pow'r Tee, 219
Practice Golf Cage, 87
Practice Golf Range, 88

Precision Putting with Dave Stockton, 186
The Precision Putting System, 51
Pro-Align, 35
Pro Golf, 121
Pro-Green, 53
Pro Practice Putting Green, 53
Pro-Swing, 21
Pro-Tater, 21
Professional-Class Golf, 122
Professional Golf Putting Cup, 52
PROTECH Golf Bag, 229
Pug-Ugly Putter, 69
Pure Silk Golf Ties, 148
Put'r There/The Putter Caddy, 229
Putt-a-Bout Auto Return Putting Green, 53
Putt-Caster, 55, 89
Putt-in-Cup, 55
Putt Master Putting Carpet, 55
Putt-R-Buddy, 56
Putt Square, 56
Putt Wizz, 56
Puttband-Swingband, 54
Putter Gripper, 229
Putter Power, 134
Putter Tie Clip, 148
Putting with Gary Koch, 184
Putting and Chipping, 186
Putting and Chipping with Paul Runyan, 187
Putting for Profit with Tom Ness, 170
"The Putting Green," 150
Putting Trainer, 56
Putting Tutor, 56
Putting with Confidence with Duff Lawrence
      and Barb Thomas, 187

QuicKnicks, 195

RagTail Golf Towel, 223
Redi Club, 230
Reed & Barton Ball Mark Repair Tool, 148
The Reel Putter, 57
Renegade 410 Golf Balls, 201
Rev-Tee, 219
Right Touch, 58
"Robert Tyre Jones, Jr., 1930," 152
Rules Master, 122
Rules of the Thistle Golf Club, 156

W. Dendy Sadler Prints, 154
"St. Andrews Caddie," 150
St. Andrews Headcovers, 230
Sand Trap Practice Net, 89
Sav-A-Scratch, 231
Saving Par from the Sand with John Elliott,
      170

Score Caddy, 205
The Secret Weapon Driver, 69
Seiko Golf Scorecard, 205
The Separator, 41
Set-Up Master, 35
Shademaster Umbrella Clamp, 209
Shag King, 89
Shake-a-Round, 123
Sharpen Your Short Irons with Jim Flick,
      170
Short Flyte Golf Balls, 89
The Short Game with John Jacobs, 181
The Short Game with Craig Stadler, 184
The Short Way to Lower Scoring with Paul
      Runyan— *Volume I: Putting and
      Chipping; Volume II: Pitching and
      Sand Play*, 187
Shotmaker Golf Glove, 32
The Shrivot, 207
Shurfire Alma Mater Putters, 70
Side Saddle Putters, 72
Sidesaddle Putters, 71
Signature Series Golf Glove, 195
Silver Scot Collector Putter, 77
Slice Repellent, 136
The Slicebuster, 36
Slim Jim Putter, 72
The Smitty, 207
Sam Snead's Power Stance Mat, 35
*So You Stand on the Wrong Side of the Ball,
      Too!* with Jay Edgar, 188
Soft-Tee, 220
Solar-Powered Ventilated Golf Cap, 196
Sony CaddyCam, 22
*A.G. Spalding & Bros.— Pre-1930 Clubs,
      Trademarks, and Collectibles*, 158
Spike Caddy, 217
The Spiro Swinger, 22
Sportech Golf Swing Analyzer, 23
The Stable Flexor, 24
Stance Guide, 37
"Stayclean" Golf Towel, 224
Stay-n-Play, 209
The Strategies, 186
Strategies and Skills, 186
Streamin' Mimi Joke Golf Ball, 136
Stretch-Aligner, 37
"The Stymie," 154
Subliminal Golf Improvement Program, 188
Super Grip Dryer/Suberaanai, 217
Super Stick Adjustable Golf Club, 72
Swing Developer, 100
A Swing for a Lifetime with Bob Toski and
      Jim Flick, 170
Swing Groover, 24

Swing-Guide, 38
Swing Memory, 24
Swing Mirror, 25
Swing-O-Meter, 25
Swing Plane Trainer, 25
Swing-R Sway Control, 37
Swing Right, 22
Swing Ring, 26
Swingrite, 26
Swingthing, 27

T-Mats, 91
Target Green Kit, 90
Tasco Golf Scope, 231
Tea-Time at the Masters, 231
Tee-Off, 27
Tee Shots and Others, 156
Tee Wizz, 90
Tempo Training Club, 28
Think Big! Golf Ball, 136
"3 in 1" Club, 74
Tiger Shark P-Squared Putter Grip, 58
Top Sight Putting Aid, 59
Top-Tips, 38
TopTan Shirts, 196
Bob Toski Teaches You Golf, 189
The Toski Trainer, 28
Total Golf with Bruce Crampton, 189
Tour Belt, 101
TourHawk Putter, 74
Tourna Grip, 202
The Track, 59
Training Grip, 32
Travels with a Golf Tour Gourmet, 232
Triple Crown Wedge, 74
The Triumverate, 154
Trouble Shots: The Great Escapes with Hank
    Johnson, 171
TRS-80 Golf Handicapping System, 123

Tru-Stroke Putting Guide, 59
TruSwing, 30
Tunstall Putter, 76
Two-Way Indoor Putting Green, 60

***The Ultimate Drive* with Art Sellinger,
    190**
Ultimate Golf, 124
The Ultimate Golf Towel, 224

Vassisdat Putter, 136
Vedoro's Ball Prospector, 211
Vision Putt, 60

Wacky Golf Cap, 137
Wacky Tees, 137
Warm-Up Practice Weight, 101
Wastepaper Golfer, 125
When the Chips Are Down with Jack Lump-
    kin, 170
Wiffle Golf Balls, 91
The Wilson 8802, 78
The Wilson 8813, 78
Wilson Golf: History-Catalogs (1931-1979),
    159
The Window-Wedge, 76
Winning Pitch Shots with Davis Love, Jr.,
    170
"A Winter Evening," 154
Wood Wand, 76
Wooden Golf Jigsaw, 126
Woods and Long Irons, 186
World Class Leader Board, 126
World Tour Golf, 127
Wrist Lock, 41
Wrist-Magic, 30

Zippo Greens Keeper, 207